"THE SOUL OF THE RHINO is unusual, fascinating, and important. It provides not only a rare insight into the personality and behavior of the highly endangered and little known Asian rhino, but an equally absorbing picture of the people who share its habitat. Hemanta Mishra is a native of Nepal, and he shares his struggle to reconcile Western conservation science, learned when he studied in America, with the cultural beliefs of his people; he attempts to combine hard facts with the mystical values of Eastern philosophy. THE SOUL OF THE RHINO is also a commentary on the way in which wildlife management can be helped or tragically hindered by revolution, politics, and the commitment, or lack of it, of those in power. Most important, it will surely inspire other young people in Asia to follow in his footsteps. I hope you will buy and read this book." —Dr. Jane Goodall, DBE, founder - the Jane Goodall Institute & UN Messenger of Peace

"Hemanta Mishra helped to establish Nepal's famous Chitwan National Park, and he has with great dedication fought for three decades to assure the survival of its rare Indian rhino. From the unique perspective of a Nepali dealing with conservation battles in his own country, he describes his contacts with everyone from poacher and foreigner to bureaucrat, royalty, and rhino. I enjoyed THE SOUL OF THE RHINO immensely for its potent conservation message, as well as its insights into a culture and the soul of the author." —George B. Schaller, Wildlife Conservation Society

"It is the first book of its kind that proves that nature conservation in Asia does not only depend upon good Western science. But like politics in America, it is an art—an art of the possible—an art that puts human needs and culture in the forefront of environmental conservation." —Lodi Gyari, special envoy of His Holiness the Dalai Lama

Hemanta R. Mishra
with *Jim Ottaway, Jr.*

The Soul of the Rhino

*A Nepali Adventure
with Kings and Elephant Drivers,
Billionaires and Bureaucrats,
Shamans and Scientists
and the Indian Rhinoceros*

WITH FOREWORDS BY
BRUCE BABBITT AND JIM FOWLER

THE LYONS PRESS
Guilford, Connecticut
AN IMPRINT OF THE GLOBE PEQUOT PRESS

The Lyons Press is an imprint of The Globe Pequot Press.

10 9 8 7 6 5 4 3 2 1

Printed in the United States of America

Designed by Claire Zoghb

ISBN 978-1-59921-146-6

Library of Congress Cataloging-in-Publication Data is available on file.

IN LOVING MEMORY OF

Mingma Norbu Sherpa (left), Tirtha Man Maskey (second

from right), and Chandra Prasad Gurung (right)—the heroes and

builders of nature conservation in Nepal and my band of brothers in

bringing the rhino back from the brink of extinction

(Courtesy: Phurva Sherpa).

CONTENTS

FOREWORD *by Bruce Babbitt*   ix

FOREWORD *by Jim Fowler*   xi

PREFACE   xv

PROLOGUE: *A Tryst with Destiny*   xxi

1   CLOSE ENCOUNTERS WITH THE
    UNICORN KIND   1

2   CHEATING YAMA, THE GOD OF DEATH   11

3   A TALE OF THE TERAI   21

4   RHINO ROOTS   29

5   CLASH OF CULTURES   35

6   MEDICINE OR MYTH?   45

7   LEARNING FROM THE WEST   57

8   WILDERNESS BLUES   67

9   POVERTY, RHINOS, TIGERS, AND
    TOURISTS IN CHITWAN   77

10 GEORGE OF THE JUNGLE   89

11 KILLING MOTHERS TO SNATCH BABIES   101

12 SCIENCE AND SHAMANISM   107

13 KIDNAPPING BABY RHINOS FOR
    AN AMERICAN ZOO   113

14 TAMING TEXAS RHINOS   123

15 POPES, KINGS, QUEENS, AND THE RHINO   137

16 PALACE INTRIGUES   147

17 ROOKIE AT THE ROYAL RHINO HUNT   157

18 RHINO VERSUS ROYALTY   169

19 PRAYERS IN THE DUSK   179

20 MOVING RHINOS   187

21 A NEW HOME FOR THE RHINOS   197

    EPILOGUE: HOPE OR UNCERTAINTY
    ON A HIMALAYAN SCALE   205

    SELECTED BIBLIOGRAPHY   217

    INDEX   225

FOREWORD
Bruce Babbitt

This book is an intriguing adventure tale, set in lowland jungles beneath the towering summits of the Himalayas in remote regions of Nepal, in which the author is seen stalking the mythical Indian rhino from atop a large, lumbering elephant. He is not, however, seen toting a high-powered rifle, and he is not searching for a trophy kill. His weapon is a tranquilizer gun, and his mission is to save the rhino from extinction.

Hemanta Mishra is a native Nepali, raised in the Hindu Buddhist tradition. Early on he decided on a career as a forester and naturalist, and along the way he became fascinated with the rhino and set out to save it from extinction. In the process he obtained an advanced degree in Scotland, studied the American system of national parks, returned to Nepal to continue field work, befriended American philanthropists, learned the ways of palace intrigue in Kathmandu, and perfected the dangerous techniques necessary to capture and transplant these creatures to extend their range and chances for survival.

Beneath the surface of these adventure tales, however, the author has an important message for those of us interested in nature conservation in Nepal and elsewhere in developing regions of the world. To save the rhino and the tiger and to preserve our heritage of biological diversity, we must acquire more than textbook knowledge. We must also listen to indigenous communities, learning their history and traditions and factoring in their needs and aspirations for the future. We must blend Western science with tradition and mythology and have the patience and wisdom to reconcile the two.

The climactic chapters of this book recount the planning and execution of the royal hunt of Tarpan, in which the king of Nepal must hunt and kill a male rhino and make a ritual offering of the dead animal's blood to assure peace and prosperity in the kingdom. When called upon to organize the royal hunt, Hemanta is repelled by the thought of killing even one rhino. Yet he must retain the goodwill and patronage of King Birendra in order to expand nature reserves within the kingdom.

Tarpan as described by the author is a primitive and bloody ritual, yet also a mystical and evocative ceremony in which participants approach and enter the rhino carcass on the forest floor, suffused with the yellow light of oil lamps, the scent of incense and flower petals, and priests chanting ancient Sanskrit verses. Finally the author resolves to partake in the ceremony, reconciling his Western education and his traditional upbringing in a transcendent moment — "I had found my soul in the body of a rhino."

In recent years Nepal has been torn by armed rebellion and political violence. Both the monarchy and the Tarpan ritual may disappear, and the fate of the rhino is once again less than certain. However, ancient myths and the beauty and instructive power of Hindu and Buddhist tradition will surely endure. And this book will continue to remind readers that to save the planet we must reconcile science and tradition and assure a future for both indigenous peoples and wildlife.

—*Bruce Babbitt,*
Chairman of the World Wildlife Fund
Washington, D.C.
March 2007

FOREWORD

Jim Fowler

From the flats below the foothills of the Himalayas, on a clear day you can see some of the highest mountains in the world looming far off as if they were a painted backdrop in an expensive restaurant. The artist, in this case, is Mother Nature, whose work can't possibly be duplicated by humans.

I was so entranced by this scene that I almost forgot I was riding on the back of an elephant in the unspoiled wilderness of Chitwan National Park in Nepal, looking for a greater one-horned Asian rhinoceros that was to be darted and tagged in order to study its movements.

The grass grows high along the floodplain and river, and it would be hard to find a rhino even from the back of an elephant ten feet up. But our guide and host, perched on the lead elephant, knew where to go. He was Dr. Hemanta Mishra, director of the King Mahendra Trust for Nature Conservation. It was 1987, and I was meeting him for the first time to make a film for the Mutual of Omaha Wild Kingdom series.

If you were to meet Hemanta in Kathmandu, Nepal's capital city, you might think he's a businessman. When in town, he usually wears a suit and carries a briefcase. You wouldn't know that he works with rhinos, but when he starts talking, you soon discover he's an accomplished scientist. Hemanta can tell you stories about his country's flora and fauna with enthusiasm, and he knows more about the endangered one-horned rhino than anyone I know.

Although Nepal is heavily populated and much of the landscape is terraced and farmed, there are still tigers, elephants, rhinos, leopards, and sloth bears living in the wild not far from crowded villages. Hemanta has spent the better part of his adult life instituting conditions that protect his country's wildlife. He has traveled and represented Nepal to many of the world's leading conservationists, scientists, and spokespeople for the natural world. His grasp of the modern concept of "eco-sustainability" and the use of economic incentive to save wildlife habitat has allowed him to help villages establish their own privately owned and operated tourist camps.

Chitwan National Park was originally created as a private hunting reserve for the rulers of Nepal, their family and friends, and visiting dignitaries. In 1987, the last time I visited Nepal, Chitwan was the only refuge of the Indian Rhino in Nepal. Few animals are more impressive than this ancient behemoth that has lived on the planet successfully for millions of years. While I was there, I thought about why it is so important for us to guarantee the continued survival of such a potentially dangerous animal and how this could be communicated effectively to the public.

These questions become more meaningful when you ponder them from the back of a pachyderm, as Hemanta and I have done. Hemanta agrees that we must not only point out how rare and magnificent the rhino is, but also link its existence to the welfare of humans. In other words, we must consider how our human "quality of life" will be affected if we destroy nature. When we destroy natural resources, we run the risk of creating societies of haves and have-nots that invariably result in dictatorships, political upheaval, and social tragedies. Hemanta found a solution for Nepal through nature-based tourism, which brought in revenue that reduced illegal hunting and poaching and convinced the locals that land with restricted access, such as a national park, was a good thing.

Using his model, we may be able to convince other nations, ours included, that it's important to understand and respect "how the earth works." It is clear that overpopulation, destruction of the land, and the creation of one-resource economies are the root causes of most social tragedies, wars, and violence today. If we can't even save the habitat of rhinos in Nepal, we may not be able to save enough healthy natural habitat for ourselves.

Last year it was reported that less than 5 percent of the American public spent more than half an hour per year thinking about the welfare of wildlife and wilderness. Apparently, politicians know that the average voter does not necessarily understand and respect the world of nature, so all too often, how we treat the earth is not a priority in their campaigns.

Hemanta's book will help save rhinos because it forms a personal connection with the reader. His story is told with the passion of personal experience. No matter whether he's working in the wild, for the World Bank, a conservation group, or the American Himalayan Foundation, he is what we need most in the twenty-first century: a spokesperson for the natural world who makes people care.

—Jim Fowler
Honorary President, The Explorers Club,
and former host of Mutual of Omaha's
Wild Kingdom
April 2007

PREFACE

I *was five years old when I first learned about the rhino's soul. I was* watching my father perform his religious duties in our front yard in Kupondole in Kathmandu, Nepal. It was a Saradya, a day of worship for the spirits of our dead ancestors. My father—a Hindu—believed that the dead have the power to influence the lives of the living.

"Babu," my father called, using an affectionate Nepali term to address me, "go and get the *khaguto* from your mother."

"Father," I asked curiously, "what is a *khaguto*?"

"Oh, my dear," my father replied with a loving smile, "it is a cup made out of a rhino horn. The souls of our ancestors will not be appeased if I do not offer them milk and water from the *khaguto* during the Saradya."

I fetched the *khaguto*, which was hidden, as if it were a precious piece of jewelry, in a compartment of a huge iron safe anchored to the floor of our attic. Yet it was only a dark, boney, lightweight cup hardly three inches in diameter and an inch deep. My father told me that the *khaguto* has been with our family for generations. For our clan it was more valuable than any earthly diamonds. Although I was five when I first touched a rhino horn, it would take another seventeen years before I saw my first wild rhino. Yet I could not help stretching my imagination about rhinos as I grew to adulthood. Rhinos have always created an aura of power and mystery in my mind—even to this day.

This book is the culmination of my three decades of work in conservation in Nepal, mostly in the Royal Chitwan National Park located in the foothills of the Himalayas—the last stronghold of the greater one-horned Asian rhino. It would not have been completed without the support of Jim Ottaway Jr., a friend, a philanthropist, a comrade in conservation, and an American with a Himalayan-size heart. Jim spent many days with me at the Yale Club of New York, reviewing, rewording, and rewriting this manuscript word by word. I am also indebted to two wonderful women who have provided me with invaluable help throughout this process. Cornelia Bessie reviewed the manuscript, provided helpful criticism, and enthusiastically showed the book to agents and publishers. Bonnie Burgoyne patiently retyped and formatted the manuscript, over many months of editing and rewriting.

I am also grateful to Bruce Babbitt and Jim Fowler for writing forewords to this book. In addition, I am grateful to my old friends Fiona Sunquist, Chris Wemmer, Lisa Choegyal at Tiger Tops, Brot Coburn, and Phurva Sherpa for permitting me to use some of their photographs. Masahiro Iijima—an old friend, a veteran of conservation in Nepal—also provided many of the photographs used in the book. Masahiro has worked with me in Nepal since the 1970s, and we have jointly produced a book on tigers in the Japanese language. The cover was designed by Georgiana Goodwin from The Lyons Press, and the map of Chitwan was designed by Karna Jung Thapa, from the World Wildlife Fund, Nepal.

Updates on rhino census and poaching data were provided by Tirtha Man Maskey, Chandra Gurung, Mingma Norbu Sherpa, and Narayan Poudyal. As described in the epilogue of this book, these vanguards of conservation lost their lives in a helicopter crash in eastern Nepal in September 2006. The sudden demise of these heroes and builders of national parks and protected conservation areas in Nepal is a great loss, not only for Nepal but also for the global conservation movement. They were my friends, partners, and band of brothers in bringing the rhino back from the brink of extinction.

My wife, Sushma, has been my soul partner for thirty-five years. She helped me collect and synthesize the data on rhinos when I was living in Chitwan. She also provided some of the photographs used in this book. My daughters, Alita and Pragya, and my son, Binayak, spent hours reading the draft manuscript. They provided the harshest yet most candid critiques of the book. Lodi Gyari, Geoffrey Ward, Brot Coburn, and Adrian Cowell were among the first to read my manuscript and suggest improvements. They also inspired me not to give up on my writing.

Some of the scientific information, particularly on the evolution and behavior of rhinos, was adopted from Eric Dinerstein's book *The Return of the Unicorns: The Natural History and Conservation of the Greater One-Horned Rhinoceros* (2003). Furthermore, the description of the first translocation of rhinos from Chitwan to Bardia in chapter 20 is based on a popular article titled "New Zip Codes for Resident Rhinos in Nepal" that Eric and I published in *Smithsonian Magazine*. Eric, a brilliant scientist, has remained my key partner in rhino and tiger conservation in Nepal for thirty years. The description of the Royal Chitwan National Park and the culture of the Tharu people are adapted from my own book, *Royal Chitwan National Park: Wildlife Heritage of Nepal* (1991) that I coauthored with Margaret Jefferies. Information on the illicit trade in rhino parts was based on outstanding work done by another friend, Esmond Bradley Martin from Kenya, particularly his pioneering publication, *Rhino Exploitation: The Trade in Rhino Products in India, Indonesia, Malaysia, Burma, Japan, & South Korea* (1983). In addition, Anup Joshi, a former colleague from Chitwan, provided much of the vital information and helped in fact checking, particularly on the impact of the recent civil war on the rhino population in Nepal. Status reports on both African and Asian rhinos are based on published information from the Web sites of the International Rhino Foundation (IRF), World Conservation Union (IUCN), Rhino Resource Center, and various publications of the Asian Rhino Specialist

Group (AsRSG). I have also relied on the pioneering works of an old friend, Andrew Laurie, and my own publications. Andrew was the first to undertake a comprehensive study of the ecology and behavior of the greater one-horned Asian rhinoceros.

The Smithsonian Institution and the World Wildlife Fund (WWF) have remained Nepal's key partners in conservation since the 1970s. In addition, the American Himalayan Foundation has supported my work in Nepal since the 1980s, including other parts of Nepal, particularly in the Sagarmatha (Mt. Everest) National Park and the Annapurna Conservation Area. Furthermore, my work in the Royal Chitwan National Park was supported directly or indirectly by His Majesty's Government of Nepal; the King Mahendra Trust for Nature Conservation; the Frankfurt Zoological Society; the Wildlife Department of Narayanhiti Royal Palace; U.S. Aid; the Australian, American, German, British, and French Embassies in Nepal; the Singapore, Cologne, and Berlin zoos; the World Conservation Union (IUCN); the MacArthur Foundation; and the Fauna and Flora Preservation Society. I am deeply indebted to many friends and colleagues in the aforementioned organizations.

The bulk of funding for my work in Chitwan, including finding new homes for the rhinos, would not have been possible without the generous donations of Edward P. Bass and Richard C. Blum.

As described in the prologue and the epilogue, there has been a major shift in the political power structure in Nepal, and the monarchy in Nepal is no longer a dominant force. Consequently, these days it is not popular to give any credit to King Gyanendra Bir Bikram Shah Dev. However, it would be wrong and an injustice to the history of nature conservation not to credit him with saving the rhinos from becoming extinct in Nepal during the twentieth century. His leadership and dedication were instrumental in generating the political will in Nepal and in gaining international support to create a network of national parks and wildlife reserves, second to none in the developing world.

By April 2007 the political and social dynamics in Nepal were changing fast. The Maoists joined the government on March 30, 2007, and took over the responsibility of saving the rhino and its habitat in the twenty-one-person cabinet. The status of the current monarchy by the time this book reaches bookstores in Nepal is at best uncertain. On the bright side many of the sons and daughters of those who poached and destroyed rhino habitat in the 1970s and 1980s have become rhino protectors and are profiting from wildlife tourism in the new millennium. Thus, to avoid ostracizing them for the past sins of their fathers, I have changed their names and apologize in advance if this book causes any distress to their relatives in Nepal. Unfortunately, the practice of "defame, demoralize, and destroy" seems to have overtaken our traditional values of respecting the dead. This is not my intention; rather it is to focus on the challenges of rhino conservation in Nepal.

Finally, I am also grateful to The Lyons Press for publishing this book. In particular, I am indebted to my editor, Holly Rubino, who helped get this book into its final shape.

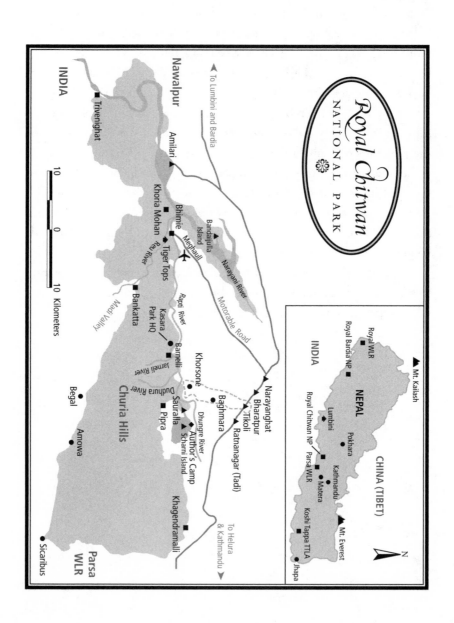

PROLOGUE:
A Tryst with Destiny

"*What have you done, my son!*" were the last words mumbled by the bespectacled God-King before he died on the dining table at a family dinner at the Narayanhiti Royal Palace in Kathmandu on June 1, 2001.

The death of King Birendra, a gentle, humble, Harvard-educated monarch was not an act of God. It resulted from a bizarre bloodbath unprecedented in the history of monarchy. In an all-in-one bloody mayhem of patricide, matricide, fratricide, and regicide, Crown Prince Dipendra massacred his whole family and then committed suicide to prove his love of a woman that his parents did not want him to marry. The carnage in Kathmandu sealed the life of a mortal monarch who is regarded, even today, to be the reincarnation of God Vishnu the Protector. It also changed the destiny of Nepal, my motherland, and with it, perhaps, the fate of the rhino—a thick-skinned unicorn that I have loved and venerated for three decades.

What a death for a gentle and humble monarch revered by his people. What a destiny for a mortal who is regarded by his people as immortal. What a fate for a nature-loving ruler who had the courage and the political will to bring the rhinoceros back from the brink of extinction.

It was the court of King Birendra that cemented my fate with the world of the rhinoceros in 1972. Back then, I was invited to serve on the Royal Palace Wildlife Committee, a body that made virtually all policy and operational decisions on wildlife conservation in

Nepal. King Birendra also assigned Prince Gyanendra, his younger brother, to chair this committee.

As a native Nepali and a practitioner of its strange Hindu-Buddhist mix of religion, I believe in fate. It was my fate that lured me to the world of the greater one-horned rhinoceros in Nepal's Royal Chitwan National Park almost three decades before the carnage in the Royal Palace in Kathmandu.

Fate has offered me a glimpse into the soul of the rhinoceros, a mystical beast legendary for its power, its sexual energy, its unpredictable temperament, and its prodigious strength. It has led me to observe rhinos from the backs of elephants and from helicopters, to participate in a royal rhino-hunt ritual that dates back to the sixteenth century, to capture baby rhinos for American zoos, to celebrate rhinos in hours of film and hundreds of still photos, and to save rhinos from becoming the innocent victims of skullduggery and political violence.

Juggling the diverse philosophies of East and West, I have tried to find a balance between my spiritual beliefs and rigid Eastern superstitions and my scientific knowledge and Western education. I have attempted to create an entirely new vision of wildlife management, one that balances scientific exactitude, spiritual values, and practical politics.

Wandering along my predestined path, I have faced many questions: What are the bonds that hold a rhino family together? How does Western science affect Eastern rituals pertaining to this animal? Where should the line be drawn between commerce and conservation? How do the royal monarchs of the East differ from the business moguls of the West? What is more valuable: a human life or the life of a rhino? My questions have taken me from my own humble beginnings in the ancient capital city of Kathmandu to the jungles of southern Nepal to the highlands and islands of Scotland. They have also taken me to a pilgrimage of the mind at the bubbling hot springs of Yellowstone National Park and to Main Street in

Fort Worth, Texas; from kowtowing to the officious whimsy of the rich and famous to hobnobbing with monarchs from Asia and Europe and billionaires from America.

Over the years the rhino has been transformed into something more than a strange and wonderful beast to me. It has become a talisman, an enigmatic creature suffused with magical force. Ugly yet enchanting. Massive yet delicate. Terrifying yet timid. Holy and revered for its mystical powers, yet a destroyer of farmlands and the farmers that it gores every year.

The rhino is a mixture of contradictions. In these contradictions, perhaps, is the secret to a healthy coexistence between human and beast.

Celebrated in myth, story, and song and slaughtered by poachers in search of its psychotherapeutic powers, the Asian rhino survives today in its greatest numbers in the Terai, the jungle area along the southern border of the Himalayan kingdom of Nepal. It was there that I trained myself in the Western sciences and Eastern shamanism and learned lessons from elephant drivers, peasants, and poets; holy men, hunters, and soldiers; moguls, monarchs, and mindless bureaucrats.

This is my story of the search for the soul of the greater one-horned Asian rhinoceros, a prehistoric Asian unicorn that still mystifies modern man.

1

CLOSE ENCOUNTERS WITH
THE UNICORN KIND

I sat fretfully on the back of Mahendra Gaz, a big male elephant in his twenties. Oblivious to my anxiety, this mature elephant trudged through the riverine forests of Chitwan as the sun was sinking over the distant hills. As we approached the Rapti River, lapwings cried stridently, cutting through the cooing of doves and the twittering of forest birds. Orange oak leaves, peacock pansies, rose windmills, and myriad other butterflies bobbed and fluttered silently as they sought moisture from damp patches of earth.

We crossed the river and reached a small meadow in the middle of the jungle. We waited there, silently, for wild animals to emerge into the open. From atop the elephant, I spotted a female bear stumbling out of the bush, following her nose toward a termite mound. A young cub, wonderfully camouflaged on her back, held on anxiously for dear life. The mother bear ripped the anthill with her long claws. With her cub clinging precariously on her back, she licked and sniffed inside the big hole in the mound, trying to suck up the insects with her extensile tongue.

While I watched the bears, a group of wild boars trotted by and melted into the brush on the other side. In the distance a wild hen called "kukuri caa." The bear suddenly stood on her hind legs to expose a big white V-mark on her mangy chest. The sight thrilled me. It was the first time that I had seen a wild bear. She was much bigger than I had imagined, almost six feet tall. Standing on her hind legs, the bear focused her eyes on the edge of the bush where a pair of hog deer stole nervously into the meadow. The deer sized up the bear and then continued grazing, their ears and torso twitching spasmodically. With no danger in sight, the bear dropped her forefeet and continued tearing into the mound. Soon a herd of chital deer, two female sambar deer, and a barking deer also made their appearance. The meadow was a favorite picnicking ground for Chitwan's wildlife.

Suddenly, two rhinos snorted and tussled out into the clearing. The deer stopped grazing. The bear ran for cover. I stared, transfixed, at these prehistoric pachyderms. It was my first sighting of rhinos in the wild. Ugly and vicious, yet, for all their physiognomic anomalies, they radiated an undeniable appeal. Grotesque, yet elegant; cloaked in the unique regalia of brownish gray, armor-plated, hairless skin covered with tiny warts. Clumsy and misshapen, yet lithe and graceful. Their sight frightened me, but I could not turn away. I was spellbound.

Hidden behind a cluster of Bhelur trees, safely ensconced on the broad back of a government elephant, I watched the two-ton creatures scuffle and snort. Their actions seemed purposeful. Shifting, gently shoving, and encircling one another, they spun in endless circles as they trotted behind one another. Huffing, puffing, and grunting "dhurr dhurr!" hoarsely, the larger male restlessly followed the female. Whistling "kuiee, kuiee!" in unchanging tones, the female jogged gracefully in front. The female seemed to be taunting the male with a gesture of "catch me if you can."

At twenty-two, I was fresh out of forestry school in Dehra Dun, India. Although any novice could have read this persistent prodding of the female rhino as sexual foreplay, I was too struck by awe and curiosity to realize that. I was not sure if the male was trying to kick, bite, or gore the female. His wide-open mouth dripped pools of saliva and exposed big sharp incisors on his lower jaw. His tail swayed gently, and his eyes were glued to the female's rear end. He caught up with the female, and then, raising his forelegs, he made a feeble attempt to mount her.

"Are they fighting over territory?" I asked Tapsi, my sullen-faced elephant driver. His leathery face was lined with the authenticity of jungle lore, a hallmark of a lifetime of exposure to the hot, humid subtropical forests of the Nepalese Terai.

"They are not fighting, city boy," he laughed disdainfully, displaying a jagged row of rotten teeth. "They are trying to mate," he added, spitting a barrage of obscenities.

My academic inadequacies proven for the moment, I did not respond but continued to watch the rhinos. The huffing, puffing, grunting, and whistling foreplay continued until, after several futile attempts, the male finally mounted the female. The female then moved forward, dragging the reluctant male on his hind legs. In this strange mating ritual, they tangoed around for ten yards or so before standing motionless for what seemed like forever. I had expected the rhinos to copulate quickly, mechanically, with impassionate detachment, as most other mammals do, yet there was no such action. They were contentedly standing peacefully still. After a long pause, the female moved again and dragged the male toward the edge of the meadow, only to nibble at a bush. The male held on tight, his forelegs firmly clasping the female's back. He held his head high and scanned the sky, swaying his head rigidly from left to right, as if in response to an ancient ancestral dance. It was a bizarre sight.

I knew from my textbooks that once the male mounted the female, the mating could take an hour or more. I also knew that male and female rhinos reach sexual maturity when they are six to eight years old. Both the male and the female had to come into heat at the same time to mate. I had read that rhinos court each other over a three- to four-day period, nuzzling and bumping into one another.

But in reality, I saw that the rhino's sex habits were rather more aggressive. As I watched four thousand pounds of rhino thrashing in the meadow in a struggle toward orgasm, I realized that no amount of academic learning could prepare me for the actual experience of close encounters with wild rhinos.

I watched the rhinos grunt and snort as they made love. I coughed nervously. The elephant trumpeted. Suddenly, the male rhino dismounted. Both rhinos turned and looked at us. Had we interrupted their mating? Were they angry? They began to move toward our elephant. Each curved horn that had earlier seemed so harmless and ornamental now threatened like a gleaming knife aching to be embedded into our soft flesh. They stepped closer, carefully. Were they about to attack?

"*Subba sahib*," I quivered, addressing Tapsi, my elephant driver, by his honorific title. "Shouldn't we back off?"

"*Boor chodiga!*" cursed Tapsi in his native tongue, equating me to the female genital. He turned around and looked me up and down, sneering at me, sitting astride the neck of the elephant. "Those rhinos aren't going to charge," he continued. "You'd better go back to the city. You'll never make it in the jungle."

He was right. The prehistoric pachyderms spared us. Obviously having more pressing matters, they eased away into the thicket—huffing, puffing, and snorting.

There were no roads or motor vehicles in Chitwan. The only way to travel through the jungle was by elephant. Moreover, the only way to travel by elephant was to work with Tapsi Subba, the chief elephant driver of His Majesty's Government elephant stable in Saurah, on the banks of the Rapti River. A man of medium height and slender build, with dark, slightly Mongoloid features, Tapsi was a Tharu, a member of the ethnic group that had traditionally inhabited Chitwan and the rest of the Terai.

Unlike my ethnic group, the Western hill Brahmins, who traditionally worked as priests or as appointed bureaucrats behind government desks, the Tharus had a reputation as tough survivors. Through drought, malaria, floods, and savage summer heat, they had survived in the Terai for centuries. They farmed rice, mustard, and other crops in small patches and fished and hunted for deer, wild boar, and birds in the jungle. The most skilled of the Tharus found employment as guides and elephant keepers for the royal family. Tapsi was known as the most skilled and toughest of the Tharus who worked in the Chitwan area. According to government protocol, I was Tapsi's supervisor, but when it came to the ways of the jungle, he was definitely my boss.

My apprenticeship with Tapsi had not gotten off to a very good start. I was encroaching upon what was obviously his domain. When I arrived in Chitwan, I found him standing near the large thatched grass shed that served as the elephant stables. I looked like a typical college-educated Nepali male—dressed in pants, shirt, and leather sandals. I could not hide the fact that, within the narrow, highly influential middle-class stratum, I had succeeded in gaining employment that, if I made the right political deference, would ensure an uninterrupted monthly salary until I retired.

The economic and social disparities of my country had never seemed as apparent to me as I stood apologetically before this wizened old man. I saw no personal insult in the disdainful looks he cast at me, in the way he spat and scratched his privates. I was embarrassed and sensitive. I saw a million bureaucratic inadequacies that had caused his caste its lamentably slow progress to a better economic opportunity. Between his rude gestures and his meticulously placed grunts, I heard the silent protests of the impoverished people of my country. As my brain rapidly processed all this information in favor of Tapsi and his tribe, I considered, for a moment, ditching it all and heading back to the capital in defeat. However, the tenacity of the middle-class mind must never be underestimated. In spite of my sympathy for Tapsi and his people, I returned to my career goals—a monthly salary, societal respect, and a hunger to succeed with the breed of people who were in a position to make a difference in ecological preservation, and, more important, to bring back the greater one-horned Asian rhinoceros from the brink of extinction.

When I first met him, Tapsi was leaning against a bamboo support, smoking a bidi, a kind of cigarette. He was bare-chested, wearing a red lungi, or sarong, that reached just below his knees. His toes gripped ascetic wooden sandals or *kharaow*.

"*Namaste*," I said, "I am Hemanta Mishra from the Forest Department." *Namaste* or *namaskar* is the traditional form of Nepalese greeting that means, "I bow to the God in you." It is usually spoken with both hands clasped in a praying posture.

Tapsi grunted, twisting his wrinkled face into an unwelcome snarl. "What do you want?" he said in Tharu, a dialect I could understand. I stared at him.

"*Haathi ke boor!*" cursed Tapsi, calling me the vagina of an elephant. "What are you staring at?" With that, he turned and walked away.

My friends had warned me about Tapsi. I retreated to my hut and then, after a while, returned to the elephant stable. "*Namaste,*" I said, attempting to gain his attention.

"You again?" scoffed Tapsi, insulting me by scratching his testicles. "I don't have time to deal with a city boy like you."

I held out a bottle of Nepalese-made Khukuri brand rum. I had been told that this was Tapsi's favorite. "*Subba sahib,*" I beseeched, my voice almost reverential. "Perhaps we should drink first and then talk."

Tapsi released another one of his trademark grunts. He glared at me but took the bottle all the same. We drank. Finally, we talked.

I respected Tapsi. Tapsi had never collected scientific data. He had never performed regression analysis. He had never read a biology textbook. He had never learned to read. What Tapsi did know about was life in the jungle. He knew the habits of the rhinos, what they ate, where they slept, how they mated. I might have possessed textbook knowledge, but he had a lifetime of laboratory hours in the wild.

We began to work together, spending days wandering the jungles of Chitwan on the back of an elephant. Often, my lack of field experience was painfully obvious. At other times, we worked together well and even played with his elephants.

One winter evening, as twilight drew its gray shades, Tapsi turned our elephant away from the river. "*Chal-chal,*" he said, "move, move," pressing his toes into the soft flesh behind the elephant's ear. The hum of insects pervaded the atmosphere; chattering flocks of emerald parakeets played in groves of curry-leaf trees and Indian rosewood. A herd of chital deer grazed on saccharum grass, their spotted coats blending with the lengthening shadows.

Riding on the broad back of an elephant, I scanned the darkening banks of the Rapti River in the jungle of southern Nepal, straining to catch a glimpse of more rhinos.

"Pay attention, you city boy," barked Tapsi. "We are coming to the Rapti, where you may see rhinos crossing the river. Learn to keep your eyes and ears open all the time," he ordered, a crooked grin cracking his dark, deeply lined face. "I will make a *shikari* out of you." A *shikari* is a hunter or a game scout.

We approached the Rapti River. A fisherman was casting his net from a dugout canoe. A few yards upstream, an egret was standing motionless on the riverbank. Nearby, a pied kingfisher hovered over shallow backwater. I watched it dive into the water but could not tell if it caught a fish.

"Look," said Tapsi, pointing to an opening in the forest that revealed the waters of the river. And there it stood, a modern-day dinosaur, a massive two-ton creature with armorlike skin, grazing on water plants in the shallows. The soft yellow glow of the setting sun lit a silk cotton tree. The rhino's large, dark shape contrasted with the gold, snowcapped peaks of the Himalayas, fifty miles to the north. This was Chitwan, a pristine Asian jungle. The land has nurtured the rhino for thousands of years.

As we got closer, the rhino moved out of the water. He walked along the riverbank, urinating backwards and spraying urine more than two yards away. I had never seen any animal pee like that. A single horn, about eight inches long, emerged from his snout. I wondered if the rhino knew that his horn was not a boon to, but the bane of, his survival. Its high price tag—in thousands of dollars—often spelled the rhino's death; it attracted poachers from all over Asia who exploited the horn for its perceived medicinal and ornamental value. Did he know that humans believe that his urine cures asthma, stomachache, and tuberculosis, and his meat is supposed to create male vigor?

This big male seemed unconcerned by my thoughts. Using his protruding lips, the rhino continued to forage along the riverbank. He reached a pile of dung and sniffed it. The sniff seemed to induce the rhino to empty his own bowels immediately. He turned around and proceeded to defecate on the pile of dung by first walking backwards, then dropping his new pile of oval-shaped dung, slightly smaller than a soccer ball. It was a strange way to defecate.

"That is the rhino's latrine," muttered Tapsi, pointing to the pile of dung with his stick. "After inspecting a latrine, rhinos usually defecate at the same place. This is how they communicate with each other and find out who is around the area. A calf will usually defecate immediately after its mother does."

As I watched night fall in Chitwan, thoughts raced through my mind. What use was my book learning when faced with a real-life rhino? How could I possibly give orders to someone like Tapsi, who had spent his whole life in the jungle? Before I could assume my responsibilities as the wildlife biologist in charge of Chitwan's rhinos, I had to become an apprentice to the people who best understood the creatures of the jungle.

On a hot afternoon in July 1968, Tapsi and I were wallowing with some of his elephants in the Rapti River. Waist deep in the water, he was scrubbing the back of Himal Kali, a female elephant, when he came up with an idea—an idea years ahead of its time.

"City boy," he muttered. "I have watched you closely. As time marches on, you will grow up, not only to be a powerful person in His Majesty's Government but also a skilled wildlife technician."

I did not know where he was going with this train of thought. Flattery was never in Tapsi's vocabulary. I stared at him. Words were unnecessary. "Please the king," he told me in a fatherly voice. "Ask him to send you abroad for higher studies. When you return to Nepal, you must find a new home for my Chitwan rhinos."

"New home for rhinos?" I questioned.

"The survival of rhinos is at best uncertain," he continued. "Currently, they are all in one place here in Chitwan. What if a disease or any other sickness wipes out the rhinos from Chitwan? We need a second home for rhinos."

"Where?" I asked, realizing that the old man was right. Trying to save rhinos only in Chitwan was akin to carrying all your eggs in one basket. Anthrax had been reported to kill wild boar and cattle, both warm-blooded mammals, like rhinos.

"Bardia, to begin with," he responded. "Bardia is remote and isolated from any human habitation and would provide a safe haven for the rhinos. If they do well in Bardia, you can move them to other game reserves such as Sukla Phanta and Koshi Tappu." Bardia was a wildlife preserve about four hundred kilometers west of Chitwan. As there were no roads, it was only accessible during the dry season.

Tapsi's speech was not consistent with his character, particularly when he did not use his choicest curse words. It was hard to tell what was driving him. But he was right. Any unforeseen epidemic, such as one caused by foot-and-mouth disease, could wipe out the rhino population in Chitwan. After all, prime rhino habitat is adjacent to villages, and rhinos often grazed together with villagers' cows and buffaloes.

I knew that a translocation of rhinos had never been done before. It was a utopian and idealistic concept, yet this uneducated elephant driver had a vision. His thinking and plans to save the rhinos from extinction were quite progressive.

I was lost for words. It was a touching moment. Though I knew it was a pipe dream, I found myself saying, "*Subba sahib*, I swear in the name of Ban Devi, the Goddess of the Forest, that I want to be the first to provide your Chitwan rhinos a new home in Bardia."

A few years later Tapsi died peacefully in his sleep while I was abroad. But his vision lived on with me. Providing new homes for rhinos became an obsession that I nurtured for a long time.

2

CHEATING YAMA,
THE GOD OF DEATH

Unlike Tapsi, I was the son of a well-to-do family in the Kathmandu Valley, in central Nepal. Mother had borne sixteen children, nine girls and seven boys. I was number fifteen and my younger brother, who was born five years later was number sixteen. Only seven, five girls and two boys, survived infancy. Having lost all five male siblings before me when they were less than six months old, my mother desperately wanted a son.

Sons are a necessity in traditional Nepalese culture. It is a son's duty to look after his parents in their old age. At their death the son is required to light their funeral pyre, which ensures a clear passage for the departing soul as it cycles through myriad incarnations. Daughters are not allowed to perform the last rites of the dead. In short, a Nepalese son provides security for his parents in their old age and facilitates the passage of their souls after they are dead. Desperate to have a son survive, my mother consulted an astrologer when I was three months in her womb.

"Go on a pilgrimage to the Temple of Manakamana, The-Goddess-That-Grants-Every-Wish," advised the astrologer. "Offer a goat sacrifice and pray in peace for a son."

Mother journeyed on foot for seven days. At the temple on top of a mountain five thousand feet high, my mother purified her body with a twenty-four-hour fast and a cold-water bath. She sacrificed a male black goat, offered libation to the Goddess, and quietly prayed for a son. The Goddess seemed to have heard her prayers— six months later, on September 21, 1945, I was born late in the evening at home. My birth was supervised by a midwife with no training in modern medicine; Nepal had no maternity hospitals at that time.

"The Praying Virgin sang religious melodies when you entered earth," my mother told me on my seventh birthday. The Praying Virgin was a deeply religious twenty-five-year-old woman with a good voice for Hindu hymns and supposed psychic powers. She was also my mother's friend.

"My joy knew no bounds when you were born," my mother continued. "I cuddled you to my breast and summoned the priests and the astrologers to chart your horoscope. Alas! My happiness was short-lived. The astrologer told me that your lifeline was similar to that of your previous siblings. He said that you might die within six months. I was scared when the astrologer predicted your karma. I threw you on the lap of the Praying Virgin and cried and cried in a corner. The Praying Virgin soothed my sorrows by singing. She also suggested a rite to cheat the God of Death."

"What happened next?" I questioned, with the anxiety of a child.

"The first thing I did was to make you a girl," said my mother, with a grin on her oval face.

"How did you do that?" I questioned with rising curiosity.

"I certainly did not castrate you," she giggled. "I left you in the hands of the Praying Virgin." Then she paused and told me the story of how Yama, the God of Death, was cheated by my birth rite.

The Praying Virgin threaded a needle with a black string. While a priest prayed, she pierced the left nostril of my nose and sewed on the black string. In Nepalese Hindu religion only girls pierce their noses to wear nose rings, a must for brides. Consequently, the Praying Virgin made a girl out of me. Then she took me from my house in the middle of the night and hid me in a bush at a point where four paths crossed. Four crossings are ill fated in Nepal. People believe that Yama, the Hindu God of Death, will not touch human people when they are in the center of a four-crossing, even when they are enrolled on his death roster.

By prior arrangement a Kasai woman, a member of an untouchable caste, picked me up out of the bush. She took me to her home and breastfed me. Then she bought me from my mother with a tiny copper coin called *chun-dam*, equal to one-quarter of a penny.

The coin represented payment to my mother for nurturing me in her womb. The untouchable woman pierced my ears with the same needle used for my nose and threaded a ring of black string through each of my earlobes. Then she sold me to a Chautaria woman, a member of a warrior caste clan, for more money—a small silver coin worth fifty pennies. After the purchase, the priest formally declared me a Chautaria and not a Brahmin, my caste at birth. The family astrologer charted a new horoscope under the guidance of the Praying Virgin, who was singing in a state of mystic frenzy. The new horoscope showed my lifeline to be longer. My mother was relieved. Her friend, the Praying Virgin, later became a popular spiritual leader in Kathmandu, known to devotees as Bhaktini Amma, the Praying Mother.

"I made you a woman and changed your caste twice so you would survive," my mother said to me, finishing the story.

The rites must have worked, and Yama, the God of Death, was fooled. I did survive, long enough to take care of my parents in their old age and to light their funeral pyres.

We lived in a large house in the middle of a rice field between the ancient cities of Kathmandu and Patan. It took only thirty minutes to walk to Darbar Square, the city center of Kathmandu. The air and water were clean, and the valley was lush and green. There were only a few cars in Nepal, and most of them belonged to the royal family or their relatives. People traveled on foot or bicycles.

My father used his horse to get around town. I never knew Father to do any work because he retired early. My mother told me that he served in some kind of intelligence work for the Ranas and used to travel to India and Tibet quite often. He talked little about his past.

Father spent most of his time at home with a stable that housed four horses, ten cows, and a big ram. He also kept about three dozen pigeons up in the attic and six pairs of quails in a dark room on the ground floor. Every morning he was at the stable, talking to and grooming his horses, while the stable boys milked the cows. Later in the morning, he was on the roof of the house to fly his pigeons. He would grab a few of his best pigeons and hurl them into the sky to watch them soar high. His best pigeons flew for hours and often somersaulted a few times in the sky before landing back on the roof. I could not understand what pleasure he got by watching a dozen pigeons soar and somersault.

On Saturdays, which are holidays in Nepal, his friends gathered in our living room for a quail fight. Two male quails fought each bout that lasted for about three minutes. Holding their best fighter quail tightly in their fists, my father's friends would squat around in a circle and gently brush their quails against their opponent's bird. Then the quails were released on the ground. The fight would start, as one of the birds would attack its opponent with a kick. The winner was decided based on the number of kicks within a set time agreed to before the match. If any quail ceased to fight or flew away, it would be declared the loser.

I also recall a ram fight in our yard. Father's ram lost. After it was head-butted viciously by its opponent, it took off toward the stable in a fright. Later that evening, as a loser, it ended up in the pot for a feast. That was the last I saw of any pet ram or pet sheep in our house. However, my father kept his quails, pigeons, cows, and horses until he died in December 1968.

We also had two dogs, a Tibetan mastiff and a Lhasa apso. They were presents from my father's *Mit*, a Tibetan trader and Father's best friend. A *Mit* is a formal friend, established through a ritual of exchanging a copper coin, a grass garland, and a never-to-lie and never-to-betray oath of honor to keep friendship at any cost. Father's Tibetan *Mit* visited Nepal at least once every two years. He and a horde of his entourage stayed with us. Then the house would be lively with music and exotic Tibetans milling about the garden. The air became rich with an aroma of Tibetan herbs and marijuana that my father relished occasionally, particularly when he partied with his friends. Alcohol is not allowed in a proper Brahmin house. My father's *Mit* disappeared around 1962, after the Chinese invaded Tibet. Using his contacts and influence through the Royal Nepalese Consulate in Lhasa, Father tried to find him; his search was futile. Yet every winter he expected his friend to walk in through the door. His *Mit* never came back.

Father made a fortune before he reached fifty, but he spent it all on his imported horses, pigeons, and quails and on his lavish parties and expensive gifts for his friends. Father died suddenly from a heart attack in 1968 at the age of seventy, surrounded by his friends and family. Even at death he had a cigarette in his mouth and a big smile on his face.

My mother was a *dharmaputri* of Juddha Shamsher, a Rana prime minister. *Dharmaputri* means "religious daughter," akin to a goddaughter but more formalized than in the West. She had her own wealth. Like my father, my mother was a spendthrift and loved to travel and entertain her friends and family. Even so, our parents left us a parcel of prime property and a legacy of love and happiness. Above all, they provided us with the best education that money could buy.

Two of my sisters were unmarried and lived with us. The other three were married before they were twelve years of age. My third eldest sister was married when she was only eight. She once told me an amusing story. Since her husband had four look-alike brothers, it took her months to figure out which one was her husband. Her husband was also a child—only two years older. Along with his brother and their wives, they played together and slept together in a row in a big room, girls on one side and boys on the other.

I went to St. Xavier's, a Catholic boarding school run by Jesuit priests in Godavari, a well-forested enclave at the eastern edge of Kathmandu Valley. At times I got into fights with kids in the neighborhood, who often yelled "*achoot Kisten, achoot Kisten*" to insult me as an "untouchable Christian." It was not only the kids but also their parents who viewed our school with suspicion. They felt that the Jesuit teachers were either spies or proselytizers who converted Hindus and Buddhists into Catholics, yet my eldest brother-in-law, Sharada Prasad, a former schoolteacher, who later became known as the father of modern education in Nepal, was a visionary. He had seen that the Jesuits provided the best education throughout South Asia. They did not interfere in local politics, religion, culture, or festivities.

Besides learning English, I also learned to swim and play hockey and soccer. The school was located at the foot of the wildlife-rich Mt. Pulchoki, the lush, green, ten-thousand-foot-high mountain southeast of Kathmandu. It was only natural that outdoor life became my passion.

After completing my junior high school at St. Xavier's, I spent two years in local public schools in the cities of Patan and Kathmandu. It was during these years that I discovered the richness and diversity of Nepalese culture. Almost every street and alley had a temple, with rusty brick buildings, overhanging porches, or richly crafted windows and a courtyard, where people prayed, sang, and danced. The culture of Kathmandu, always vibrant, was centered on these ancient temples. Here people sold, traded, and bartered goods and services and talked at great length. During the Dasain, a religious Hindu festival that celebrates the victory of the good over the evil, I visited Kot and watched hundreds of goats and buffaloes being sacrificed. Kot is a sequestered courtyard in the center of Kathmandu, where in 1846 a nobleman named Jung Bahadur Rana massacred hundreds of members of the Nepalese aristocracy and established himself as the de facto ruler of Nepal, leaving the Shah kings as puppets. His family, the Ranas, ruled Nepal for 104 years until they were overthrown in 1950. It was during the Rana regime that Kot was declared a ceremonial site for sacrificing goats and buffaloes to celebrate the Dasain festival.

Goats were mostly sacrificed by slitting their throats, after which their blood was sprinkled in the courtyards. Buffaloes were beheaded with one swipe of a big *khukuri*, the traditional Nepalese machete. It was also during the Dasain that I flew my kite and had many fights, particularly with my sisters and many cousins. My younger brother was too small to play with us or join my many visits to the temples of Nepal during the festival season. The valley of Kathmandu is full of temples and shrines that draw Hindu and Buddhist devotees from all over the world. On the birthdays of Lord Buddha, I trekked to Swayambhu Nath temple, perched on a hill west of Kathmandu. There, I fed the monkeys on the long uphill steps before paying homage to the Buddha amid chanting monks and pilgrims who came from Tibet.

On the days of Shivaratri, the Night of God Shiva, I visited the Pasupati Nath Temple with my friends. Shivaratri is one of the most auspicious festivals for the Hindus. It is celebrated on the fourteenth day of the fading moon in the Nepalese lunar month of Magh-Falgun (February-March in the Gregorian calendar) at Pasupati Nath, one of the holiest shrines of God Shiva located on the banks of Bagmati River in Kathmandu. On Shivaratri, pilgrims from all over the world visit this temple to take a dip in the Bagmati River and worship Shiva. These pilgrims include the Nagas (naked ones) that belong to a sect of Sadhus. *Sadhu* is a loose Hindu term for a person who has given up the four human quests: *Kama* (Pleasure), *Artha* (Wealth), *Shakti* (Power), and *Dharma* (Duty). Though the Nagas are a minority among the thousands of pilgrims, they are the most uninhibited sects in Hinduism, and their practices are believed to date back to 1500 BC.

The Nagas also believe in absolute freedom of mind and body. They openly smoke hashish in the belief that it pleases Lord Shiva. Although some use flimsy loincloth or a wooden structure to cover their private parts, many of them cover themselves only with *vbhooti*, a sacred ash from the *dhuni* (fireplace) of Yogis (holy men) that is believed to have powers to drive away all evils. According to the *Puran*, one of the oldest Hindu scriptures, all sins will be forgiven if one takes a pilgrimage to Pasupati Nath temple on the day of Shivaratri. Though the sight of bearded and stark-naked Sadhus covered with ash amused me, my pilgrimage to the holy places in Kathmandu was also a rite of passage for me in the mid-1960s.

By the late sixties, a new breed of pilgrims started flocking to Kathmandu. Unlike the naked Indian Sadhus, they were the well-dressed twentieth-century Western tourists. They also introduced into Nepal the nasty habit of poking their cameras at people who were doing their normal chores or were at religious shrines. Soon the tourists' children followed. But these children were different from their parents. They sported long hair, wore gaudy clothes, and rarely carried a camera. Like the Indian Sadhus, they cherished marijuana and hashish, which were cheap and legal in Nepal. By the seventies Kathmandu had become a haven for the hippies of Europe and America. In the city center, the sound of music, drums, and prayers were soon replaced by the loud voices of street hawkers selling hashish and fake Tibetan and Nepalese artifacts and exchanging American dollars for Nepalese rupees on the black market. Tourism had come to Nepal to stay in the 1960s and became its largest industry.

As a youth I had enjoyed nothing more than exploring the fields and woodlands in the Himalayan foothills, hunting birds and butterflies. My parents expected me to follow my uncle's footsteps and join the diplomatic service of His Majesty's Government of Nepal. But my love for adventure and outdoor life led me to study biology in Nepal and forestry in India, even though it was not regarded as a prestigious profession in Nepal. After graduating from high school, I enrolled at Tri-Chandra College in Kathmandu to study biology. There I learned to smoke cigarettes and to dissect frogs and cockroaches for my biology class. After graduating with a bachelor of science degree in 1964, I disappeared from Kathmandu for three months. I was bored and restless at home and had been looking for excuses to visit remote parts of the Nepal Himalayas. Consequently, I joined a clandestine British television crew, which illegally crossed Nepal's northern frontiers. We trespassed in a restricted area to film Tibetan guerrilla fighters waging hit-and-run warfare against the occupying Chinese forces. This film captured a handful of Tibetan Khampa warriors blasting several Chinese military trucks and killing a dozen Red Army soldiers. For the first time this film showed the outside world an internal uprising of poorly armed Tibetans against the mighty Chinese occupant army. I was nearly thrown in jail by the Nepalese government on my return to Kathmandu after the filming expedition. General Sher Bahadur Malla, military secretary to King Mahendra and father of a friend of mine from St. Xavier's School, saved me from being thrown into prison for covert acts against the national interests of Nepal. The good general believed my story of the happenings across the Himalayas. He realized that I was merely a careless and innocent youth who had been in the wrong place at the wrong time.

In 1965 I left Nepal for two years to study forestry in the Indian Forest College in Dehra Dun. Upon graduation in 1967, I took a job as a wildlife officer with Nepal's Ministry of Forests. I was twenty-two years old and full of energy.

One of my first assignments was to explore Chitwan, a remote jungle in southern Nepal, also known as the Terai.

3

A TALE OF THE TERAI

It was a cool and typical Terai evening with a clear sky and a big bright December moon in 1968. We were squatting around a campfire near the Chitwan elephant stable, on the edge of a forest, when Tapsi began his folktale.

"The creator was not drunk but stoned when he made the rhino," said Tapsi, gazing deep into the burning logs and sipping his favorite rum.

Tapsi claimed that God Brahma gave life to the rhino more than ten million years ago. The Hindu God, who created the universe, enriched the earth with every form of plant and animal life but was still not content with his creations. He summoned Viswakarma, his master designer.

"Viswakarma," commanded Brahma, "make me a new and perfect creature. It must not resemble any beast in this world in shape, size, or personality."

"Yes, my Lord," uttered Viswakarma. What choice did he have? His master, the creator of the world, had hit a creative impasse. Now he had to come up with something to avoid the wrath of Brahma, his master.

Tapsi lit a bidi and exhaled a cloud of smoke. After a short pause, he continued with his story.

Viswakarma decided to travel across seven seas, seven mountains, and seven lands in search of an inspiration. After wandering for eons through forests, river valleys, and mountains, Viswakarma reached Mount Kailas, the abode of Lord Shiva, God of Gods.

Shiva was in deep meditation. All of his eyes, including his third eye in the middle of his forehead, were closed. Viswakarma then stood on one leg, folded his palms, and prayed nonstop for ten thousand years, chanting, *"Om Namo Shivaya Om Namo Shivaya Om Namo Shivaya,"* a Sanskrit prayer that means "Praise the eternal sound of Shiva's name."

Viswakarma's devotion impressed Shiva. He finally opened the third eye and roared, "Viswakarma! I am pleased with you. Why are you here? What can I do for you?"

Thrilled and relieved, Viswakarma kissed the earth, folded his palms, and cried at the top of his lungs, "O Lord of thirty-three million gods, preserver of the truth, destroyer of the demons, I traveled through many lands, crossed many oceans, and drank from many rivers to seek your blessing."

At this point, Tapsi paused, coughed, and cleared his throat, before spitting out a gob of thick saliva into the fire. Then he washed his throat with a shot of rum from a glass in front of him before going on with his story.

Viswakarma told the story of his journeys, spicing things up a little, before he got to the point: "O God of Gods, my Master Lord Brahma has ordered me to make a new creature, something that has never been seen before on earth. What am I to do?"

The Almighty's advice was short and simple: "Create an animal as elegant as Biphanke Ghoda, the flying horse; as holy as the River Ganges; and as fat, strong, and arrogant as Nandi, my bull."

Shiva placed his right hand on Viswakarma's forehead and blessed him. "Even humans shall not destroy the new animal you create," proclaimed Shiva. "They shall preserve your extraordinary creation forever."

"But how shall I go about creating such a beast?" inquired Viswakarma.

"That is your concern, not mine," retorted Shiva, before he settled back into meditation.

"Oh, my gods," thought Viswakarma. "I'm no better off than I was when I started out."

To stoke his mind, Viswakarma smoked marijuana nonstop for twenty-one thousand years, at which point his efforts were rewarded with visual grace. Viswakarma started hallucinating a solution to his problem and went right to work.

He picked the best parts of many animals on earth and stitched them together. The result was beyond his expectation, a masterpiece of the art of imperfection. His creation had the skin of an elephant, the hooves of a horse, the ears of a hare, the eyes of a crocodile, the brains of a bear, the heart of a lion, and horns like Nandi, Shiva's bull. In his zeal, Viswakarma creatively twisted, molded, and further modified these parts, even fusing two horns into one.

Viswakarma then took his invention to Brahma.

The beast was clumsy and ugly. But its clumsiness concealed a wonderful gracefulness. And its ugliness hid an elegant beauty. Brahma was pleased. He breathed into the creature the elixir of life and freed the beast into the forests of the Terai under the watchful shadows of the Himalayas, the abode of God Shiva. He gave it the name *"Gainda,"* meaning "fat and stubborn."

Tapsi ended his story with a ring of high-pitched laughter. My thoughts were more sobering, however. I was reflecting on how ironic it was that the Almighty had not foreseen the turn of events in the twentieth century. Poachers and the growing population of Nepal have destroyed the rhino and its habitat, yet I was fascinated by Tapsi's fable. I thought that the fable of Viswakarma's rhino also echoed some scientific truth. When scientists began classifying the world's creatures in the eighteenth century, they were unable to assign the rhinoceros to any existing family in the animal kingdom.

Consequently, they classified the rhinoceros as a separate and distinctive family of its own, the *Rhinocerotidae*, which means "nose horn."

One of the five surviving species in this family is *Rhinoceros unicornis*, the greater one-horned Asian rhinoceros of the Himalayan kingdom of Nepal, the sequestered land of Tapsi's tribe, the Tharus.

Tapsi was a great storyteller. But Tapsi did not know the history of his own people any more than he knew the prehistoric origins of the rhino. What he knew about Chitwan he had learned with his own eyes, his own ears, and his own nose. He was ugly, foul mouthed, and insubordinate. He was a lowly, uneducated Tharu. I was a college-educated Brahmin. But in the jungles of Chitwan, on the back of an elephant, questions of social status seemed irrelevant. It was a relief for me. It released me from the tight strictures of my traditional Kathmandu upbringing. Tapsi did not give a damn if I was a Brahmin, a Tharu, or a king. If I wanted to learn about the jungle, I would have to do it on his terms. Often, I could not help but feel that Tapsi himself was like a rhino. Beneath the rough exterior hid a graceful master of the jungle. If I was ever going to do my job correctly, I was going to have to follow Tapsi's ways. I was going to have to close the textbooks on wildlife biology, open my eyes, and search deeply to understand the people and the culture of the land of the Tharus.

Most of present-day Nepal was formed fifty million years ago, as the Himalayas began to rise to form a barrier between the cold, windswept Tibetan highlands and the sun-baked plains of India. Yet not all of Nepal is rugged and mountainous. Along its southern border with India are flatlands, where the river valleys are broad and gentle. Here the altitude averages about three hundred feet above sea level to form an extension of the Indo-Gangetic Plains. This is the Terai. Hot and humid, this steaming tropical jungle is rich in wildlife. Chitwan is the heart of the Nepalese Terai.

Chitwan's natural history is unique in South Asia. Akin to a safe depository in a Swiss bank, the grasslands and forests are repositories of biological diversity. Consequently, the land of Tapsi Subba's people, the Tharus, was a sporting ground for big-game hunting for the powerful and the privileged. It was known as the Royal Shikar Reserve—the hunting grounds of the royal family.

Massive royal hunts were more than just a diversion. They served as relaxed venues for making important political decisions. In this way, the royal rhino hunts were similar to corporate-sponsored hunts in the United States, where business deals are struck far away from the pressures of the office, while the participants squint down the barrel of a loaded gun at doves, pheasants, or deer.

Strangely enough, the tradition of the royal hunt did a great deal to protect the wildlife of Nepal. The hunts were infrequent. They were also rotated to different parts of the country, so that the carnage of each individual hunt never endangered the total population of any animals. To facilitate the hunts the rulers of Nepal established royal hunting preserves, complete with permanent stables for the elephants. They prohibited cultivation to protect wildlife habitat and prevented poaching.

The job of protecting Chitwan was also made easier because the Terai was not an attractive place to live. Summers were hot. Extensive wet areas within the jungles and grasslands provided breeding grounds for malaria-carrying mosquitoes. The disease-infested forests were so dangerous that they served as an efficient barrier against the British and other potential invaders from India to the south. In short, the rulers of Nepal realized that protecting the forests of the Terai helped them protect their kingdom, and they relied on Tapsi's people, the Tharus, to protect the forests.

Tapsi had served as the elephant driver for kings and prime ministers of Nepal during many great hunts. He had done his job well and had earned a reputation as a top elephant driver who could position hunters for their best shot at a rhino or a tiger. Tapsi was a legend in his own right. Stories about him were common in the Forest Department of Nepalese government.

One described how he lost his teeth. That day Tapsi drove the elephant of Prime Minister Juddha Shamsher Rana for a tiger hunt in Chitwan. He worked his elephant into a position for the prime minister to have a chance at an enormous trophy tiger. The prime minister had the tiger in his sights. The elephant moved as he squeezed the trigger. The prime minister missed his shot and his chance to take home a trophy.

"You idiot!" the prime minister screamed in anger and frustration at Tapsi Subba. "You ruined my shot." Tapsi shrugged. He did not say a word. But his expression implied, "Don't blame me or my elephant if you can't be quick and shoot straight."

Furious, the prime minister lifted his rifle and slammed the butt into Tapsi's face, breaking most of his teeth. The unfair and unprovoked blow made a lasting impression on Tapsi's spirit as well as his smile. Princes. Kings. Dignitaries. College degrees. Fancy clothes. So what! Tapsi did not give a damn. He had been hired and fired from his job a dozen times. There was no one who matched Tapsi's skills in the jungle. He held the power in Chitwan. And he knew it.

During the seven years I lived in Chitwan, I grew fond of the Tharus. I found them to be nonaggressive, egalitarian, and proud of the rhinos in their homeland. They also have great skills in turning local grasses, canes, and timber into beautiful household items like baskets, ropes, mats, and elephant saddles. Though I had many trusted Tharu friends, such as Tapsi, I had little knowledge of their tribal history.

On some evenings I enjoyed sitting around a bonfire with the Tharu elephant keepers, forest rangers, and Tapsi. We shared food, drinks, and stories around our campfire. It was in the evenings that I learned a lot about the Tharu way of life.

The Tharus are shy and unobtrusive and live in harmony with their land and forests. Dwelling on the forest edge, they use it for grazing their cattle and for fruits, vegetables, firewood, and game. Tharu society is strongly influenced by Hinduism. Their religious organization generally operates on three levels: district, village, and family. The Rajgurau, on the top tier, is the district high priest. He holds a hereditary position that is believed to be linked with old Tharu kingdoms in the mountains. In the old days they were given a royal seal by the rulers of Nepal that permitted them to practice religious rituals. During such rituals, many goats, chickens, and pigeons were sacrificed to please the deities, and the high priests attained a trancelike state. On the village level, shrines are located in the center of most villages. These are usually represented by pieces of stone or wood to symbolize various gods. The main god is Brahamaawaa, who is supposed to relish goats and pigeons. In contrast, one of the lesser deities, called Parihar, likes pigs, while Jakhim prefers chickens and is supposed to provide good harvests. Dihacandi, a goddess, along with god Jogi Haawaa will destroy the community if not worshiped properly. Likewise, the local village god Thanagaidi is linked to the forests; he provides protection from wild animals.

Village rituals often involve the whole community. They are performed by the gaongarau, or village priest, and are held on fixed dates based on the Hindu lunar calendar. Each household also has its individual ghargurau, or house priest. This position is not hereditary but is chosen by the individual family members. An important service performed by the ghargurau is associated with women. Like ancient Greeks and Romans, Tharus believe that deities can be good or evil. After marriage, bad influences generated by deities from a woman's natal home move to her husband's house, causing sickness to her husband's family. A key function of the house priest is to appease deities, to curb their evil, and to bring out the good in them.

In the past Tharus married at any age. Occasionally, arranged marriages took place between unborn children. However, such marriages were annulled if both turned out to be of the same sex. Now, new laws have made these practices illegal. Unlike orthodox Hindus, Tharus can divorce and remarry freely. Polygamy is not practiced, but levirate, where a man marries his brother's widow, is acceptable. This practice ensures that the children remain within one joint family.

Besides the Tharus, ethnic groups such as the Bote, Musahar, and Kumal have lived in Chitwan for hundreds of years. Botes are fishermen. They make a living by selling or bartering fish or transporting people across rivers in their dugout canoes. Musahar means mouse eater. After the rice harvest, Musahars track the field mice that have stolen their rice and stored it in underground dens. They dig out the dens and recover the grain stored underground. They also trap and barbecue the thieving vermin and eat them as a form of delicacy. Kumal are potters. They supply the village with clay pots and other household items.

Mass migration of the hill people to Chitwan began in the late 1950s and peaked in the 1970s. These migrants include almost all of the ethnic groups from the hills and lowlands of Nepal. They include Mongoloid races such as Gurungs, Rais, Tamangs, and Magars; Caucasian or mixed races such as Brahmins, Chettris, and Newars; and the Madhesis, the darker Terai Nepalese such as Yadavs, Thakurs, and Kayasthas.

Some social scientists speculate that the Tharus migrated to southern Nepal from northern Nepal and Tibet about a thousand years ago. Others believe that the Tharus fled to southern Nepal from Northwest India during the Islamic invasion of the subcontinent in the fourteenth century. Like the Tharus' roots, no one is sure about the origin of the greater one-horned Asian rhinoceros of Nepal.

4

RHINO ROOTS

Twenty-five million years ago, giraffes, eland, kudus, chimpanzees, baboons, hippopotami, and a wide variety of other animals inhabited the swamps and forests of the Indian subcontinent. One of the animals was a massive pachyderm that looked like a cross between a modern-day giraffe and a rhinoceros. It stood eighteen feet tall and measured twenty feet long. This ruminant, aptly named the giant giraffe rhinoceros, was the largest land mammal ever to live on earth. Based upon studies of fossils in the Siwalik Hills to the south of the Royal Chitwan National Park, some scientists believe that the progeny of the rhinos in Nepal was a pachyderm called *Rhinoceros unicornis fossilus*. This descendent of the giant giraffe rhinoceros is believed to have been common in Chitwan about a million years ago.

As the Himalayan Mountains began to rise as a result of geological shifts, the climate in the Terai changed gradually, making it impossible for many species to survive. *Rhinoceros unicornis fossilus* also became extinct. But it is believed to be related to the five living species of *Rhinocerotidae* that dwell in isolated patches on the hot and humid grasslands of Asia's tropical forests and the open, dry savannas of Africa.

The rhinos of Nepal are also known as Indian rhinos, yet the name rhinoceros does not come from India but from Greece. *Rhino* means "nose," and *ceros* means "horn" in Greek. Likewise, in Latin *uni* is "one," and *cornis* is "horn." However, the one-horned species of Chitwan is not the only surviving species of rhinos. Today, five species of rhino exist on the earth: two species in Africa and three species in Asia.

The two-horned African square-lipped or white rhinoceros is not actually white but dark. The names come from the Afrikaans word *weit*, which describes the wide mouth of the animal. Early English settlers in South Africa confused the word *weit* with "white" and named it the African white rhinoceros. Next to the elephant, it is the largest living land mammal. There are two discrete populations of this species: the northern African white rhinoceros and the southern African white rhinoceros. The former is almost extinct. A relict population of twenty to thirty individuals survives in the Garamba National Park in the Democratic Republic of the Congo. However, their future is threatened, as a brutal civil war clouds this former Belgian colony, once named Zaire.

The southern African white rhinoceros, as its name implies, is mostly restricted to an area south of the Zambezi River in southern Africa. Hunting by European colonials reduced the population from millions in the eighteenth century to less than a hundred by the first half of the twentieth century. Nevertheless, with effective conservation measures, largely by the South Africans, its population has rebounded to more than eleven thousand individuals. The success story of the southern African white rhinoceros demonstrates the resilience of the rhino and its ability to bounce back with effective protection from poaching and habitat destruction.

The other species of African rhino, the two-horned black rhinoceros, is smaller and more widely distributed than the African white rhinoceros. In the 1950s more than sixty-five thousand black rhino roamed throughout Africa. Today, less than thirty-five hundred rhinos are left in the African continent, most in Kenya, Tanzania, South Africa, Zimbabwe, Namibia, and Malawi.

Asia has three species of rhinos. Two of them, the Indian and the Javan rhinoceros, have only one horn. They are also related, as they belong to the same genus, *Rhinoceros*. The third species, the Asian two-horned rhinoceros or Sumatran rhinoceros, is distinct and belongs to the genus *Dicerorhinus*. It is related to the woolly rhinos and other unicorn-like creatures that roamed the earth more than a million years ago. Both the Javan and Sumatran rhinos are dwellers of the dense tropical rainforests, whereas the Indian rhino prefers grasslands of the floodplains and likes to live close to watercourses.

The smaller, one-horned species of Asian rhino, the Javan rhinoceros, is aptly named the lesser one-horned Asian rhinoceros, in contrast to the greater Asian one-horned or Indian rhino. Recognized as Asia's rarest mammals, only fifty to sixty Javan rhinos currently survive in the Ujung Kulon National Park in Java, Indonesia. Another small population of ten to fifteen individuals has recently been reported from the Cat Loc Nature Reserve in the Dong Nai region of Vietnam. They have disappeared from Thailand, and their status is unknown in Laos and Cambodia, which still have some pristine tropical rain forest suitable for rhinos. As most of Cambodia is heavy with land mines from the Khmer Rouge, extensive ground surveys to confirm sightings in that country have not been possible.

The two-horned Sumatran rhino seems to be doing better than the Javan rhinoceros. Between one hundred and two hundred individual rhinos belonging to the *sumatrensi* subspecies are found on the island of Sumatra; their population is scattered mainly over three sites: Kerinci Sabalat, with a population of sixty to seventy; Gunung Leuser, with fifty to sixty, and Serbojadi, with fifteen to twenty-five rhinos. Other populations numbering fewer than ten individuals are reported in sites such as Lokop and Torgamba. Besides those in Indonesia, some eighty to ninety

Sumatran rhinos are found in peninsular Malaysia, mainly the Endau Rompin and the Taman Negra National Parks. In addition, sixty to seventy rhinos are reported in the State of Sabah and ten in Sawarak, in Malaysia.

These hairy pachyderms, with bristlelike hairs on their back, were also once widely distributed in the foothills of the Himalayas in Bhutan and Eastern India and throughout Burma, Thailand, and Indo-China. Currently, there are only a few unconfirmed reports of their existence in Cambodia and Laos. However, a decade-old report from a scientist of the World Wildlife Fund indicating the possibilities of their existence in Vietnam generated big excitement in the media in the 1990s. Some newspapers even implied that these rare rhinos were resilient to the carpet bombing by the US Air Force, particularly the heavy usage of defoliating agents during the Vietnam war.

Two hundred years ago the Chitwan species, the Indian rhino or the greater Asian one-horned rhinoceros — *Rhinoceros unicornis* — roamed widely over the Indian plains from the banks of the Indus in present-day Pakistan in the west to Burma and South China in the east. By the 1960s they were found only in Nepal and India, with the largest concentration in Kaziranga in Indian Assam and in Chitwan in Nepal. Lesser populations of fifty or so existed in Manas, Jaldapara, Gorumara, Orang, and Pobitora in Assam and West Bengal in India. Elsewhere in Asia, the Indian rhino is extinct.

A similar fate for the rhinos of Chitwan was the last thing I wished when I began my work in Chitwan in the late 1960s. I wanted to ensure that Chitwan remained a key stronghold for rhinos in Asia, yet I had no idea how many rhinos were left in Chitwan. I did not know if Nepal still had a viable breeding population. We needed a good census.

In February 1968, I was able to carry out the first scientific survey in Chitwan and count rhinos together with Dr. Graeme Caughley, a wildlife expert assigned to Nepal by the United Nations.

He was one of the world's leading experts on the population dynamics of wild mammals.

I not only learned how to count rhinos from Caughley, but I also learned my first lesson about the clash of cultures during the rhino census.

5

CLASH OF CULTURES

It was a sunny but pleasant morning in the month of March 1968. I was in Itcharni, a patch of riverine forests at the eastern end of the rhino reserve. Hanging high on the branches of a Bhelur tree, obscured by green foliage, I watched a mother rhino and her calf as they grazed on imperata grass, using their prehensile tongues. I was close enough to see the round, warty tubules on the mother's hairless leathery hide. Her single horn was a mass of fibrous hair. It was not attached to the skull but rooted firmly on an enlarged nasal bone. The horn was about six inches long with a broken tip. Even though it was slightly damaged, I knew that the horn would keep growing throughout the thirty to fifty years of the rhino's expected lifespan.

The horn is the rhino's distinctive feature, yet its actual purpose is unknown, as the rhino does not use its horn for fighting. It is also very different from the horns of deer and antelopes. Rhino horn is not made of bone but rather compressed hairy fibers made of the same protein as in human fingernails. The rhino's chief weapon is a pair of tusklike teeth protruding from the lower jaw. Since both males and females have horns, it is unlikely that it is an ornament to attract the opposite sex. Some biologists say it is a vestigial organ, which has lost its function through evolution.

As I watched, the rhino stopped grazing. She was alert. She made a surprisingly quick turn and charged nimbly toward the bushes with her calf nervously following her. Like all rhinos, she had poor eyesight and could see no farther than a few hundred feet. But she had sharp hearing through her elliptical ears. She also had a good sense of smell. She was very protective and nervous, like all mother rhinos with their calves. Although adult rhinos have no predators, tigers have been known to kill calves on occasion.

The mother rhino I was watching resumed her grazing, as the danger she had perceived no longer existed. The calf stayed close. It looked like a three-hundred-pound puppy. I estimated its age to be three to six months, as I had read that a calf weighs one hundred to one hundred fifty pounds at birth. The calf shook its head playfully as it grazed side by side with its mother. The mother, more serious, moved her two-ton frame gracefully across the landscape, using her tongue to grab succulent shrubs, but she continued to keep a watchful eye on her playful calf. She was not as large as some of the males, who could reach six feet high at the shoulder. But she was impressive nonetheless.

In the year of 1967, after I met Tapsi Subba, I lived, breathed, ate, and slept rhinos. I tracked them from the backs of elephants and viewed them hidden in the branches of Bhelur trees. Even the Bhelur trees where I hid connected me to the rhinos. Rhinos cherish Bhelur seeds; in return, they ensure the survival and propagation of the Bhelur plant. Their digestive juices break down the seed coverings, and when rhinos pass the seeds in their dung, they are ready to germinate. Soon after, new Bhelur trees sprout. Since many rhinos habitually use the same spots to defecate, Bhelur saplings often mark rhinos' favorite toilets.

Later, in 1968, I was able to observe rhinos from high above the Bhelur trees, sticking my head out from the door of an American helicopter with a weather-beaten-faced New Zealander. The face belonged to Graeme Caughley.

Graeme and I spent hours crisscrossing Chitwan by air in an effort to make a comprehensive census of the rhino population. For our aerial census, we used a small Bell helicopter that belonged to a US company called Arizona Helicopters. It was in Nepal under contract to the US government's Agency for International Development to ferry US economic-development experts to remote parts of roadless Nepal. Besides the king's Russian-made helicopter, it was the only helicopter available in Nepal.

The pilot of our helicopter was a lanky, parrot-nosed American named Tom Pieffer. Tom sported dark glasses and a baseball hat. His outfits made him look like an American spy in a third-rate Indian movie popular in Kathmandu. It was perhaps Tom's look that triggered rumors in Kathmandu that the helicopter company was a front for CIA operations in Nepal. But Kathmandu thrives on rumors. If a foreign resident was white and well dressed, he had to be a spy, either CIA or KGB, who resided in the Himalayan Heights, an expensive gated housing community near the United States Aid headquarters. The British and French did not count any more in the spy game during the height of the Cold War. Only the Russians and Americans watched each other in Nepal in the late 1960s.

In addition, if the man in question was white and shabby, he was presumed to be a dopehead or an idol smuggler from Maru, a narrow street in the heart of Kathmandu. Maru's name changed from Pig-Alley to Freak Street in the sixties as the aroma of hashish replaced the smell of pig dung. White women did not count in the male-dominated culture of Kathmandu. Single white women were considered loose in character, and it was a game to see if they could be picked up. I dated an Anglo-Indian girl, a schoolteacher and a staunch Roman Catholic. We raised more eyebrows in my own orthodox Hindu community than did any Western resident in Nepal's capital.

Resident Europeans and Americans lived in fancy houses with high walls and many servants. They also partied together, rarely socializing with the Nepalese. Thus, they were named the "white

Ranas," after the feudal class that ruled Nepal for over a hundred years. However, my friend Graeme Caughley was an exception. His small, quaint brick house on the edge of the city was open to all: Nepalese, Indians, Europeans, Americans, and Tibetans, regardless of color, caste, or creed.

It was at one of Graeme's parties, that I met Tom Pieffer, the Bell helicopter pilot. Tom was a wildlife buff with a yen for rhinos and tigers. It did not take long for Graeme to sweet-talk Tom into counting rhinos in Chitwan from his helicopter.

Graeme Caughley, a skinny, bespectacled, red-headed New Zealander, had counted elephants in Zambia in the early sixties. In 1967 he was assigned by the United Nations to assist the government of Nepal in wildlife conservation. He was the first biologist to predict that the elephants in Zambia were seriously overpopulating their habitats. He recommended drastic reduction of elephant populations by culling both males and females. This created an uproar in the wildlife world. At the behest of European elephant lovers, Sir Peter Scott, a prominent British conservationist, intervened directly with President Kenneth Kuanda of Zambia. Caughley's recommendation was quashed, forcing him to move to Nepal from Zambia.

Unfortunately, Graeme's assessment proved correct. In the early seventies, Zambia lost more than a third of its elephant population within five years, as the overpopulated herds devastated their own habitat. However, by the eighties it was not overpopulation but poachers that drastically reduced the number of elephants in Africa. They also did not spare the African rhinos. By the seventies Africa had lost more than 90 percent of its rhinos, as prices for rhino horns soared and agricultural expansion destroyed their habitat. Both Graeme and I were concerned that this trend would reach Nepal, where human population was also soaring.

For our 1968 rhino count in Nepal, Graeme and I divided the Chitwan Valley into four sectors. We needed to get a complete picture of rhino population. We cruised over these sectors systematically in the Bell helicopter, counting rhinos from the air. We did two counts each day, one in the morning and one in the afternoon. We flew low, gliding over the treetops. We could easily see not only rhinos but also other wildlife. The way our flight lines were organized made it unlikely that we would double count any individual. In total we counted only seventy-three rhinos. However, we were certain that we had missed a few from the air, particularly in the dense forests and tall grass. Therefore, we supplemented our helicopter observations with ground census, using Tapsi's elephants.

The ground-check operation was marked by an interesting clash of cultures. Graeme was a Western scientist with Western values. I was a Kathmandu civil servant. We were working with Tapsi Subba, a self-trained man of the forest with his own style and prowess in the wild. I found that I was spending as much energy trying to bridge the gap between Western and Eastern values as I was trying to learn about the rhinos. When Caughley wanted something, he wanted it immediately. Ceremonial rituals did not matter to him, just results. This worked fine with someone like an American helicopter pilot. But when it came to an elephant and an independent-minded elephant driver, conflicts inevitably arose. Tapsi would never saddle an elephant without imposing his own methods of organizing his elephants and his junior staff. He liked to parade and bark orders at his subordinates, while he talked and stroked the trunks of all the elephants in the stable.

Graeme was an "on-time" Westerner, whereas Tapsi and his elephants operated on "Nepal time." An hour or so either way was not tardiness but flexibility to changes in weather or social obligations. Graeme equated time with money. To Tapsi and his men "time came, and time went." In any case the elephant drivers did not wear watches. They operated on their own daily rhythms or the rhythms of their elephants.

One day Tapsi had promised to deliver two elephants to pick us up at seven in the morning. We were scheduled to make a reconnaissance along the Churia foothills some ten miles from our camp. Seven, seven fifteen, seven thirty, and finally eight, ticked off the watch. But the elephants were nowhere in sight. Graeme was getting impatient. He circled around the tent as he chain-smoked several long American cigarettes. At eight thirty, Graeme blew his top. "What's going on?" he fumed. "Where are the fucking elephants?" I shrugged. It made him madder.

"I'm packing my bags," he yelled. "I will leave for Kathmandu. You and Tapsi can count the fucking rhinos by yourselves in your own sweet time. I'm fed up with the Nepalese lack of any sense of time."

I had never heard Graeme use such language. I did not respond. I left him and walked toward the elephant stable.

The elephants were tethered to their posts. A dozen Tharu girls dressed in white saris were singing and dancing in a circle around the elephants. Tapsi was squatting on the ground. He was beating a flat one-sided drum. A dozen of his men were throwing red powder at each other and the elephants. They grabbed me and painted my face with red, powdery vermilion. Suddenly, I recalled that it was the first day of Phaguwa, a Tharu festival; there was no way we could get any work done that day. Tapsi and the dancing girls were rehearsing for the day ahead. I saw no point in arguing about elephants with Tapsi, so I walked back to our camp, with a string of elephant drivers tailing me.

Back at our camp, the elephant drivers grabbed Graeme and rubbed red powder on his face. Graeme was perplexed. He relaxed only after I explained that the act of the elephant drivers was symbolic for his welfare and a holy gesture to wish him a long life. Tapsi then invited Graeme to join his men to celebrate the Phaguwa festival. He cooled off and went to the elephant camp to join Tapsi in the drum beating.

A stream of dancers visited our camp during the day. They danced around us in a circle and left only after I gave them a cup of tea and a rupee coin. Later Graeme and I joined the elephant drivers for a bath in the Rapti River to wash the red dye from our faces. In the evening, we feasted with Tapsi and his men at the Saurah elephant stable.

The Phaguwa festivities broke the ice in Graeme's behavior. Despite cultural gaps, our work progressed well. Like most of the Nepalese, Graeme smoked cigarettes. He shared his long, slender, made-in-USA Pall Mall cigarettes with Tapsi and his crew. He was also generous with his imported White Horse Scotch Whisky. In return they taught him to drive an elephant, which Graeme managed to master better than I did. Slowly, we forgot the color of Graeme's skin. He became one of us. However, living with a New Zealander in a Tharu community had its amusing moments.

Since most of the villagers in the interior of Chitwan had never seen a white man, Graeme attracted a crowd of onlookers wherever we camped. Most of the time, the onlookers were men or boys; no women. Tharu women were more reserved. They ignored men without any discrimination, Nepalese or foreigners.

"I need a bath," said Graeme, after we had pitched our tents on the outskirts of the village of Pipra. It was the first day of our camp, and we had had an easy day. Leaning against an old Jamun tree, I was relaxed and reading Nepalese short stories by Bhiviniti Tiwari, a well-known Nepalese writer. Graeme, however, was restless.

"No big deal," I responded, raising my eyes from my book. I pointed to a well-water pump on the edge of the village and added, "Take off your clothes. Squat under that big tap. I will ask Thaga, one of Tapsi's sidekicks, to pump and splash you with water."

Graeme and Thaga strolled toward the water pump. The usual fleet of spectators tailed him. I went back to my book. Suddenly the air was filled with Thaga's scream: "Nai—nai!" meaning "No—

no!" A loud chorus of laughter followed Thaga's angry shriek. I looked up from my book. Villagers were giggling and scrambling away from Graeme in all directions. Graeme was stark naked, sitting in a lotuslike position under the tap as if he were a white Buddha. Thaga was madly throwing clothes at him. I, too, burst into laughter.

Graeme had taken me literally when I told him to take off his clothes and squat under the tap. When he reached the tap, he looked around and, seeing no women, took off all of his clothes and looked forward to bathing in the nude. Because he was a New Zealander and also had lived in Africa, nudity in the company of the same sex was not taboo for Graeme. He had not realized that most Nepalese men, even in the company of other males, never expose themselves in total nudity. Exposing genitals without a loincloth, no matter how flimsy, is regarded as an insult. Some also view nudity as a bad omen.

Thaga took Graeme's innocent behavior as an insult and did not speak to Graeme for almost a week. Peace between the two was restored only after they had shared many stiff whiskies. Memory of Graeme's naked bathing posture remained a source of amusement for all of us as we continued collecting data on the Chitwan rhinos.

It took Graeme and me a month to complete our rhino ground survey in Chitwan in 1968. As we synthesized the results of the air and ground census, we realized that the rhino situation in Nepal was extremely serious. We estimated that the rhino population of Chitwan had fallen from more than a thousand in the early 1950s to between ninety and one hundred and eight animals in 1960s. The real shocker was that mothers with calves made up only 5 percent of the population, indicating that the rhino population was in a downward spiral.

As one of the world's leading experts on population dynamics of large wild mammals at that time, Graeme came to a sobering conclusion: he predicted that if the trends were not reversed rhinos would be extinct from Nepal by the end of 1980. We reported to the Nepalese government's Ministry of Forests that Nepal's rhino population was dangerously small. A copy of our report was discreetly passed directly to King Mahendra, through the help of one of my father's friends. King Mahendra was the all-powerful absolute monarch who ruled Nepal with a firm grip. He was also the king that would later send me abroad for higher studies in wildlife management. Alerting this wildlife-loving Nepalese king was the only way of getting quick action in the slow-moving bureaucracy of Nepal. King Mahendra had to know that the rhino population was shrinking due to rampant habitat destruction and poaching for the supposed Eastern-medicine markets in East Asia.

In the sixties King Mahendra took extreme action to save the remaining forests of the Terai. He resettled twenty-two thousand people outside the designated area of the Royal Chitwan National Park area. He set aside more than eighty thousand acres of land as an exclusive rhino sanctuary. He also deployed a strong garrison of armed guards, called Gainda Gasthi or the Rhino Patrol Unit— well-trained ex-military men stationed in the field. However, these efforts only bought time.

In our rhino census report, we demonstrated that the efforts of King Mahendra, though timely and vital, were not enough to save the rhinos in the end. We made the daring and provocative predictions that the rhino might be extinct from Nepal by the late 1980s. This message generated a lot of publicity that alarmed bureaucrats and political leaders. The rhino was an important national symbol of Nepal. It was even embossed on the one-hundred-rupee bill, the highest denomination of Nepalese currency at that time. Besides Mt. Everest, the rhino was the best-known icon of Nepal. Nepalese often say, "We have Mt. Everest. We also have rhinos and elephants."

NATIONAL PARK NOW OR NEVER beamed the headlines of newspapers in Kathmandu, the power center of Nepal. Consequently, the government, led by King Mahendra, launched an aggressive plan to save the rhino and its habitat through more effective legislative and administrative antipoaching measures by adopting the concept of a national park.

6

MEDICINE OR MYTH?

Before 1950 the poaching of Chitwan rhinos for their horns or other body parts was a rarity in Nepal, particularly when compared to other countries in Asia and Africa. In Nepal the rhinoceros had been given full protection by Jung Bahadur, the first Rana prime minister, who declared the rhino a "Royal Animal" in 1846. However, the decree also allowed the ruling family and their state guests the exclusive right to continue to hunt rhinos. Consequently, hundreds of rhinos were killed during the royal *shikars* (big-game hunts) over the course of a century. After the hunt the remains of the rhinos were often distributed to the royal courtiers, who used them for religious purposes.

In contrast Nepal's neighbors in China and India had been buying and selling all parts of the rhino's body for much longer, as they believed that this was a panacea against any form of illness. For example, both Indians and Chinese still believe that a ten-gram dose of powdered rhino horn mixed with cinnabar is an instant cure for any kind of fever. Dried rhino tongue, powdered and mixed with milk, is believed to cure children with speech difficulties. Rhino meat is supposed to increase male strength. Rhino urine is taken as a cure for asthma. Even rhino dung is valued as the best fertilizer for growing hot chilies. A rhino tail placed under the pillow of an expectant mother is supposed to ease labor pain. Powdered rhino penis is ingested as a cure for impotence. From the tip of its tongue to the end of its tail, there has always been a lucrative market for rhino body parts in most of Asia.

In the 1960s East Asia—particularly Taiwan, Singapore, Macao, and Hong Kong, with its large ethnic Chinese population—emerged as the key hot spot for the burgeoning black market in rhino parts. This clandestine transnational trade flourished, as there were yet no concerted or coordinated international efforts to curb trafficking on endangered species. Alarmed by the escalating illicit trade on not only rhino products but also other endangered species, such as tigers and musk deer, the International Union for Conservation of Nature (IUCN) and Natural Resources World Conservation Union made a bold first move to curb this transnational trade at their eighth General Assembly in Nairobi, Kenya, in September 1963. Then, IUCN—a global wildlife watchdog created in 1948 in Fontainebleau, France—adopted an unprecedented resolution that created an international covenant to regulate the trade in wild animals and plants.

Yet it took ten years for this resolution to move from words to action. On March 3, 1973, in Washington, D.C., eighty countries signed an international treaty aptly named the Convention on International Trade in Endangered Species of Wild Fauna and Flora (or CITES for short). A total ban on the trade in rhino products, in addition to the mechanisms necessary to monitor their trade, were at the top of CITES's list of priorities. But effective enforcement of this international agreement remained elusive, largely due to a paucity of empirical information on the trade in rhino horns and other body parts.

In 1976 IUCN and the World Wildlife Fund created an additional specialist group to oversee the trafficking of endangered species. This new group, TRAFFIC (an apt acronym for Trade Records Analysis of Fauna and Flora in Commerce), targeted all five species of rhinoceros.

In early 1978, as an honorary consultant for IUCN, Dr. Esmond Bradley Martin, an American geographer who lived in Kenya, ventured the first investigative study on the trafficking of rhino parts. I first met Esmond in September 1975, in Kinshasa, the capital of Zaire, when I was the only one from Nepal attending the twelfth IUCN General Assembly. Given our common interests in rhinos, it did not take long for us to become good friends. Esmond, who donned expensive suits and sported a crop of puffed-up blond hair, was the last person I would have expected to undertake this kind of covert investigation—an exploration that stretched from Africa to the Middle East to Asia.

Risking his life among smugglers and black marketers, Esmond traveled for months from the main streets of Sa'ana in Yemen to the back streets of Bangkok, Rangoon, Hong Kong, Macao, Jakarta, Singapore, and Taipei to the remote provinces of China. There he appraised the trade on rhino body parts, both covertly and overtly, in his meetings with sellers, buyers, and intermediary dealers. In 1979 he published a comprehensive monograph on the illicit trade in rhino parts, a report that had far-reaching implications. This report revealed that the international trade on rhino parts was much more widely spread than presumed by conservation biologists. It was not only practiced in impoverished states such as India, China, and Yemen but also in affluent nations such as South Korea and Japan.

Esmond's report also dispelled the belief that the Chinese used rhino horn extensively as a sexual tonic, indicating that this belief was merely a myth exaggerated by the European colonials to degrade the image of the Chinese people. On the contrary, it was not the Chinese but some of the eastern Indians who superstitiously believed that the rhino horn was an aphrodisiac. Occasional sightings of the rhino's hours-long copulation in the floodplains of the Brahmaputra River seemed to have triggered these myths. In addition Esmond's studies revealed that almost 40 percent of black-market rhino horn, amounting to about 22,645 kilos, was used in

Yemen for making dagger handles and not as an aphrodisiac for the Chinese. Curiously, Yemen, the poorest country in that region, was the only Arab nation that prized rhino-horn handles for their *jambiyas*, or traditional daggers.

By 1980 Taiwan had become the largest market for both Asian and African rhino horns. Tihua Street in the city of Taipei, the capital of Taiwan, with its booming economy, was a major trading center of rhino horns, tiger bones, and other parts of endangered species from all over the world. This street in downtown Taipei was not only a retailing outlet but also became a major center for the wholesale distribution of rhino horns from Asia and Africa, with their export extending beyond the Taiwan Straits into mainland China. Taiwan's secretive trade in rhino parts remained closed for many years to any international scrutiny. Because of Taiwan's strong anti-Communist and free-market-oriented regime, Taiwan was a darling of the Western world during the Cold War. The media covered mostly Taiwan's economic success and its stand against the Marxist dictatorship of the People's Republic of China. Stories of the trade in rhino horns did not sell newspapers in the East or the West. Even the United States, which has championed the cause of endangered species, remained a passive bystander largely because the gravitas of the situation in Taiwan was not well-documented.

Throughout the seventies and the eighties, Taiwan's role in the clandestine trade of rhino parts was immune to public criticism. During the 1980s, the Environmental Investigative Agency (EIA), a small but effective London-based wildlife watch group, launched a daring campaign publicizing Taiwan's consumption of rhino parts. They produced a powerful advertisement that called Taiwan "Diewan." Their video showed a Taiwanese-made computer screen dripping with blood. The advertisements that aired mostly in Britain linked Taiwan's burgeoning export earnings with the killing of rhinos. It also called for boycotting Taiwanese products. The Americans did not want to be left behind the British in bashing Taiwan. By the end of the 1980s, the Americans threatened Taiwan with trade sanctions.

The reaction of the Taiwanese government was largely mixed. In 1989 Taiwan passed its Wildlife Conservation Law with a lot of publicity and fanfare in conservation circles. However, this law was stringent on paper but loose in practice. Its implementation was only halfhearted; the Taiwanese never believed that the United States would impose a sanction against one of their staunchest anti-Communist allies in Asia. Nevertheless, the Taiwanese government created some high-profile legislation that was largely cosmetic and mainly designed to generate publicity to deflect criticism from the international nongovernmental organizations now zeroing in on Taiwan's involvement in black-market trading.

To prove that they were enforcing the laws seriously, the Taiwanese government even arrested Princess Deki Wangchuck, a powerful member of the ruling family of Bhutan with diplomatic immunity, in a sting operation in Taipei's Chiang Kai-shek International Airport in 1993. The princess was caught red-handed with twenty-two illegal rhino horns in her expensive suitcase. Using her royal privilege, she was smuggling the rhino horns for a major distributor in Tihua Street. She was lured to Taipei by an informant, who did it in exchange for immunity for his own crime of dealing in illicit rhino horns.

Most of the horns came from Indian rhinos poached in Assam. They were easily smuggled into Thimpu, Bhutan, because customs checks between India and Bhutan were very loose. From Bhutan the princess took Druk Air, the Bhutanese airline, to Bangkok. No one dared to check her luggage at Paro International Airport in Bhutan. She did not clear customs and immigration at Bangkok's Don Maung International Airport but transited instead on a Thai Airways flight to Taipei. In any case it was unlikely that the customs people of the Kingdom of Thailand would inspect the baggage of an Asian princess. The Taiwanese sentenced her to ten months in jail.

However, her cousin Prince Namgyal, a South Asian royalty of unimpeachable reputation, bailed her out of prison. To his credit King Jigme Wangchuk of Bhutan did not interfere in the proceeding. On the contrary His Majesty disowned his cousin and lifted the princess's diplomatic immunity.

Back in Taiwan the Bhutanese princess's arrest generated a lot of publicity for the central government in Taipei. But their propaganda machinery could not fool the United States, which had vigilantly continued to monitor the trafficking of endangered species in Taiwan and mainland China and found that the trafficking in rhino and tiger products continued unabated, albeit more discreetly. Using a lesser-known provision of their law—the Pelly Amendment to the Fishermen's Act (1967)—the Americans imposed a trade sanction on Taiwan in 1994. This amendment authorizes the US president to stop importation of any goods from any country as a means for achieving international conservation objectives. As the first signatory of CITES, the Americans had always prided themselves on their global role in saving endangered species. Thus, with pressure from nongovernmental organizations, Washington used its most powerful tool for the first time since the Pelly Amendment was promulgated.

And Taipei finally got the message. The Taiwanese government was forced to stringently enforce their own laws against the trade in rhino horns. Within one year, they cleaned up their act. Consequently, in 1995 President Clinton lifted the trade sanctions.

The action of the US government was a flag to the international conservation community to reinvigorate their attention on the plight of the rhinos, particularly in places like Chitwan, where I was working. The government was forced to take serious actions as foreign attention and foreign assistance began to trickle into Nepal.

In Taiwan the government tightened its grip on the illicit trade in rhino horns on Tihua Street. But things were not over yet. Like any illicit trade, the clandestine business muscled into another venue. By the mid-1990s the center of the trade in rhino horns had moved from Taipei to Haikou on the island of Hainan off the shore of Vietnam. Far from Beijing, yet close to rich Asian markets, including Hong Kong, a free-for-all capitalism was flourishing on this tropical island of Communist China. It was natural that the illicit trade in rhino horns and body parts of other endangered species would flourish in Hainan. The other key market is Hekou in the Yunan province of Southern China. Remote and isolated from most of China, Hekou is a short boat trip across the Red River from Lao Cai in Vietnam, which by the late 1990s was surging as the center for trade in endangered species, including rhino parts.

Being curious about how Nepalese rhino horn from Royal Chitwan National Park ends up in the back streets of Taiwan, I once interviewed a man named Som, who was a rhino poacher and was serving five years imprisonment in a jail in Bharatpur, the district headquarters of Chitwan. He was caught red-handed with a rhino horn. Tirtha Man Maskey, the superintendent of the Royal Chitwan National Park, arranged this interview for me in 1978, back when I was just getting started learning about rhino poaching. Poor and raggedly dressed, Som hailed from the hills of Makwanpur District, which is adjacent to Chitwan in southern Nepal.

At first Som refused to talk. I bribed him with a generous offer of one thousand rupees (about forty dollars), a fortune in the seventies and almost equal to a month's salary for me.

Som was at the bottom of the poaching ladder and therefore took the most risk and did the dirtiest work, yet he was the least paid in the illicit trade in rhino horns. Using a muzzleloader, he shot an old male rhino late in the evening on the fringes of a farm near Amaltari—a village across the Narayani River in an isolated western section of the Chitwan Park. He hacked the horn off and calmly walked away from the scene of the crime in the cover of darkness, with the rhino horn hidden under one arm. He laid low for about two weeks in his village before attempting to sell the rhino horn to an undercover agent in Hetura, a bustling town some four hours drive from the site of his kill. He did not know that his arrest was a setup.

Using funds donated by the Fauna Preservation Society of Britain, the national-park superintendent had launched a sting operation using the set-a-thief-to-catch-a-thief technique. Som was unaware that the warden was offering cash rewards to informers whose information led to the arrest and conviction of rhino poachers. Many poachers and illicit traders found it profitable and safer to help finger their partners in crime than to enter the forests and shoot a rhino.

Som had been a poacher for three years, yet this was only the ninth rhino that he had poached. He told me that he was paid two thousand Nepalese rupees at the most for each rhino horn. This was less than eighty US dollars at that time, but it was enough to supplement his income to feed his wife and five children. He sold the horn to a middleman whom he refused to name. Ironically, it was his middleman, Neel Nath, a petty timber thief and the owner of a small sawmill, who had betrayed Som in exchange for immunity and a reward of five thousand rupees, more than double what Som was paid for the horn.

Neel Nath was supposed to sell the rhino horn to an Indian trader who contacted him once or twice a year through an intermediary. He did not know the Indian trader's whereabouts because the intermediary changed frequently. However, he suspected that the main distributor was someone with strong connections in both India and Nepal. Like a drug kingpin, the distributor raked in most of the profit when the rhino horn ended up in retail Eastern-medicine shops in Southeast Asia. The retailer would cut, grind, and mix powdered horn with other ingredients. He sold them as small pellets or in powder form to the practitioners of Eastern medicine. The price was $90 per gram of rhino-horn pellet in the late 1970s.

Though I have examined bodies of many poached rhinos, I have never had any close encounter with rhino poachers in action except once. Moreover, he was a dead poacher shot in the act.

I was camped in Chitwan Park at a place called Simri Ghol, about half a mile from the edge of a village. It was a cold, clear, moonlit November night in 1971. I was fast asleep after a long day of erecting demarcation pillars to separate the park boundary from the village land. It was around ten in the evening when gunfire awoke me. I rushed out of my tent and ran toward the gunfire, with a fleet of elephant drivers and laborers in tow. In about ten minutes I reached a big wallow in the middle of a meadow—a popular rhino grazing site. I stopped to wait for my colleagues. Being unarmed, I was afraid of walking directly into the barrel of a poacher's gun. Suddenly, out of the bush emerged a man dragging a human body. He was also carrying two guns. I panicked. A sigh of relief overcame my fears as I recognized the armed man. He was Tilak, a crack member of the Gainda Gasthi, the Rhino Patrol Unit set up by King Mahendra—an armed-guard unit deployed with a shoot-on-sight license to combat rhino poaching.

Tilak was also relieved to see me. He kicked the bloodied corpse he was dragging, switched the two rifles he was carrying to safety mode, and dusted off his khaki shirt.

"I have been stalking two poachers since dusk after I stumbled into their camp near the village of Bhimpur," he said with excitement. "We played hide-and-seek as I followed them to the edge of the village of Bhawanipur. It was there that they spotted me. I dived for cover and crept towards a demarcation pillar that you had erected this morning. Both the poachers fired at the demarcation pillar thinking it was me. At night the pillar looked like a human being."

I lit a cigarette and gave it to him. He took a long pull and continued his story. "I was scared for my life. Even scared to breathe. There were two of them against me. I kept my gun aimed at the direction of their fire. After a long wait, one of the poachers stood up and exposed his body. I felled him with one shot. The other ran away. I fired at him. But in my excitement I must have missed him."

It was a long night. We walked over an hour to Tikoli, the Rhino Patrol Unit's headquarters, and reported the shooting. The next day an inquest was held at the bullet-riddled demarcation post. We had no idea who the poacher was. Surprisingly, this poacher's weapon was also a 303 rifle, the standard weapon of the Rhino Patrol Unit antipoaching patrol—but no rifle had been reported missing or stolen in the last three months. I knew of no members of the Rhino Patrol Unit involved in poaching.

Nobody came forward to claim the body. The next morning the poacher was cremated on the banks of the Narayani River. Colonel Thapa, the commander of the Rhino Patrol Unit, issued a strong verbal reprimand, warning Tilak against going solo on patrol. The colonel also promoted him to sergeant, ignoring rumors that Tilak was not on patrol but visiting a girlfriend in Bhimpur when he encountered the poachers.

Except for Tilak's dead poacher and a few others in jail, I have never encountered rhino poachers. However, based upon circumstantial evidence, I have learned about their operational methods in the jungle. They usually operated alone or in a group of not more than three, traveling light and rarely spending more than a night at each campsite. Their bases were nearby villages, where they bribed a few accomplices, who reported on the movements of the armed guards of the Rhino Patrol Unit. Poachers did not always use bullets for killing rhinos. At times, they trapped rhinos in large pits they had dug along trails frequented by the animals. Some of the poachers were also involved in other criminal activities, particularly armed robbery.

Poaching was not the main cause of the decline in rhino numbers—from one thousand in 1950 to one hundred in 1968. Habitat destruction was the prime cause. Before 1950 virtually all of the Rapti Valley in Royal Chitwan National Park, except for a few hamlets, was covered with pristine forests and grasslands. By the sixties, more than 65 percent of rhino habitat was lost to agricultural encroachment. Likewise, the human population of Chitwan increased from a few thousand to more than a hundred thousand by 1969. Before 1950 a few Tharu cattle used to graze in the forests, with little or no competition with rhinos. By the time we carried out our rhino census in 1969, we estimated that there were at least twenty thousand domestic cattle grazing in rhino habitat.

It is also paradoxical that the United States, a champion of saving rhinos in the nineties, was mainly responsible for destruction of rhino habitat in Nepal in the fifties and sixties.

Nepal's Rana regime collapsed in 1951, triggering drastic changes all across the country, particularly in Chitwan. Throughout the 1950s the government in Nepal, though still a monarchy, was in a state of flux. Because of Nepal's strategic geographic location, the US government tried to take advantage of the political situation. In order to gain influence in the Himalayan kingdom, US Aid for International Development (USAID), then called the United States Operation Mission (USOM), launched a successful program to eradicate malaria, to expand farmland in the Terai area of southern Nepal, and to settle people from the rugged mountains of northern Nepal. The US government also financed a huge sawmill in Hetura, which was an outpost in Chitwan. Within a decade, settlers and lumbermen had destroyed 65 percent of the forests of Chitwan and fed them into the American-funded sawmill. Most of the sawn timber was exported to feed the Indian markets. Ironically, the American-funded Timber Corporation of Nepal exported some of the prime-quality lumber to the Soviet Union through an intermediary in India, to be used as railway ties to expand and improve railway tracks for use by the Russian military-industrial complex.

The net effect of the American-funded malaria eradication, sawmill, and settlement program was a drastic decrease in the rhino population and a dramatic increase in the human population. Besides the rhinos, tigers and other animals also suffered. One species, the swamp deer, became extinct. Its former habitat is now the district headquarters of a township in Bharatpur. Because USAID paid for the development of a new township, US taxpayers inadvertently financed the extinction of the swamp deer in Chitwan.

However, the Americans did not dictate or design their program in a vacuum. These projects were specifically requested by His Majesty's government of Nepal to undertake this endeavor. Resettling the hill people in the Terai was a priority program that had the full blessing of King Mahendra, who wanted to provide free land to the poor people of the Nepalese hills. Some say that the king was terrified that the escalating population of Indians from across the border would settle in Terai after malaria was eradicated, as there were no restrictions on the movement of people between Nepal and India. Furthermore, many Indian leaders viewed the Nepalese Terai merely as an extension of the Indian plains.

King Mahendra was a staunch nationalist, but he was also a realist. He believed that Nepal, a small country sandwiched between India and China, Asia's two antagonistic giants, must learn from the West the art of preserving national sovereignty. He knew that Nepal needed a core of trained and educated staff to implement his nation-building programs. He was among the first Asian leaders to invite the American Peace Corps, to alleviate the shortage of math, science, and English teachers. In addition he sent hordes of young Nepalese to the United States and Great Britain for higher education. I was one of them.

In late 1969 I was provided a scholarship to study wildlife management at the University of Edinburgh in Scotland and to return to Nepal to practice what I learned.

7

LEARNING FROM THE WEST

I landed in London's Heathrow Airport on a Quantas Australian Airlines Boeing 707 jet from Delhi on a cold October morning in 1969. It was my first visit to Europe. I was anxious, curious, and intimidated by the big jet. It was a fifteen-hour flight, with the plane stopping in Tehran and Rome.

I was worried that I would get lost in the sea of humanity that converged into Heathrow. But unlike airports in Nepal and India, the signs were prominently placed, and they were clear, simple, and idiot proof. Customs and immigration was smooth and efficient. No one jostled or jumped the queue. In the 1960s I had not experienced this kind of efficiency in India or Nepal—the only two countries I had visited at that time.

From Heathrow, I took a double-decker bus to London's West End Air Terminal. A petite, middle-aged woman with a yellow armband greeted me with a warm smile and a firm handshake as I picked up my suitcase. The armband was an indication that she was from the British Council, which takes care of foreign students arriving in Britain. I was too tired for any conversation. She was not.

"I am Mrs. Hoare," I heard her say with a big smile on her elliptical face and a sparkle in her dark blue eyes. "Welcome to Britain. Hope you had a nice flight."

It was hard to control myself from an outburst of laughter. I never expected to meet someone with such a name on my first day in Great Britain. But Mrs. Hoare was no loose woman; she was a volunteer, helping foreign students to adjust to life in Britain. I liked her. She took me in a taxi to a small bed-and-breakfast place in Russell Square, a district with lots of trees and quaint houses. The place had no name. A chubby, pug-nosed retired British army officer ran it. He spoke English like a BBC newsreader and gave me a single room with a shared bath.

The next morning Mrs. Hoare escorted me to the British Council in Davis Street. There a young woman greeted me in a tiny room with an overflowing desk. She was Mrs. Cox, who was a foot taller than Mrs. Hoare and half her age. She had long dark hair and brown doe eyes and sported a very short tartan skirt that barely covered her undergarments. I was in culture shock. Nepalese women rarely exposed their legs beyond the ankle.

"Do we have a warm coat?" she said, emphasizing the word "we." "How are we doing with some English currency?" I did not know why she used the word "we" instead of "you," and it made me a bit ill at ease, but I later realized she was only trying to be polite. I responded that I had warm clothes and that I would buy a warm woolen overcoat. Stressing the word "I," I also told her that I had fifty British pounds given to me by my government as a clothing allowance.

Mrs. Cox coached me on living in Britain as a foreign student. She advised me to open a bank account as soon as I reached Edinburgh. Her information would help me manage the United Nations scholarship that was given to me at the request of His Majesty's government of Nepal. I had never had a bank account before, as I came from a culture where cash up front was the king, not check or credit card. She also told me that I would get a stipend of 120 pounds a month. That was over three hundred dollars. I felt rich. I also got my marching orders to report to the British Council in Bruntsfield Crescent in Edinburgh as soon as I settled in the Scottish capital. Mrs.

Cox handed me my air ticket to Edinburgh and loaded me up with lots of touristy material about London and Scotland.

After Mrs. Cox left, I was back again in the company of Mrs. Hoare. We walked the streets of London. She took me on a quick tour of the British Museum, which was nearby, and for lunch at a pub called the Hawk and the Hound. There I learned how to order beer and say "please" and "thank you," words most uncommon to Nepalese when they converse in English. My English was not bad, but I still had a lot to learn. After lunch we took the London Underground to Notting Hill Gate, from where we walked a few blocks to the Royal Nepalese Embassy at 12A Kensington Palace Gardens. There I signed the visitors' book and called upon Ishwari Raj Pandey, the first secretary. He noted my contact address and gave me a large mug of tea and a small sermon.

"Don't do drugs," he preached. "You will be deported in twenty-four hours, and there is nothing we can do about it. This is the law of the land." He dismissed me after warning me in a cynical voice, "Don't return to Nepal with a British girl. They never last long in Nepal," and added after a short pause, "Furthermore, you will be cast out of your family."

With my formal duties over, I walked with Mrs. Hoare to Barkers, a huge department store in Kensington High Street. I had never seen such a huge bazaar. I was totally bewildered and had no idea what to do. But the good Mrs. Hoare taught me how to shop and how not to break a queue, as was common in Nepal, when paying for my purchase, a Harris Tweed overcoat.

After Barkers, we were back on the pavement of the streets of London. We cruised through Hyde Park and had tea at a place called the Ceylon Tea House in Oxford Street. After tea she escorted me back to my bed-and-breakfast lodging in Russell Square to bid goodbye. I had learned a lot in a day from Mrs. Hoare. To express my gratitude I presented her with a small wooden rhino that I had purchased at a tourist trap in Kathmandu.

That evening, I walked alone to Piccadilly Circus. The neon lights and the stream of people rushing in and out of the underground station fascinated me. I was mesmerized by the bright and colorful lights of the city. Later I dined at an Indian restaurant called Veraswamy's in Bond Street. The food was good, spicy, and expensive. However, with a monthly stipend of 120 pounds, I was content as I rode in the spacious black London taxi to my digs.

Next day I took the British European Airways flight from Heathrow to Edinburgh. Mrs. McIntyre, a Scotswoman, met me at the airport. She had a heavy but pleasant Scottish accent. She took me to another bed-and-breakfast called St. Margaret's in Mayfield Road near the University of Edinburgh. Another Scottish woman, named Mrs. Macdonald, ran it. All of my encounters in Britain had been with women. I wondered what the men did in Great Britain. As in Nepal, women in Britain seemed to work harder than men did. Nepalese men spent their free time playing cards. Perhaps men in Britain spend their time in the pub, I thought, as I checked in to my single room in Mrs. Macdonald's digs. This lodging would remain my home for the next two months, before I moved to a student dormitory called Moncrief House, an all-male student house managed by the University of Edinburgh.

The next morning I walked ten minutes to a tall, ugly building that housed the Department of Forestry and Natural Resources. There I met James Lockie, my supervisor, who enrolled me in the two-year master's-degree program. James also introduced me to Dr. Charles Taylor, director of education. I told Dr. Taylor that I might need English classes to improve my vocabulary.

"Rubbish," he responded with a mild Scottish accent. "The best way to learn English in Scotland is to watch television; read the *Scotsman*, Scotland's premiere newspaper; and date English, not Scottish or Nepalese girls, if you can find one from your own country." His advice was meaningless, even if it was meant as a joke. There were no Nepalese girls in Edinburgh at that time.

Over the next two years James Lockie coached me well. Above all, he taught me how to think and be analytical, as there are no simple answers to complex issues of nature conservation. I learned how the British had managed to resolve conflicts on land use, particularly between sheep rearing and managing red deer on the same parcel of land. I also learned about the principles of animal ecology and wildlife management based upon works in the Lake District of England, the forests of Galloway in southern Scotland, and the moors of Sutherland in northern Scotland.

I completed my academic requirements by writing a master's dissertation on the ecology and behavior of the roe deer, a small European herbivore that weighs twenty to thirty kilograms. During my two-year study, I returned to Nepal and visited the Chitwan for a "reality check," especially on the rhinos, to analyze not only what was desirable to do from my Scottish education but also what was doable given the realities in Nepal.

Despite many newspaper reports of "skinheads" harassing Asians and racial slurs made by a British member of Parliament named Enoch Powell, I never felt any discrimination during my two-year stay in Britain. Ironically, I learned a lot about Nepal in Scotland. The British were an inquisitive lot; they asked too many questions, forcing me to do research and update my facts on Nepal. Their queries also taught me to look objectively at my motherland from a distance. I also developed a taste for haggis and learned to cherish single-malt Scotch whisky. Though I was from Nepal, the country of the highest mountains in the world, I learned climbing in the highlands of Scotland. However, I never reached the summit of Ben Nevis, the tallest mountain in Scotland. I chickened out on my first attempt, as I was unable to stomach a blizzard when I was halfway up to the peak.

With money saved from my stipend, I traveled overland through Western Europe, starting in France and ending up in Sweden. I also visited Canada and the United States for two weeks and expanded my understanding of Western culture. These visits helped me shed many of the preconceived biases and prejudices about the West that were entrenched in my mind from my Eastern upbringing. People were people, no matter to which country they belonged. Traveling in the West also taught me to look into the good and not the bad in humans.

In October 1971 I earned my master's degree and returned to Nepal. There I threw myself into work in Chitwan, as required by the pact I made in order to receive the scholarship to Edinburgh.

Working in the field, I soon learned that for many old residents and recent migrants, large mammals such as rhinoceros and tigers were not objects of revered curiosity but were pests and sources of conflict. Crop damage from wild animals, mainly rhinos, ranged from 10 to 90 percent of the harvest. Villagers tried to deter this by yelling at marauding animals from raised platforms scattered throughout the fields, but many of their sleepless nights had only limited success against wild pigs and deer and were often futile against rhinos. Crop-raiding rhinos usually crossed into farmlands under cover of darkness. Perched on their feeble platforms, the villagers created pandemonium, beating their pots and pans and shouting "haat—haat" at the top of their voices. Most rhinos ignored the humans and continued grazing.

In the wild, the rhinos spend fifteen to twenty hours a day consuming about 120 to 150 pounds of forage daily. Not all wild vegetation is palatable, however, so rhinos move a great distance, even as far as 3 to 5 kilometers to get their required diet from the farmland. Cultivated farmlands provided easy and palatable feed in the form of succulent rice, wheat, and mustard plants. Here rhinos could maximize their intake with a minimum amount of time spent on feeding. Like most herbivores, rhinos are nutritionally wise. They know how to maximize calorie intake, expending the least amount of energy.

Settlers from the mountains farmed the once-prime rhino habitat, indiscriminately bringing people into direct conflict with this wild animal. The rhinos ate the crops that grew on their former forging grounds, and tigers preyed on the cattle that grazed in the jungle. More people were killed or mauled by goring rhinos than any other animal—even the lethal cobras. Once I treated a woman whose back was slit by the rhino's incisor teeth as if by a razor-sharp blade. While cutting grass near her village, she had an eyeball-to-eyeball encounter with a female rhino. She had tried to run away; however, the rhino was faster. My next gruesome experience was stumbling upon a disemboweled villager. A rhino attacked him without any provocation while he was tilling his mustard field. Humans are not natural enemies of rhinos, yet death is the ultimate expression of conflict between man and beast. Thus, it is not surprising that angry farmers often retaliate by helping poachers kill rhinos or destroy their habitat by expanding agricultural land.

For me, the greatest challenge for conservation in Chitwan was linking human welfare to saving the rhino. Though my methods to face these challenges changed, my mission remained the same for more than three decades. How was I to help rhinos and humans live as good neighbors? How was I to make a live rhino worth more than a dead one? How was I to develop schemes that provided direct economic benefits to the local people? For wildlife managers these questions are still as valid today as they were thirty years ago and are applicable to all endangered species.

Back then I still had to learn new methods that were practical and pragmatic and were not yet available in Nepal. I needed more training and exposure.

To that end, in 1972 I left the jungles of Chitwan and went to Yellowstone National Park in the United States. Established in 1872, Yellowstone is the world's first national park and has been, with its legal and administrative frameworks, the forerunner of a global movement for the creation of national parks. Besides the legislative and technical characteristic of a national park, I also wanted to learn the social and human aspects of the building of a national park—particularly how to resolve human–wild animal conflicts.

As the world's first national park, Yellowstone is a sacred place to me. My journey to Yellowstone was also a pilgrimage of the heart, much like a Muslim's to Mecca, a Catholic's to the Vatican, a Buddhist's to Lumbini, or a Hindu's to Benares. Yellowstone is where the fundamental charter of a national park first became legalized.

The cones and terraces of hot springs mesmerized me as I watched the brilliant coloration of algae thriving in boiling hot water in Yellowstone National Park. The beauty of Yellowstone's three thousand geysers and hot springs and the marvels of the forest, meadows, waterfalls, and canyons of the Rocky Mountains captivated me. Yellowstone's expansive river gorges and pristine mountainous woodlands brimming with elk, bison, coyotes, and other wildlife fired my imagination. I was struck most deeply by the Americans' vision of legally protecting large areas of valuable land for the enjoyment and benefit of future generations, particularly when there were still wide-open spaces in the Wild West. Yellowstone National Park broadened my horizons particularly in understanding the ethics behind the concepts of a national park—a purely American invention of the last century.

I learned three key lessons in Yellowstone. First, national parks have not only aesthetic or recreational values, but they also have spiritual values, as they connect humans with Mother Earth. Second, no national parks will be successful without the support of the people that live in the neighborhood. What is good for a national park must also be good for its human neighbors. And third, building a national park is an ongoing and continual process that requires constant vigilance. Good park managers must keep their eyes and ears open at all times for any unforeseen problems. These unanticipated problems range from poaching and habitat destruction from roads, dams, and mining to government policies that could adversely impact the park's infrastructure development.

On the last day of my visit, I purified myself by sprinkling the chilly water of the Yellowstone River all over my body. Later in the afternoon I watched Old Faithful shoot a dense column of steam and water more than 150 feet up in the air. I prayed to the unseen and unknown deities of Yellowstone and said to myself, "If the Americans could do it in the nineteenth century, why can't we, the Nepalese, do it in the twentieth century?"

In July 1972 I returned to Nepal to continue my work in building Nepal's first national park in Chitwan.

8

WILDERNESS BLUES

A melancholic voice crooned in the middle of the night. "Kakuwa queu kala hai? Bakula queu gora hai? Sab Bhagwan ke lila hai." The song was sober but high-pitched. "Why is the crow black? Why is the egret white? This is the game that God plays."

I crawled out of my tent and looked around. A full moon lit Ravi Rahut, my elephant driver—a former apprentice of my friend Tapsi. He was squatting next to Manju Kali, a female elephant that was tethered to a sal tree. At the top of his voice, Ravi was singing his favorite three-line blues. The Jarneli River flowed quietly barely ten feet away. At a distance, the Churia Hills rose in the jungle of Chitwan.

I was camped in the middle of a sal forest, where I was building roads and bridges to connect Saurah in the East to the banks of the Narayani River in the Western part of the Terai. I had returned home from Yellowstone in 1972, pumped up with energy and the resolution to make Royal Chitwan National Park not only a haven for rhinos and tigers but unique among the world's wildlife sanctuaries.

I started overseeing the building of basic infrastructures such as roads and guard posts to house rhino antipoaching units. I worked with a small crew of twenty Tharus, moving camp constantly as we cut a dirt road through the thick elephant grasses and jungles. We did not have any surveying or engineering tools; we were forced to improvise with the help of the elephants. Our work was full of fun, folly, and at times danger. We used the sun and the elephant's tail to align the roads, but we often wound up in the middle of a swamp, wasting days of work. Sometimes a good road followed the will of the elephant, not the will of any human engineer, making the road longer than required but following the easiest route.

One time I was startled by a sloth bear fifteen yards from my tent. She had a cub clinging to her back. *"Bhalu! Bhalu!"* ("Bear! Bear!") I yelled to warn the road crew. She scared the living daylights out of me as she stood up on her hind legs and looked straight at me. I backed off slowly and crawled into my tent to watch her from a safe place. Recognizing that I was no threat to her or her cub, the sloth bear trotted into the bush. Even to this day, I do not know what a sloth bear with a cub was doing so close to our camp, noisy with men and elephants. Another time, two rhinos in heat huffed and puffed through our camp. They caused pandemonium as we ran in all directions looking for trees to climb to safety. The big male rhino was oblivious to our panic and continued chasing the female into the forest.

But the most frightening incident happened at noon during a hot day in April, when I was mobbed and manhandled by a group of villagers in the middle of the day. I was alone in the camp, writing notes, with my back resting on a Semal tree. Hidden by tall grasses, the road crews were some three hundred feet away. Out of nowhere a dozen villagers appeared, yelling, *"Sarkari chor, Chitwan chod!"* ("Government thieves, get out of Chitwan!")

Kishan Kumar, an unsavory politician and a reputed timber thief, led the mob. The mob ransacked my camp and kicked our pots and pans as if they were footballs. Then they grabbed me, put a jute sack over my head, and dragged me to the river. There they forcibly dipped my head in and out of the river. I was drenched by the cold water and shivered with fear. I screamed at the top of my voice, *"Guhar! Guhar!"* (Help! Help!").

Suddenly the mob released me. I pulled the jute sack from my head and threw it into the river. As I turned around, I saw my Tharu friends converging to rescue me. They were fast on their feet and were equipped with axes and crowbars. Some of them were chasing the mob that was dispersing at random toward the village. I gathered my courage and joined the chase to catch Kishan, the ringleader. When we caught up with him, he was hiding in a small gully near the bank of the Rapti River. We tied him up and left him on the ground, moaning and groaning, for the next three hours. None of his cronies came to his rescue—my perfect revenge.

It was almost five in the evening when I gave him a dose of his own medicine. As he had done to me earlier, I covered his head with a jute sack, dragged him into the river, and dipped his head in and out of the river until he choked a few times. Then we took him across the river and left him to walk to his village with his hands still tied to his back. The politician never bothered me again. Later I found out that he had incited the trusting villagers to believe that the establishment of a national park would curtail their traditional rights of movement. This was not true. The thieving politician did not want any new roads or guard posts in his domain because they would stop his lucrative but illegal trade in sal-tree lumber.

This incident reminded me of an essential lesson that I had learned from the Americans in Yellowstone. A good national park needs to be backed by good laws that are easily understood by local communities. Good laws also must be enforceable. Proper law enforcement needs cooperation and not suspicion or antagonism from the people who live around a national park. Yellowstone had taught me that generating local political support backed by a strong legal and administrative organization is a prerequisite for establishing a national park.

A week after the mob attack in Chitwan, I returned to Kathmandu to focus on getting Nepal's first National Park and Wildlife Conservation Act approved by Rastriya Panchyat, the legislative assembly of Nepal. There I worked with John Blower, a United Nations advisor, and Bishwa Nath Upreti, a Nepalese civil servant, who later became the director general of the Department of National Parks and Wildlife Conservation. Both Blower and Upreti were talented. But the two did not get along.

Blower was a tall, bald Briton who dressed in khaki cotton shorts; knee-length, thick, pale green woolen socks; a khaki shirt; and desert boots. He belonged to the old school of the British Empire, the East African colonial type. Rumors among Kathmandu's expatriate community said that Blower was kicked out of Ethiopia in 1970. Apparently, he called Emperor Haile Selassie "His Imperial Majesty, The Ethiopian Dwarf," after he had downed a dozen stiff gin and tonics in a diplomatic reception in Addis Ababa, the capital of Ethiopia. Selassie was a diminutive monarch, standing less than five feet tall, yet he was believed to be the descendant of the biblical King Solomon and the Queen of Sheba and ruled Ethiopia with a firm grip until he was deposed by a Communist-led coup d'etat in 1974.

In contrast, Bishwa Upreti, who mostly donned traditional Nepalese dress, was a high-caste east Nepal Brahmin and the son of a high-court judge. He also prized his two degrees, one in forestry and one in law. Years of service in His Majesty's Government of Nepal's bureaucracy had honed Upreti's handiness in establishing a pecking order for all, Nepalese and foreigners. Nothing moved Upreti except memorandums written on the Nepalese government's official pad.

Upreti found Blower to be an old colonial, best suited for the British Museum and not for a free and independent kingdom. Blower thought Upreti was an incompetent desk jockey and a paper pusher, unfit for new ideas and ideals. I remained neutral. I needed both of them.

My first task was to link Upreti's expertise on the legal framework in Nepal with John Blower's years of experience in building national parks in developing countries. I engineered their reconciliation by inviting both of them to my camp in Chitwan.

One evening during the hot summer of 1973, we were resting on the Dhungre River. I walked down to the river and fished out half a dozen bottles of Nepalese Star beers that I had left underwater for cooling. As we sipped our beers, I asked Upreti, "What does it take to get a new act on national parks and wildlife introduced in Nepal?" The question was dovetailed for his legal background. Upreti guzzled a long drink of beer and systematically explained the byzantine process. He described the paper trail that started at his desk and snaked through a maze of committees before being approved by the Nepal legislative assembly for final promulgation by the king of Nepal.

Smoking his pipe, a vestige of his colonial days in Kenya, Blower listened attentively. He seemed to be impressed by the depth of Upreti's knowledge on the legislative procedures in Nepal. Blower scratched his bald head and asked gently, "Mr. Upreti, how long will the process take?"

Blower and Upreti had not become close enough to use each other's first name. "Anything between three and five years, Mr. Blower," Upreti responded courteously, puffing his big nose, and added, "at the minimum."

"That long?" moaned Blower, blowing smoke out of his pipe. "Then I am wasting my time in Nepal. I'd better go back to England."

"But," said Upreti, with a mischievous grin on his triangular face, "like anything in Nepal, there is a shortcut. If we can get a blessing from King Mahendra, the rest is merely rubber stamps."

"I am impressed," chuckled Blower, "by your pragmatic views for fast-tracking in Nepal."

Clearly Blower had not realized that Upreti too was action oriented. Like all of us, he wanted to bypass the bureaucracy in order to create a national park and save rhinos. Their conversation continued, with Blower explaining to Upreti the salient feature of the national parks and wildlife act in Kenya and Uganda. It seemed to be the first time they had communicated amicably.

Without the overshadowing officialdom of the Kathmandu bureaucracy, they sorted out their differences in the serenity of the jungle as they shared elephant rides and watched rhinos over the course of the next three days. Their joint visit also helped us develop a strategy to grab the attention of decision makers. We fed the news-hungry Kathmandu media by stretching information as far as we could without distorting the facts on the status of rhinos and tigers in Chitwan.

To catch their attention, we had spiced the report with an alarmist scenario of doom and gloom, claiming that rhinos would be extinct in Nepal within ten years. Bad news sold newspapers and also brought attention to the cause of conservation, a tactic that is still prevalent in a few conservation circles. We also printed a leaflet and mailed it to all the members of the Nepalese legislative assembly. The flyer read that it was not only rhinos that were endangered in Chitwan but that there were no more than ten tigers in Chitwan, and that most of Nepal's unique wildlife was marching toward extinction. The media reports, coupled with our leaflet, caused an uproar in the Rastriya Panchyat (Nepal's legislative assembly). Several members called for quick legal action, particularly a new and comprehensive wildlife preservation act. This was precisely what we wanted.

We also got the blessing we needed from King Mahendra, Nepal's absolute monarch. He issued a high-priority royal directive to the Ministry of Law and Justice to draft Nepal's first National Park and Wildlife Conservation Act and submit it for approval by the Nepalese legislative assembly.

The king needed no motivation to set aside large tracks of land for wildlife, particularly if it could save Nepali rhinos and tigers. There are many anecdotes told by Nepalese about King Mahendra, some good, some bad, and some amusing. One particularly popular story amuses wildlife lovers, both Nepalese and American. It describes his snubbing the American ambassador, Henry Stebbins, who recommended agricultural expansion in the Terai, including Chitwan, by converting large tracts of virgin forests and grasslands into farmlands.

"We are not keen on any human settlement in the forests or grasslands of Chitwan, Bardia, and Sukla Phanta," the king told the American ambassador. Bardia and Sukla Phanta are two game reserves west of Chitwan in southwest Nepal.

"Why, Your Majesty?" questioned the American ambassador. "These areas are good for agriculture, and the United States has helped your country eradicate malaria. In addition, in accordance with your directives, we have helped your government settle many of your poor citizens from the eroding hills to the fertile plains of the Terai."

"I like hunting there," curtly answered the king, with his flair for regal pomposity.

The American ambassador was not prepared for such a blunt response, particularly from the monarch of a tiny sequestered kingdom. After all, Chitwan, Bardia, and Sukla Phanta had valuable and extensive flatland, water, and other qualities best suited for agricultural development in a country of rugged mountains. The United States was Nepal's biggest donor. Agricultural extension was one of the major programs financed by American aid. It was also consistent with the Nepalese government's general policy to provide arable land to the poorer hill people.

However, King Mahendra vetoed this proposal to expand farming in his three favorite game reserves because they were also the last remaining habitat of Nepal's wildlife wealth. The story of the king and the American ambassador did not end there. It ended with King Mahendra charming the American ambassador by inviting him for a tiger hunt in Chitwan.

King Mahendra was a poet and a musician. Few people knew that he was the anonymous composer of many popular Nepali songs praising nature. The king also had a passion for hunting. He was one of the foremost practitioners of jungle statecraft. He believed that it was much more effective to conduct delicate negotiations surrounded by forests and wildlife rather than by the walls of the Royal Palace in Kathmandu, which had many ears.

I had met King Mahendra one year earlier when he made a surprise visit to my jungle camp on the banks of the River Dudhaura in Chitwan. My first reaction when I met him was fear. He was the most powerful person in Nepal, a ruler who had solidified absolute power of governance in the hands of the monarchy.

On his surprise visit, the king approached my tent on an elephant. He was wearing a topi, or traditional Nepalese cap, and a khaki hunting outfit. His eyes were hidden behind dark glasses with thick black frames. As he dismounted from his elephant, he waved his finger, commanding me toward him. With prayerful palms I approached him and bowed. *"Jaya Sarkar"* ("Long live Your Majesty"), I uttered in a shaky voice.

The king placed his right hand on my shoulder and said, "Tell me what you are doing." His voice was soft, almost a whisper, and his gestures were relaxed and casual. I felt less nervous. Picking up a stick, I first drew a map on the ground, taking advantage of the fresh and flat patch of the road I had just constructed. I showed him the location of the park boundaries and the alignment of the road I was building. I also pointed out to him the strategic points to locate antipoaching guard posts. He asked a few questions and then walked around my tent.

"Gain the confidence and trust of the local people, particularly the Tharus," commanded the king, who had a soft side for the Tharus. "I will return in a few days. I want to spend more time to see how you are getting along."

I never saw him again. The king died the next day on January 31, 1972, of a massive heart attack in his modest bungalow on the eastern bank of the Narayani River, eight miles from my jungle camp. His death at the young age of fifty-two shook the nation. Like most male citizens of Nepal, I shaved my head as a sign of respect for the dead monarch. I was also concerned that Chitwan and the rhinos might have lost an ally. Fortunately, his son Birendra, who took the throne, did not change his father's policy but followed it with even more vigor.

King Birendra had the political will to make nature conservation a top priority in his blueprint for Nepal's national development agenda, as a model that other developing countries could follow. He declared Chitwan Nepal's first national park in 1973, exactly 101 years after the United States declared Yellowstone the world's first national park. It was a day for me to celebrate, yet I was sorry that King Mahendra had not lived to see that great day.

Tirtha Man Maskey, a young Nepali Forestry Officer, was appointed as the first warden (superintendent) of the Royal Chitwan National Park. As his supervisor I continued my works on the technical and scientific side of national-park protection and management. We established park headquarters at Kasra, an old concrete lodge built in 1939 for Britain's King George V's rhino hunt. After long negotiations, a contingent of the Royal Nepalese Army was also deployed to operate the thirteen antipoaching guard posts that encircled the park.

King Birendra assigned his younger brother, Prince Gyanendra, the responsibilities of creating a network of national parks and wildlife reserves in Nepal. In 1974 the prince ordered me to work with Sir Edmund Hillary, the conqueror of Everest in 1953, to create the world's highest national park, the Sagarmatha (Mt. Everest) National Park. I also was given various assignments to survey and help develop eleven more nature reserves. In between these assignments I returned to Chitwan frequently, to nurture Chitwan as an exemplary model of a viable national park in a poor country such as Nepal.

9

POVERTY, RHINOS, TIGERS, AND TOURISTS IN CHITWAN

"*ink saving rhinos with reducing poverty in Chitwan" was a mantra* that was constantly preached by Prince Gyanendra, the brother of King Birendra, from 1973 on. "Human welfare must be central to our strategy to develop and sustain the Royal Chitwan National Park." He was right. That was precisely the key lesson that I had learned from the Americans in Yellowstone.

We decided to follow a three-pronged strategy. The first way was to provide direct income to the local people through tourism. The second way was to link saving rhino habitat to wise and sustainable sharing of resources, such as thatch, reeds, and elephant grasses. These rapidly renewable resources were much needed by the local people for their households. At the same time they were also required by rhinos for food and cover. The third way was to remove problem animals that destroyed the life and property of the local people. All these solutions required constant consultation with the local people who dwelled in the neighborhood with the rhinos. We needed their trust and confidence, particularly from the Tharu people, to make saving rhinos not antagonistic to but symbiotic with their needs.

In 1978 we started the *pancha vhella,* a public-hearing and public-consultation process. This gathering of village leaders provided a

venue for the community people to air their grievances. It also provided us an opportunity to reach consensus in addressing their concerns and in building partnerships.

Mallu Mahato, a seventy-year-old Tharu man from the village
of Saurah, was our key partner in conservation. A respected village
leader, Mallu opened the doors for me to have a meaningful dialogue with the community. I was a frequent guest at his house,
where he helped me build bridges with key members of his tribe
that were against the National Park.

I convinced Mallu and his fellow villagers that even though not
all tourists who visit Nepal are rich, there was money to be made by
catering to visitors at the lower end of the tourism market. We
hatched a small scheme, which later became a popular tourism
mantra in Saurah: *Sano bidayashi paisa garib janata laai*, which means
"Small foreign money to the poor people."

Mallu was the first to practice what we preached. He converted his house in Saurah into an inn for those who traveled with
tight budgets. It was managed efficiently by one of his sons and
soon became popular with young people who travel the world for
less than ten dollars a day. Mallu named his five-room inn "Wendy's
Lodge," instead of choosing a name affiliated with Chitwan or the
rhinoceros. I did not know who this Wendy was. It seems that he
chose a short, simple Western name to attract Western tourists; his
lodge was a commercial success. Soon Mallu had many copycats
and many competitors. In no time, a number of lodges with the
words "rhino," "tiger," "Rapti River," "jungle," or "crocodile" in
their names sprouted all over the village of Saurah, transforming a
sleepy Tharu village into a bustling tourist center in the Terai.

Mallu moved forward to make more profits from tourism. We
helped him revive and market the traditional Tharu "stick dance"
for entertaining tourists in the evenings. It is not known when this
dance originated, but as it is traditionally performed during the
Phaguwa in the lunar calendar month of Falgun (mid-February to

mid-March), some say it could date back to the eleventh century, an era when the Tharus first settled in the Nepalese Terai and fought other tribes with their bamboo sticks. This dance, like most Hindu dances, also signifies the victory of good over evil. Accompanied by a drum, a dozen men danced counterclockwise, twisting, turning, and fencing with their yard-long bamboo sticks in a rhythmic beat.

Tourism was both good and bad for Chitwan. On the positive side, it boosted the economy of poor and impoverished villagers. However, it also introduced several bad elements that influenced the environment and culture of Chitwan. More tourists meant more disturbances to the natural environment of Chitwan. Driven by the market economy, many local communities also lost their traditional value systems. The order of the day was not the generosity and hospitality of the Tharu culture but how to extract the last dollar out of a gullible tourist. When questioned by critics, I often justified my efforts by saying, "I would rather have a national park with a lot of rhinos and a few unsavory tourists than have no national park with no rhinos and no tourists." But I cannot turn back the clock. For good or bad, I feel responsible for the rapid expansion of low-cost tourism in the once-isolated and remote sleepy village of Saurah.

Expanding tourism to Chitwan was easy compared to my second goal, which was to link saving rhino habitat to the sharing of resources needed by the local people. Based upon consultation with the local community, we developed a scheme to allow villagers to harvest thatch grasses from protected rhino habitat. These wild, tall grasses are much used as roofing material by the local people. However, this scheme needed a royal decree from the king of Nepal, as it entailed a major paradigm shift from the "no extraction of any resources" policy to a "sustainable-use" practice. With King Birendra's blessing, the national park rules were amended to allow the residents of Chitwan to harvest the fast-growing thatch grasses once every year. Villagers could take as much as they wanted within a period of thirty days. They also took the reeds and stems of elephant grasses to use as walling materials during the grass-cutting season in the months of February and March.

In two years' time we were surprised by the success of the grass-cutting scheme. Each year more than one hundred thousand people used this free concession. Field studies of this scheme indicated that more than one million dollars' worth of grasses were removed every year. The poorest villager benefited most, as motorized vehicles and even bullock carts were prohibited from the area in order to discourage the forming of monopolies by the rich landlords, who owned heavy equipment. But there was no restriction for the poor to sell to the rich and profit from their labor. The area was burnt once the grasses were harvested. By the next season the grasses had rejuvenated, with some species reaching heights up to thirty feet immediately after the monsoon rains.

Like any good scheme, the practice of annual grass cutting also had its bad points. With the daily movements of more than a hundred thousand people for a month, the park had a carnival-like atmosphere, causing severe disturbances to the flora and fauna. No one knows what happened to some of the ground-dwelling creatures, such as the Indian cricket frog, the East Asian tortoise, and the grass owl, from constant trampling and burning of their nesting sites, as there has been no scientific investigation to study these rarely seen creatures. Nevertheless, the scheme helped to maintain the grasslands, the prime habitat for the rhinos. It also benefited the people who dwelled in and around rhino country. In short, it was a practical and pragmatic trade-off.

Our third objective to resolve wildlife-human conflicts in Chitwan was mainly focused on the tigers. My aim of removing problem tigers that destroyed human life and property of the local people proved to be a moral dilemma. I did not like killing tigers, yet I was compelled to kill one tiger and one tigress that had eaten more than seven people. My only consolation was that I never used a bullet but put these magnificent animals to sleep by using drugs. I also captured three more man-eating tigers and moved them to Jwalakhel Zoo and the Gokarana Safari Park in Kathmandu, where they remained confined behind bars for the rest of their lives.

But there was little that I could do about crop-raiding rhinos. I urged the government to provide compensation to the local people for rhino damage by using government revenue from park-entry fees for tourists. Since it is rare that any government wants to part with the money in its coffers, the Nepalese government ignored my recommendation. They could not see the nexus between human welfare and conservation, which was gaining momentum as a key spinner of revenue.

One of my key coworkers was Ram Prit Yadav, a forest ranger who reported to me. Dark and handsome, Ram Prit also had a nickname—The Professor. He earned this title for lecturing Murli Bhakta, an aggressive and loudmouthed politician at one of our public hearings. The key agenda of this town-hall-type meeting was to discuss the ways and means to minimize conflicts between rhino conservation and human needs.

Murli, a potbellied politician with catlike eyes, was a powerful but corrupt man with the gift of gab. A recent migrant from the central hills of Nepal to the Terai, he claimed that his family was indigenous to Chitwan. He stood up on his chair, waved a fist at Ram Prit, and yelled, "Are rhinos more important than the people of Nepal? Why can't we graze cattle in the forest as our forefathers have done for years?"

The politician had long been seeking the suspension of restrictions on cattle grazing in prime rhino habitat. We were totally opposed to this idea.

"Absolutely," rebutted Ram Prit calmly. "Rhinos are more important. There are less than two hundred rhinos and more than 20 million people in Nepal. You tell me which is more important!"

Suddenly, this gathering of nearly five dozen people hushed into silence. This incident occurred on a hot, humid afternoon in

May 1979 in the town of Bharatpur, the district headquarters. The politician and his henchmen had expected Ram Prit to be on the defensive and to waffle with rhetoric on the "intrinsic values" of rhinos to the world at large. In the past Ram Prit had always been subtle. He also avoided confrontation, particularly on issues regarding human-wildlife conflicts. Today he was different.

"The rhinos are the crown jewels of Chitwan. Chitwan is the heart of Nepal. People pay big money to visit Chitwan," Ram Prit said emphatically. "Saving rhinos creates jobs for the people of Chitwan. It also provides revenue to the government."

The meeting ended with the politician losing face and Ram Prit winning the debate and earning his title of "professor" for his candidness. A few years later people from all over the world would come to see our rhinos. By the early eighties the Royal Chitwan National Park emerged as one of the most popular tourist destinations in Asia.

Although I was a catalyst in the expansion of tourism in Chitwan, I cannot take credit for introducing it. The seeds of tourism in the Terai were sown not by the Nepalese but by a Texan in 1963. He was a wildcatter and a big-game hunter from Dallas. In the autumn of 1963, this American, John Coapman, came to Chitwan to hunt tigers with another Texan named Toddy Lee Wynne. They bagged their trophies, returned to Kathmandu, and got drunk with a Russian named Boris Lissanevitch. Boris ran the Royal Hotel, then the most expensive hotel in Kathmandu, where the Texans were staying. Over several stiff vodkas, the Texans hatched a scheme to develop tourism in rhino country. They wrote the deal on a napkin—to build a jungle lodge in Chitwan, and Boris the Russian hotelier signed off as a witness. Their deal making was sparked by a realization that shooting tigers in Chitwan was too easy. It would be far more thrilling to stalk rhinos from elephants during the day and watch live tigers from a hideout at night. They believed that there was money to be made by bringing wealthy Americans to stalk big game, not with guns but with cameras from the back of an elephant.

Coapman approached the Nepalese government with his ideas. The authorities thought he was nuts. Who would want to go to Chitwan? Above all, only a fool would invest in a tourism project in the malarial floodplains of the Terai. Back then Chitwan was not even a national park but more than a thousand square miles of inaccessible steaming tropical jungle. The cynicism from the Nepalese government made the Texan more adamant. Using Boris the Russian hotelier as a go-between, Coapman befriended Prince Basundhera, King Mahendra's younger brother, and convinced the prince of the validity of his project. The prince intervened. His Majesty's Government of Nepal happily gave Coapman a concession to build a jungle lodge and a monopoly of fifteen years to develop tourism in Chitwan. The government also charged the Texan a token concession fee of five hundred dollars per year.

Coapman built a rustic but comfortable lodge in the middle of the Chitwan jungle, using all local materials such as thatch grass, reeds, and wood. He also built an airstrip out of a small forest opening in Megauli, an old hunting campsite used by Britain's Queen Elizabeth II for her tiger hunt in 1961. His clients flew in from Kathmandu on a Second World War DC 3 and were met by a fleet of elephants at the airstrip. Consequently, Megauli became the only airport on earth where international visitors were directly transferred from an aircraft to elephants.

From the airport Coapman's guests rode to the jungle lodge on elephant backs in the old hunting style of the British Raj days in India. They stalked rhinos and watched other big game on their way to the lodge. Their safari provided an aura that was once exclusively reserved for royalty.

Coapman named the lodge "Tiger Tops" to give it a resemblance to a famous tourist lodge in Africa—the Treetops in the Abedare National Park in Kenya. The lodge had two wings. One wing was built around a big silk cotton tree to mimic the Treetops lodge in Kenya. The other wing was built on stilts cut out of sal tree trunks. Each wing had fourteen rooms, with double beds and an attached Western-style bathroom. Between the two wings was the "roundhouse," a room with a conical roof thatched with grass. The roundhouse had a well-stocked bar and served as the dining hall. Coapman wined and dined visitors there while he told many tales of the jungles of Nepal, as his clients increased the bar sales and waited for news about tiger sightings.

Coapman baited tigers, using buffaloes—an old hunting technique—to attract the predators. The bait sites were located near the lodge. When a tiger took the bait, one of his tiger trackers, a smartly dressed ex-Royal Nepalese Army sergeant with a solemn face, would walk up to whisper in Coapman's ear. The ex-soldier's expression and gestures generated an air of anxiety. Following a hush-hush conversation with his tiger tracker, Coapman would gracefully announce, "Ladies and gentlemen. The tiger has arrived. Please stop eating and drinking. I shall personally walk you to a hideout. There you will see a tiger feeding on a fresh kill. We guarantee your safety. But I demand absolute silence. No shoes. No talking."

Then he walked his clients in small groups of seven or less, in a single file. His clients would be very excited by the silent walk through a dense jungle in the middle of the night. Their excitement would climax when they reached the hideout and watched a majestic tiger tearing at its kill under the illumination of a light generated by an old truck battery. Sometimes the tiger growled when it felt disturbed by the light or the sounds of tourists in the hideout. This in turn stretched the visitors' imaginations and sent shivers through their bodies. Later the visitors would have quite a story to tell friends and families back home.

Tigers were not the only attraction for Coapman's clients. During the mornings and evenings, his clients, riding high on the backs of elephants, continued to stalk rhinos. During the day, some tourists floated down the Narayani River in a dugout canoe and watched the gharial crocodiles basking on the riverbank. Others went on a jungle walk or a bird-watching trip. Some of his clients preferred the quietness of a nearby lake where they could watch waterfowl and the marsh mugger, a common crocodile.

Some of Coapman's clients did not see any tigers. But they did not care; searching for the rhinos in the tall, swampy grasslands north of the lodge thrilled them with a sensation of a once-in-a-lifetime adventure. Many of these clients made an annual pilgrimage to Tiger Tops or recommended a visit to the rhino country to their friends and families. Either way Coapman had a string of clients and made lots of money. However, his money did not last long.

Besides his love for tigers and rhinos, Coapman was known to have two other weaknesses. The first was women — not American or Nepali, but British. Apparently, their accent captivated him. His second weakness was worse. He was a spendthrift. He was very generous to his staff and his girlfriends. He rewarded his girlfriends with expensive jewelry and his staff with goats and bottles of rum every time they showed his clients a tiger. Many goat feasts and much rum flowed in the jungle during the diamond- and gold-studded parties of the Coapman era.

"In the end Coapman got royally screwed by his English friends, with whom he often partied a lot," said P. B. S. Pradhan, a forestry officer who had befriended the American. "In 1971 his English pals squeezed him out of Nepal. They snatched his lease in a hostile takeover. Coapman was in too much debt to fight back."

Coapman would have made a fortune if he had not spent himself deep into debt. The hidden hands of fate guided the British to reap the fruits of the daring venture of an American. But for all his weaknesses in money management and his taste for English women, most Nepalese credit Coapman with pioneering adventure tourism in Nepal. He was a genius and a visionary, the first entrepreneur in Asia to use traditional methods of big-game hunting to lure tourists. And he could not have chosen a better country. Today the Royal Chitwan National Park is the top revenue spinner and the biggest employer in the whole District of Chitwan. Wildlife tourism that mainly revolved around rhinos, tigers, and elephants has become a new economic reality in the once malaria-infested jungles.

The new British management that took control of Tiger Tops in the mid-1970s continued to follow Coapman's footsteps and centered their tourism on rhinos and tigers. Jim Edwards, a Briton who had lived in Nepal in the 1960s, took over as the managing director of Tiger Tops. He retained all of Coapman's staff, as they were well trained. However, having worked for the marketing department of Pan American World Airways in New York, Edwards was also as innovative as the Texan was. He introduced two new elements to tourism in Chitwan. First, he constructed a Tharu Village Lodge in the heartland of Tharu country on the banks of the Narayani River to attract tourists to the rich and exotic Tharu culture that is estimated to date back to the eleventh century.

Second, in 1982 he introduced the game of elephant polo to attract the rich and the famous to Tiger Tops. Initially, it was largely a promotional campaign funded jointly by Tiger Tops and the then-popular but now bankrupt Pan American World Airways.

My friend Ram Prit Yadav became one of the world's best elephant-polo players. He set a world record for scoring the highest number of goals in a world championship match in 1985 against an international team of Hollywood celebrities. The Hollywood team was sponsored by Cartier, the famous French designer-watch company. Ringo Starr, the British pop star of Beatles fame, was the captain of the Cartier team. Ringo's team featured Hollywood celebrities, including his actress wife, Barbara Bach; Billy Connolly; Margaux Hemingway; and a cheering group of tall, thin, tinseled blondes, brunettes, and redheads from Hollywood.

I was the captain of the King Mahendra Trust for Nature Conservation Team, the only Nepalese team that participated in this high-society event. Ram Prit was my ace player. Our team was also known as the poor man's team. Unlike other teams, we could not afford fancy polo outfits. Instead of proper silky white breeches, we wore the Nepalese *surwal*, a kind of cotton jodhpur. We did not have any long, expensive leather boots, so we wore cheap tennis shoes. Instead of a designer polo jacket, we donned a long white shirt and a cheap cotton jacket, blood red in color. Our headgear was nowhere close to the standard polo solar hats—we wore traditional black Nepalese caps. However, our lack of proper uniforms did not diminish our spirit and our will to win.

Elephant polo was first played by the maharajas of Jaipur in western India in the early half of the twentieth century. The game vanished as India became independent in 1947 and the maharajas lost their titles and privy purses.

The rules of elephant polo are similar to those of horse polo. Each side has four players. However, unlike horse polo, in which the player also has to steer his horse, the elephant-polo player has the benefit of having his elephant driven by a trained elephant driver. This frees him to shoot the ball with his polo stick from his saddle. The polo stick measures between ninety and a hundred inches, depending on the height of the elephant. Another difference is that elephant polo is played in two chukkas of ten minutes each, while horse polo consists of four chukkas of seven minutes each. The ball used for elephant polo is similar to that used in regular horse polo, but compared to horse polo, elephant polo is slow, clumsy, and often hilarious, largely due to lack of coordination between the elephant driver, the polo player, and the elephant. At times it is the elephant that does the playing by kicking the ball or rolling it with its trunk.

The night before the championship match, the staff of Tiger Tops kept Ram Prit surrounded by leggy women and entertained him with premium Scotch whisky until the wee hours. They had high hopes that Ram Prit would be overcome by the booze and the blonde beauties and would be unable to play well against the Hollywood team. The British management of Tiger Tops was desperate for the Hollywood team to win the match. For global promotional reasons, the Cartier team and the Hollywood celebrities were more important to them than our local Nepalese team. News about Western celebrities grabbed the attention of the American media and helped in the promotion of Tiger Tops and Pan American World Airways. Nepalese national-park staff, no matter how talented, were not newsworthy.

Next morning Ram Prit shattered their plans by scoring all five goals for our team against the two for the Hollywood team. He also established a world record by scoring the highest number of goals ever in elephant polo. Our easy but joyous victory was a humiliating defeat for the Hollywood celebrities and their promoters. Clearly, the management of Tiger Tops grossly underestimated Ram Prit's intelligence and our will to win.

Ram Prit lived in Kasra, the park headquarters. It was twelve miles west of my camp in Saurah, but he was a frequent visitor to our jungle camp for drinks and dinner around our campfire. However, he was not the only one. We also had another visitor, a nocturnal nonhuman visitor. His name was George of the Jungle.

10

GEORGE OF THE JUNGLE

A *full moon rose above the treetops as a drone of insects buzzed* through the jungle. Otherwise, it was unusually quiet. A dozen of us huddled around a campfire in Saurah in the heart of Nepal's Royal Chitwan National Park. I gazed at the crackling flames of the sal wood and quietly sipped a "Cheapy Charlie," a cocktail of cheap Nepalese rum and good Darjeeling tea. The cocktail was invented by an Australian tourist to express his disapproval of the lack of cold Australian beer in the village market.

I was not, however, the only one sunk in deep thought. The others were also quiet, as if the night were too precious to be disturbed by a human voice. Gathering around a fire was a normal routine in our camp. There was little to do in the jungle after dark. No electricity. No television. And nowhere to go. It was December 1978, and I was at our jungle camp on the banks of the Dhungre River.

George was barely visible and motionless at the edge of a forest opening. But we knew that his eyes were also glued to the campfire, as he had been a frequent visitor to our camp for the past twelve months. Yet George was no human but an old male rhino chased out of his natal areas by other, younger rhinos. George usually stayed close to humans and rarely ventured deep into rhino country to avoid harassment from his younger counterparts. He hung around our camp, particularly in the evenings, to graze in our yard.

As I gazed into the fire, I remembered the night my wife, Sushma, woke me from a deep sleep and whispered, "There is a rhino in the yard. I need to go down to the toilet, but I am scared."

It was her second night in Chitwan. The sky was clear, and our camp gleamed in the full moon. The toilet was a few feet away from our thatched hut, which was built on stilts with a small balcony. She had to climb down the balcony and pass George to reach the toilet.

"Piss from the balcony as most of us do," I snapped back and went to sleep. Sushma hesitantly went out to the balcony. She moaned, groaned, and threw my shoes at the rhino. The rhino stared at her for a few minutes but did not budge. Finally, as nature's call became intolerable, Sushma gathered courage and walked down a few steps. As if it were precision timing, George quietly melted into the bush in front of our house, allowing Sushma some privacy. After this incident, she came to respect George.

Like Sushma, all of us who gathered around the fire cherished George. Our relationship with him was symbiotic. George was gentle, reliable, and part of our jungle life. George depended upon us for his safety, and we needed him to amuse our guests. George was the prime exhibit for tourists, children, and visiting dignitaries. Many of our visitors had neither the time nor the patience for a long stay. They were certainly not keen for a hike in the jungle or a close encounter with wild rhinos.

On one occasion I was ordered to show rhinos to a visiting dignitary, a high-ranking general of the Indian army on an official visit to Nepal. He had only thirty minutes for a jungle safari. Thanks to George, the task was easy. I took the general on top of my elephant for a quick tour of the patch of forest next to my hut. Instead of taking him directly to George, I meandered with him through the jungle and the tall grassland. During this safari, I showed him George from three different angles from opposing sites. He was so excited that he never stopped bragging about how he saw three rhinos within thirty minutes. I made no effort to correct his illusion.

George also had a local Nepali name, *Dahine Kum Chandra Khate Bhale*, which translated to "Crescent-Scar-on-the-Right-Shoulder-Old-Male." The Nepali name symbolized his last dispute over a female. Since Westerners found Nepalese names complicated, this Asian rhino was assigned a European identity. His Nepalese forest guide named him George, after a euphoric English tourist who had bought a goat for the guide to feast on. The goat was a reward for the guide, who had fulfilled the Briton's childhood dreams of a close encounter with a wild rhinoceros. Later it became fashionable for tourist-lodge owners to copycat us and name their resident rhino George.

George moved toward our elephant stable as the silence of the jungle was broken by the "*whuk-whuk-whuk*" alarm calls of the chital, a common spotted deer of the forest. "*Kai-kai,*" wailed a peacock perched on a tree above the campfire. "*Phrrr-phrrr,*" grunted George the rhino. "*Brrrr-brrrr,*" rumbled our camp elephant to warn George not to venture too close. The sounds of the forest prompted Ram Lotan, the chief elephant driver, to talk. "I think there is a tiger on the prowl," he finally said. "The predator must be stalking the chital."

Ram Lotan, a protégé of my old friend Tapsi, was in charge of all the elephants after Tapsi died, five years earlier. The others remained silent. I too was quiet but was shifting my attention from George to the men in front of me silently drinking rum. I knew the alarm call of the chital was music to their ears. Next morning some of them would sneak into the jungle and search for the tiger's kill. Meat was expensive and a luxury in the jungle, particularly as hunting and trapping were banned in Chitwan. However, stealing a tiger's kill with the help of trained elephants, even when prohibited by the national-park bylaws, was a normal practice. Few would think it prudent to challenge the nonwritten traditional practices of the elephant drivers that had been common for nearly a century. Trying to stop that practice would cause a revolt in our jungle establishment.

The chief elephant driver stared at the fire. He was nearing sixty but looked many years younger, with a crown of thick jet black hair, which he swore was natural and not dyed. Like my old friend Tapsi, he too was a Tharu. He had also followed in Tapsi's footsteps, joining the Royal Elephant Stable when he was ten. He climbed the ranks to be the superintendent of Hatisar, as the government elephant stable is called in Nepali.

Elephants and the elephant drivers were vital to our work. In 1978 I was back in Chitwan to lead a Smithsonian Institution–funded research project that was studying the ecology of the tiger and its main prey, the deer. I worked closely with American scientists, and one of my key tasks was to bridge the theory of Western science with the pragmatism of park management in a developing South Asian country. As a part of our research, we had to affix radio collars on tigers. But first we had to catch them.

Combining old Nepalese hunting techniques of the early nineteenth century with modern American medicine of the twentieth century, we mastered the technique of catching the elusive tiger. This operation consisted of three steps. First, we surveyed an area for the presence or absence of a tiger, using telltale signs such as footmarks, droppings, or scents of its urine. Then we laid out a series of baits consisting of live young domestic buffalo, tethered to wooden poles in the tiger's domain. After killing the buffalo, the tiger would snap the rope and drag its kill a few yards into cover. After feeding on part of its kill, the tiger would move to a nearby stream for a drink. After quenching its thirst, the cat would then rest near the kill to return to feed again later. The next morning after baiting, we would survey the area again, study the direction of the marks showing where the tiger dragged its kill, and estimate the location of the tiger.

Then, using elephants, we would lay *vhit* cloth in a V shape to locate the position of the tiger in the center of the V. The *vhit* cloth was a three-foot-high wall of white cotton cloth stretched about

GEORGE OF THE JUNGLE

one-half mile on either side. A small opening at the narrow end gave the *vhit* a resemblance to a large funnel. About a dozen elephants spread out at the open end of the funnel. Equipped with a drug-loaded dart gun, I would take my position hidden in a tree at the narrow end of the V.

Once I was in position, the men and the elephants moved forward, shouting and thrashing the vegetation. This caused the tiger to move toward me. The tiger was certainly able to jump over or crawl under the thin barrier of the *vhit* cloth, yet either fear or some instinct forced the tiger to avoid it. It would slowly move toward my tree. When it got under my tree, I would shoot it with the drug-loaded dart and put it to sleep for the next three hours. Then I would affix a radio collar and wait at a distance on the back of an elephant for the tiger to wake and disappear into the jungle. Later we would track the tiger from the back of an elephant or from inside a single-engine aircraft.

As they were for big-game hunting by kings and emperors, elephants were vital for our scientific research. All of us had our favorite elephants and elephant drivers. For catching tigers, my favorite elephant was Mel Kali. He was named after a bearded and bespectacled Minnesotan named Melvin Eugene Sunquist, a former Smithsonian Institution scientist who studied tigers in Chitwan. Like his namesake, Mel Kali was cool and was rarely panicked by rhinos or tigers. So was Badai, a Tharu, who drove this elephant. Badai also doubled as our resident shaman. He was known as the chief Smithsonian elephant driver because the Smithsonian Institution provided funds for the purchase and support of five elephants. These elephants, under Badai's command, were exclusively reserved for our research. In addition to the Smithsonian elephants, we also had access to twenty elephants at the Nepalese government stable under command of my friend Ram Lotan.

Normally, two handlers would control each elephant. The elephant driver would sit on the neck with his feet spread on each side of the head. Then he would steer the elephant with his toes placed directly into the cavities behind the elephant's ears. An assistant would stand on the elephant's rump, clutching a rope extending from the base of the elephant's saddle. The elephant driver would maneuver the elephant with his feet. The back rider is called the *pachuwa*, and his job is to spot game. At times, the *pachuwa* also assists in controlling panic-stricken elephants by beating the animal to a halt with a wooden dumbbell-like tool called the *loha*.

In the 1970s the elephant driver in Nepal was not called a *mahout*, as he is in India. Calling him a *mahout* or *mahoutay*, the general term used in Nepal, would be considered an insult. In Nepal *mahoutay* ranks lowest on the pecking order of the elephant stable hierarchy. All elephant drivers started out as *mahouts*; their chief duty is cleaning the elephant's stable. Even the imperious Ram Lotan, the chief elephant driver, started his career at age ten by spending years knee deep in elephant manure. Cleaning elephant dung is a rite of passage for all elephant drivers. It took Ram Lotan forty years to become a *subba*, the highest-ranking elephant driver. Before his death, my old friend Tapsi had also been a *subba*. He too started his career as a *mahoutay* when he was barely age ten.

The next rank above *mahoutay* is the *pachuwa* or the back rider. Above the *pachuwa* is the *phanit*, a rank that entitles him to drive an elephant in all formal functions. It takes a *mahout* at least five years to graduate to *pachuwa* and up to another five years to be a *phanit*. Above the *phanit* are the ranks of *rahout* and *daroga*, both of which carry administrative duties in the elephant stable.

Different colored belts with matching sashes worn over the khaki uniform — a knee-length shirt and a jodhpur — signified the various ranks of the elephant-stable personnel. A red belt and a red sash were exclusively reserved for *subbas* like Ram Lotan. *Darogas* donned green belts, while *rahouts* wore light yellowish colors. *Phanits* were assigned bright saffron, and *pachuwas* wore brown green. *Mahouts*, who ranked the lowest in the pecking order, wore white. These uniforms, introduced by King Birendra in 1977, were worn only during royal hunts or for a jungle safari of state guests and dignitaries.

Before 1950 the job of elephant driving was exclusively reserved for the Tharus. Though the positions were still dominated by the Tharus in the 1970s, some new hill migrants to Chitwan such as Newars, Gurungs, and Magars have taken this profession. For royal hunts, Nepal's Ministry of Forests maintained five *hatisars*, or elephant stables, containing more than one hundred elephants. Each stable, even today, is in a different game reserve of southern Nepal, a legacy of the hunting tradition enjoyed by Nepalese rulers. Since royal hunts in modern times are quite infrequent, the government leases its elephants to tourists for sightseeing and to Nepalese citizens for important ceremonies, including weddings. Besides government elephants, a few tourist lodges in Chitwan maintain their own elephants. Tourist elephant wranglers did not have the same prestige as royal elephant drivers or the staff of the Smithsonian project.

Besides five elephants and fifteen caretakers, the Smithsonian Institution also supported thirteen game scouts or *shikaris*, two cooks, and a camp caretaker for my research project in Chitwan. The head game scout was Prem Bahadur Rai. His favorite elephant was called Kirti Kali, named after a Nepalese scientist. Though I was his boss, it did not keep him from showing off different ways to mount an elephant.

One morning, when we were getting ready for our jungle excursion, Prem approached Kirti Kali, patted the elephant's trunk, and said, "*Dhey-dhey-dhey*" ("Give-Give-Give"). Responding to his call, the elephant rolled up its trunk and bowed its head. Prem grabbed the elephant's ears and placed his right foot on the jumbo's trunk. The elephant lifted him up in the air. Prem sailed smoothly in the air and climbed to the elephant's back with ease. From the top of the elephant, Prem waved at me. His gestures taunted me not to be a wimp and mount an elephant when it is in a sitting position but to mount a standing elephant the hard way, the way he had done. I had to save face. I walked up to Mel Kali and mounted her head-on exactly as Prem had done. But it took me three tries before I finally succeeded.

Most people mount when elephants are flat on the ground in a sitting position. This position is slow, as it takes time for the elephant to lay flat on the ground on its belly and stand up again. But this technique is easy for humans, who have only a short climb up to the elephant's back. Mounting a standing elephant head-on is tricky, as it is easy to slip from an elephant's trunk and fall flat on the ground. After he saw that I was as good as he was, Prem stopped showing off.

Before joining the Smithsonian project, Prem served King Mahendra as a *bagh shikari* (tiger hunter) in His Majesty's Royal Hunting Department. Upon retirement from the palace service in 1965, he worked for Tiger Tops jungle lodge for the next ten years as a tiger tracker, which is where I met him in 1972. In 1973 Kirti Tamang, a Smithsonian scientist, lured him to join our project with an offer of more money, more responsibility, and a more prestigious position. Prem's main task was to teach us the techniques of catching tigers. A veteran of the jungle, the fifty-year-old Prem was short and skinny, and his furrowed face almost hid his small, slant, jet black but very sharp eyes. These sharp eyes once saved my children's lives on a bright and sunny winter morning in January 1979.

Our two daughters, Alita and Pragya, had just arrived from Kathmandu to join us in the jungle. Our son Binayak was not yet born. Alita was six and Pragya was four. It was their first visit to Chitwan. I was busy writing notes inside my hut. Suddenly, I heard my wife scream, "Alita! Pragya! Stop! Come back!"

I ran out to the yard to find out what had caused all the fuss. I saw Alita and Pragya walking toward the edge of the forest. Five yards to their left was a big rhino. The rhino was browsing, with its back toward our daughters. Both of them were carrying a bundle of cabbage leaves in their hands. They were too close to the rhino. I panicked, but I did not know whether to scream, run, or walk fast to rescue them. Suddenly, from the corner of my eye, I saw Prem sprint toward the girls. He grabbed both of them and brought them back into the house in a flash. The girls did not understand the commotion. But when they saw a combination of relief, anger, and fear in their mother's eyes, both began to cry.

"We were only trying to feed the water buffalo," moaned Alita in a low and shaky voice. Suddenly the mystery was clear. Since the girls had never seen a rhino, they thought it was some kind of domestic water buffalo—a docile and domesticated animal they had frequently seen carrying kids on its back.

Clearly, the girls needed to be educated in the ways of the jungle. We assigned this task to James L. David Smith, or "Minnesota Dave," as he was called. He was from St. Paul, Minnesota, and was studying the ecology and movement patterns of the tigers. Dave was my American counterpart, yet he was as Nepali as any of us. He could outswear us in Nepali and outeat any Nepali in hot and spicy meals. He was also known for his sense of time, or rather lack thereof. Like the Tharu elephant drivers, Dave operated on Nepal time and became known as "Never-on-time-Dave." But he was one of the world's experts in radiotelemetry, the science of radio tracking. Dave and I tracked radio-collared tigers from a small Swiss Pilatus Porter aircraft as well as from the ground. In fact, it was our findings that later became instrumental in the decision of the Nepalese government to enlarge the size of the national park in 1980, from 210 square miles to 360 square miles.

"Uncle Dave" took the girls on elephant rides and not only taught them to distinguish a rhino from a buffalo but also how to recognize the four species of deer common in Chitwan. Soon the kids also learned to recognize some common birds, plants, and animals, including the sloth bear and the two species of crocodiles. Dave had no qualms about taking my children on many of our tiger-capture expeditions. They also flew with us when we radio-tracked tigers from the air.

Dave was good at the art of playing safe in the jungle, yet like my daughters, he also had a close encounter with a rhino only a few yards from our house. Unfortunately, unlike my daughters, Dave did not escape unscathed.

It was a hot, sweaty, hazy morning on May 7, 1988. After a long absence from Nepal, Dave had just returned to Chitwan with his wife Franci, his five-year-old son Alex, his three-month-old son Charlie, and his wife's parents. On this fateful morning, he took Alex for a short jungle walk using a narrow path that I had cut in front of my hut. They had hardly strolled ten yards inside the forest when they stumbled upon a rhino and her calf resting in the bush. Dave was surprised. It was rare that a rhino with a calf would rest so close to a human encampment. The rhino was startled by this sudden encounter with humans, and she stood up and charged at Alex. Dave wanted to save his son at any cost, even at the risk of his own life, so he ran in front of the rhino to block her from his son. The rhino gored Dave.

Alex kept his cool. He ran back to the camp, screaming for help. Our camp staff, mostly game scouts, rushed to rescue Dave. The sound of the running *shikaris* panicked the calf, which ran away toward the river. The mother rhino, which was kicking and biting Dave, followed her calf, leaving the bloodied and motionless Dave out cold on the ground. The game scouts thought he was dead. No one could possibly survive an ordeal like that. But miraculously, Dave was still breathing, though it was doubtful that he could survive. The game scouts took Dave to a hospital in the town of Bharatpur, some 10 miles away. But this rural hospital had neither the equipment nor the doctor to treat Dave. Most of his bones were crushed, and he had many deep and complicated cuts caused by the rhino's sharp incisors.

I had left for Kathmandu to attend a religious festival two days before Dave's ordeal with the rhino. Fortunately, Vishnu, one of the game scouts, had the presence of mind to call me. Within the next hour, I had fetched a Royal Nepalese Army helicopter to bring Dave to the United Mission Hospital, the best in Kathmandu.

Without swift and proper treatment, he could have bled to death or developed gangrenous wounds that would require his limbs to be amputated. The Kathmandu hospital provided Dave with emergency treatment, but it was not equipped to deal with Dave's multiple fractures and multiple wounds. In three days' time, he was flown out of Nepal for treatment in the United States. It took him six months to recover fully. Dave has visited Chitwan a few times after his almost lethal incident with the rhino, and he has never failed to admire the presence of mind of his son Alex and the swift action of our game scouts, the *shikaris*.

We could not have operated without the backup support of the *shikaris*. They are a breed of thorough professionals, even though none of them had any formal schooling. They learned their trade in the jungle through a learning-by-doing process.

Except for Prem, the head *shikari*, a member of the Rai tribe with roots in the mountains of eastern Nepal, and two others, all of our *shikaris* were Tamangs. They all came from the same village of Toplang, just a day's walk south of Kathmandu. Quiet, shy, and gentle, the Tamangs were know to have a natural flair for tracking game and were recognized as among the world's best game scouts. The Tamangs are the largest but among the poorest of the numerous ethnic groups in Nepal. They have Mongoloid features and dwell throughout Nepal from the Nepal-India border in the south to the kingdom's northern border with Tibet. Their culture and customs vary, as the Tamang people are tolerant and adapt easily to changing environments.

Our Tamang game scouts worked hard and played hard. They love to drink and dance. As research assistants they have helped many Nepalese and American scholars with their Ph.D. research and studies in wildlife ecology, yet they rarely sought glory or credits for their contribution to science. They are inherently a content and peaceful group.

The two non-Tamang *shikaris* in our group were Ram Kumar and Keshav. They belonged to ethnic groups totally different in caste and creed from the Tamangs. Ram Kumar was a Brahmin, a caste of priests who usually preferred desk jobs. It was very unusual to see a Brahmin working as a game scout. Keshav was a Giri. The Giris were supposed to be the descendants of sages and hermits who gave up celibacy and hermetic life after discovering worldly pleasures and sins.

I lived with the *shikaris* and the elephant drivers in our modest camp. The camp had two mud-and-wood buildings that Dave and I occupied. It had another five-room wooden building we called the "long house" or the Saurah Sheraton. It was reserved for visiting scientists, friends, and guests. Fifty yards across a big lawn were living quarters for the game scouts and the elephant drivers. They were mud-and-thatch huts. In the center of the lawn was our open fireplace, where all of us huddled every evening.

It was around the fire in the evening that we discussed our field operations. It was here that we planned and charted our course of action as we gazed at a big bonfire glowing against the rhythm of the jungle. It was also around our fire that I learned how, in bygone days, elephant drivers captured rhinos in the wild and delivered them to zoos in the city. It is not a happy story. Yet it needs to be told.

☀

11

KILLING MOTHERS TO
SNATCH BABIES

The evening was dark and damp, with dew dripping down from the wintry sky in the middle of January 1986. We had difficulty getting a good fire going. It was also an exceptionally quiet and somber night as Ram Lotan told us his story. His narrative describes the grisly task the elephant drivers were ordered to carry out as a part of their "service to the country and the king."

"Our worst nightmare," began Ram Lotan, "was in 1956, as we were preparing to march fifty of our elephants over the mountains to Kathmandu for King Mahendra's coronation. We had an unusual hailstorm that night, when the king's hunters arrived at the elephant stable and read out our orders to assist the royal hunters to catch two rhino calves, a male and a female, and walk them to Kathmandu with the coronation elephants.

"We gave the royal hunters food, alcohol, and marijuana to soothe their tiredness. The royal hunters told us that Kathmandu badly needed a rhino for its zoo. The government expected thousands of hill people to descend to the Kathmandu Valley for the coronation. They would be disgruntled if they saw no rhinos in the nation's only zoo.

"While the hunters went to sleep, the elephant drivers got to work. The elephant stable bustled with activity. Tapsi, who was young then, was my boss. He barked orders nonstop and organized the elephants, ropes, and capture nets. At dawn we lined up fifty elephants and marched them across the Rapti River to the island of Itcharni, a small island in the Rapti River, just across from the elephant camp.

"Two royal hunters were on the back of my elephant. Those days, Itcharni, like the rest of Chitwan, was crawling with rhinos. There were no human settlements in Chitwan, except a few Tharu hamlets. We did not have to go far to find Ram Krishna, a mahout, from our elephant-stable staff, perched on a Bhelur tree. He pointed us to a big female with a curvy horn. Next to her and camouflaged was a female calf browsing in the bush."

Abruptly, Ram Lotan became silent. He stood up, circled the fire, fished a cigarette from my packet, and lit it. He puffed the cigarette and blew a mist of smoke into the fire.

"We circled the rhinos from a distance. There was absolute silence except for the movements of our elephants. Hasta Bahadur, one of the king's crack shooters, packed his muzzleloading gun with heavy shells. Without dismounting from my elephant, I helped him climb a tree. Then I moved five yards to the east and helped Sukh Man, the second hunter, climb another tree. They were armed with antiquated muzzleloaders, and both needed a clean shot at close range.

"As the hunters took position, we reorganized our elephants and encircled the mother rhino and her calf. We then moved all the elephants to drive the rhinos toward the hunters. Our biggest elephant, a male tusker, Prem Prasad, led our drive. No rhinos scared this tusker. Slowly, slowly, we drove the rhinos toward the hunters' trees. We were cautious and avoided spooking the mother rhino and her calf. The drive was slow, short, and silent.

"Suddenly, the shots thundered through the jungle. Both the king's hunters had fired simultaneously. The jungle rose toward the sky as birds swarmed upwards in frenzied flights. Elephants howled and hooted in chaos. Langur monkeys scrambled and bounced from tree to tree. We constantly had to whack the elephants hard on their heads to freeze them in their tracks. We let the commotion die down before moving toward the hunters. I moved my elephant toward the trees where I had parked the hunters. As I approached, I spotted the mother rhino flat on the ground in a big pool of blood. Her calf was lying next to her with her head tucked under her mother's belly. The calf too was motionless."

At this point, Ram Lotan paused. His face was somber as if his memories were haunting him. He stared at the fire a long time before continuing his story.

"'Oh, my God,' I burst out at the top of my voice. 'The ugly morons have shot the calf, too,' recalling that there were two shots fired simultaneously. But thank heavens, I was wrong. The calf was alive. She moaned as I got closer. I took a long breath, as I was very relieved to find that the king's hunters had not shot the calf dead, but instead both shot the mother simultaneously.

"We formed a tight circle of elephants around the motionless rhinos. The scene was painful. The mother slept peacefully in death. In contrast, the young calf was preoccupied with pushing her mother with her snout as if pleading with her to wake up. I felt like a criminal. I was very touched as I watched the baby rhino's futile attempts to rouse her mother lying in a pool of blood. We scanned the scene for a long time with a heavy heart. My boss, Tapsi, barked in a weepy voice and reminded us all that our task was to deliver a rhino for the king's coronation. Soon the call of duty overruled our emotions, and we were compelled to get on with the job.

"We threw sticks at the mother rhino to make sure she was dead. We then assembled half of our elephants in a funnel shape. Dozens of our team got to the ground and stretched a long net at the narrow end of the funnel. We moved the elephants to close the funnel and corner the calf. The calf charged. She was entangled in the net but managed to get out of the tangle before we could force her to bay. She ran back to her dead mother and nudged her with her nose. We tightened the circle and closed the gap. The rhino calf was in a rage and charged at the net, only to be entangled once again. Two dozen men scrambled over the calf and used brutal human force to bring her to submission and tie her legs. But the calf fought back with equal ferocity. She bit and kicked her captors and again broke out of the scramble. We backed off our elephants to let the calf soothe her temper.

"The calf moved to her mother once again. She shoved her mother several times with her snout and finally sat down next to the mother to rest. It was a painful sight."

By this time Ram's voice was teary. "I need to attend the call of nature," he said. He walked a few steps away and urinated into a small bush. I wondered if he walked away deliberately to hide his emotions. When he came back, I gave him a short glass of rum, which he downed in one gulp. He took a deep breath before speaking again.

"'Awaii-awaii,' called the calf in distress. But the calf did not know that her mother would never come to rescue her from the clutches of a fleet of elephants and hundreds of humans. With our hearts heavy, we tightened the ring again and finally entrapped the rhino calf in the net. During the process, one of our staff tumbled from an elephant to the ground. The calf hammered him with her head and stepped on his hand. The man ended up with a cracked forehead and a fractured finger.

"After much struggle, we finally exhausted the calf. We anchored all her legs with a long rope. Ten men were tethered at each end of the rope. They kept the rhino at bay by pulling and releasing the rope in synchronicity. The pull and release of the rope matched with the calf's movement. The work was hard, but we managed to centralize the rhino at a safe distance. After a long struggle, the rhino gave up trying to cut loose from the rope. Then we allowed her to rest."

Ram Lotan scratched his forehead and adjusted his cap. Then he extended his glass for another shot of rum, which I gave him. I poured myself a shot of rum and lit a cigarette. Ram Lotan kept silent.

"*Dai*, what happened next?" I asked curiously, addressing him as "elder brother" as a sign of respect.

He took a small sip of rum and continued his story somberly. "We placed Himal Kali, our calmest female elephant, ten feet in front of the rhino calf. The elephant was positioned with her butt end directly pointed towards the calf's head. The elephant's job was to act as a surrogate mother. She had to navigate the rhino calf to our camp half a mile across the river. The men who were anchored to the forelegs of the calf nudged the rope gently until she was up on her feet. She tussled and tried to reach the female elephant in front of her. The elephant moved forward. The calf followed and took a few steps toward the elephant. The men anchored at the rear end tightened the ropes and stopped the rhino from moving forward. After a brief pause, they loosened the grip to let the rhino calf move forward toward the elephant, which was also walking forward. We repeated the process of walk, pause, and walk. The walk was slow, as we allowed the calf to rest frequently. It took us more than an hour to reach the camp and imprison the calf in a pit while it got used to us humans.

"Except for a fractured skull and a broken finger of one of our staff, we had no problem. A few of our elephants that had panicked when the mother charged were lost in the forest several hours. We were pleased that the calf survived and none of our men was badly hurt. In the next two days, the hunters killed another mother, and we snatched a male calf using the brutal force of men and elephants. Our orders said two baby rhinos, a male and a female.

"We hated that job," said Ram Lotan, ending his story with a "*ke garne?*" *Ke garne* is a commonly used Nepalese expression that means "What to do?" It denotes hopelessness or an inability to control a situation.

Except for the crackling sounds of the burning logs, the camp was silent. I was mesmerized as well as disgusted to learn how zoos used this cruel and gruesome technique to get their rhinos. It was a horrible piece of information that I wished I had not known. Yet the question that haunted me was whether I would use this traditional yet brutal technique if I were in Ram Lotan's shoes. After all, following orders and serving my country and my king without any qualms or questions were all part of my job description.

Later I was told that the Khasi tribes in Assam, India, developed the technique of using elephants as surrogate mothers to entice baby rhinos to follow them to camp. They believed that baby rhinos followed elephants mistaking the elephant for their mothers. Apparently, the art is to keep the rhino close but far enough from the elephant to avoid spooking either of them. Like most mammals, elephants resent being approached from behind. They could easily crush a baby rhino if it became entangled in the elephant's legs. The elephant and the driver must be well trained, calm, and quiet.

I faced the test a year later. Following a royal sanction, I was ordered to catch and deliver a pair of baby rhinos to an American zoo as a gift to the American people from King Birendra. This test required me to blend modern science with ancient shamanism.

12

SCIENCE AND SHAMANISM

"*Drinking from one end and pissing from the other,*" *I muttered.* "Farting and shitting in between." I wanted to relieve the tension. We had a long, hard day of capturing rhinos ahead.

My elephant driver laughed. I told him that elephants ate as much as two hundred pounds of food, drank up to fifty gallons of water, and produced about eleven gallons of urine and 170 pounds of dung every day. "No wonder they urinate and defecate frequently," he giggled.

We had just reached the bank of the Dhungre River, hardly three minutes from our camp, and stopped to water the elephants before our long adventure ahead. We watched a convoy of twenty elephants drink water and urinate in the Dhungre River—almost simultaneously. Some elephants passed gas and some discharged dung. The oval-shaped elephant droppings, almost the size of soccer balls, bounced down the river in rhythm, carried by the ripples of the tumultuous river. The morning was cool and comfortable.

A chattering flock of emerald parakeets flew noisily from tree to tree, overriding the sounds and songs of other forest birds. Along the riverbank, a group of lapwings and plovers fluttered their wings as they hobnobbed among the egrets and herons. A group of langur, or black-faced, monkeys nervously gazed toward our camp from the top of a silk cotton tree.

The sound of a motor vehicle in our camp had made them jittery. The sound was from our tractor, our rhino-transportation vehicle. Kuber, our tractor driver, had to drive a mile upstream to cross the Dhungre. Unlike our elephants, his tractor could cross the river only at shallow sites upriver. Kuber and his tractor were vital to our being able to cart our first rhino, destined for an American zoo, back to the camp. That is, if we could catch it!

I started the morning at dawn with our camp wakeup call—a strident series of shrills that sounded like a mad woman shrieking in hysteria. The call came from no human but rather our resident brain-fever bird, the common hawk cuckoo. "Brain fever, brain fever, brain fever," it continued, the noise of each shrill call doubling each time.

"Late to rest, early to rise, and dead at best," I often cursed the cuckoo. "This nasty bird needs neither rhyme nor reason to disturb my sleep." I generally hated this bird, but this morning was an exception. I was glad that the cuckoo had awoken me early, for I had a long day ahead hunting for our first rhino for the Fort Worth Zoo in Texas.

Our operations combined both shamanism and science, with shamanism topping the priority list, as it was part of the Tharu tradition and part of my own belief system. This ancient ritual required us to seek permission of the Ban Devi, the Goddess of the Forest, before venturing into the jungle to catch any wildlife. Badai, the chief Smithsonian elephant driver, performed this ceremony. He was content with this role and felt proud of his skills as a shaman.

He also enjoyed his role of "chief Smithsonian elephant driver," because all five elephants provided by the Smithsonian Institution were under his direct command. Badai, a medium-sized Tharu with sharp facial features and slight hearing loss, was also our camp's dramatist, shaman, and priest. Badai was an expert in rounding up rhinos and tigers for our capture operations. He handled his job quietly and calmly without showing any excitement, despite the tension of our capture operations.

Our jungle rites started as the first rays of sunlight broke out across the sky. I followed Badai as he dragged a black goat to an old silk cotton tree in the middle of the forest, fifty yards from my hut. Walking behind me was Gyan, his deputy, a short, flat-nosed Tharu with deep sunken eyes. Gyan had a red rooster tucked under his arm. Following behind Gyan was Brij Lal, third in the pecking order from our elephant stable. Brij had two white pigeons clutched in his hands. Man Bahadur, the head *shikari*, who was in charge of all our game scouts, and Vishnu, his deputy, followed him. They were carrying the equipment and drugs that scientists from the Smithsonian Institution had trained me to use to sedate rhinos.

The equipment I used had three main components. The first was a rifle that shot a feathered aluminum syringe loaded with drugs. This rifle went by the misspelled trade name "Capchur Gun." But we called it a dart gun. The dart gun came with a few accessories, such as tiny chargers that resembled rifle bullets. The drug we used to sedate adult rhinos was two milligrams of M:99 mixed with two milligrams of a drug called Acepromizine (the dose for young rhinos was half of this amount). M:99 is an extremely potent morphine derivative, which is lethal to humans but safe for rhinos. The effects of M:99 can be completely neutralized by two milligrams of antidote called M:50:50. We used this antidote to wake up a sedated rhino.

I followed Badai to a silk cotton tree, the incarnation of the Goddess of the Forest, who is believed to be everywhere but nowhere. A group of men squatted around the tree in a semicircle. In the middle of the semicircle were a bucket of water and a bottle of *rakshi*, a rice liquor, the equivalent of American moonshine. A pile of cow dung, which is considered holy, and two stainless-steel trays were in front of the tree. One tray contained a reddish mixture of vermilion, rice, and yogurt; three pellets of camphor; one oil lamp;

and a tube of incense. The other contained strips of red ribbon, black sesame seeds, oats, and two tiny bowls with water from the Rapti, a river that defines the northern boundary of the Royal Chitwan National Park.

Badai cleaned the base of the tree designated to be the abode of the Goddess of the Forest. He spread a mixture of cow dung and water around the base before pulling out his *khukuri*, a curved, sharp Nepalese machete, from his belt and penetrating two inches of the blade into the ground. The razor end of the *khukuri* faced the tree trunk. Its wooden handle protruded toward the sky. The position of the machete signified the need to drive away any bad spirits that may have been floating in the air. Then Badai decorated the base of the tree with flowers, red stripes of ribbon, and other items on the trays. He blew air from his mouth three times at the base of the tree in the name of the Hindu Trinity of Brahma the Creator, Vishnu the Preserver, and Maheshwar (Shiva) the Destroyer. After that, he lifted the dart gun and the equipment, placed them on the ground to face the tree, and circled the gun with vermilion. Then he drew another circle on the ground using more vermilion, placed a syringe, the accessories of the dart gun, and a bottle each of M:99 and M:50:50 inside it, and blessed all these capture tools by sprinkling them with a mixture of rice, vermilion, and yogurt.

Badai was now ready for the sacrifice. He dragged the goat three times around the tree to worship the Trinity. Two of his deputies followed him. One held the red rooster, and the other clutched the two white pigeons. Then Badai sat in a lotus position, facing the tree. He lit three camphor pellets, the oil lamp, and a handful of incense sticks and worshipped the tree, chanting hymns in a monotonous and quivering voice and scattering the base of the tree with flowers, rice, and vermilion.

"Time to shiver the goat!" yelled Badai after he said his prayers. Getting the goat to shiver was a lengthy sacrificial ritual. Badai splashed water from the Rapti River in the goat's ears, on its body, and on its genitals to induce the goat to shiver. It took nearly five minutes for the goat to cooperate. Finally it shivered and shook the water from its body. The shaman ceremony required Badai to wait for the animal to shiver its head and body. No goat could be sacrificed without the ritual of a goat shiver, which is a signal of permission from the goat to be sacrificed. Badai pulled the *khukuri* out of the ground and cleaned the dirt off it. He chanted his mantras and sacrificed each animal without any hesitation: the goat, the rooster, and the two pigeons in that order. He placed their heads in a row on the ground facing the Goddess tree and sprinkled the base of the tree with the animals' blood and rice liquor.

"Please circle the tree three times," Badai beckoned me. "Pray to the Goddess for protection." I did as I was told, as I did not question these rituals, some of which dated back to 200 BC. I had no qualms about Badai's performing the jungle rites. The other camp staff members followed.

Badai garlanded all of us with the red strips of ribbon. He marked our foreheads with the mixture of rice, blood, yogurt, and vermilion offered to the Goddess. Later we would feast on the meat of the sacrificed animals, chasing the meat with the *rakshi* moonshine. For the time being, our shamanistic ritual gave us a license to hunt for a rhino calf.

But I had a second ritual to perform, which was not shamanistic. It required me to follow strict scientific instructions for loading the drug in the "Capchur Gun."

We walked back to the camp, where twenty-one elephants were lined up in front of my hut. The number twenty-one is considered lucky because it symbolizes Lord Ganesh, often called the Elephant-God. Ganesh is the Hindu god Shiva's son. He is often worshipped for the initiation and successful completion of any major task. He has a human body with a bulging belly and an elephant's head.

Parked behind the elephants was a tractor with a huge open trailer for transporting the rhinos. Kuber Gurung, the national-park mechanic and the tractor driver, was at its steering wheel. Badai garlanded him with a red ribbon. He also sprinkled the tractor and the elephants with the vermilion-rice mixture.

A large table stood in front of the elephants. The table was covered with a white bedsheet. And at one end was a blue plastic bucket full of water. I walked up to the table and spread out all our ritually blessed capture equipment in an orderly manner. As the drug M:99 is deadly to humans, loading the drug into the aluminum syringe of the dart gun is risky. A tiny speck of this highly concentrated morphine on the skin or a tiny spurt in the eye causes instant death. I was told that more deaths occurred during the loading and unloading of M:99 than from any encounters with wild beasts during capture operations. Thus, I followed the loading procedure in strict sequence and always used the same people for loading drugs into the dart gun, calling out each step as I performed the task.

We checked and ensured that no parts of our skin were exposed. We wore long-sleeved shirts. Our hands were protected by surgical gloves. We also wore large goggles that covered our faces. It made us look comical, but it kept us alive. Vishnu, the deputy head *shikari*, stood behind me with a glass syringe loaded with the antidote M:50:50. His task was to jab the antidote into my butt if there were any mishaps. But he would have less than thirty seconds to save my life.

After much of the morning was spent performing the ritual and loading the dart gun without any incident, we mounted our elephants and headed into the jungle to kidnap a baby rhino for an American zoo.

13

KIDNAPPING BABY RHINOS
FOR AN AMERICAN ZOO

A large patch of grassland stretched along the bank of the Dhungre River. It was scattered with a mosaic of trees resembling an African savannah. The morning was bright and warmed by a November sun. Half a dozen Griffin vultures soared high in the azure sky searching for carrion on the open riverbank.

I scanned the grassland with my binoculars from the top of my elephant. A dense riverine forest stretched from the eastern edge of the grassland. Almost a mile south of us was the home of the rhino we had named Bangi Naq Pothi, or "Crooked-Nose-Female." I knew she had recently weaned a healthy daughter. My commission was to catch, tame, and ship a pair of young rhino calves as a present from the king of Nepal to the city of Fort Worth, Texas, in the United States.

We crossed the river on elephants, marching in a single file, and traversed the grasslands' high bank at the edge of the forest to higher ground. Now, hidden from the grassland, we meandered south through the forest until we found Harkha Man Tamang, a seasoned *shikari* or game scout. He was perched on a branch of a small Bauhinia tree. I dismounted from the elephant and climbed Harkha's tree. From the treetop I got my first view of two rhinos, a mother and a calf, foraging peacefully, side by side.

"It is Crooked-Nose-Female and her daughter," whispered Harkha. "I have been watching her for nearly an hour." I focused my binoculars on the rhinos. The mother rhino's prominent snout proved that he was right. Harkha and I got down from the tree to make final preparations for the kidnapping.

"We will drive the rhinos quietly into the forest in a northwest direction," proposed Harkha, using a stick to sketch his plan on the ground. "Dart the mother first from a tree," he suggested. "Then we will take care of the daughter later."

I looked around to find a tree. The other *shikaris* huddled as they planned the drive, surrounded by our twenty-one elephants. I climbed a ubiquitous Bhelur tree with a bifurcating branch. I could rest my back on the trunk of the tree, which would free my hands to aim my dart gun.

Hidden under the cover of leaves and branches, I watched the *shikaris* organize the drive. Forming a crescent shape, they encircled the rhinos with their elephants. Then they moved forward, closing the gap between the rhinos and the elephants. When they were about ten yards away, the rhinos stopped grazing and moved toward my tree, stopping five yards short of the edge of the forest. Then the mother turned around. She faced the elephants, holding her head toward the sky to smell the air. Rhinos have bad eyesight but a good sense of smell. Her daughter moved behind her, tucked her snout between her mother's hind legs, and nudged her gently. It was as if she were daring her mother to charge the elephants.

The head *shikari* raised his right hand and waved all the elephants to a halt. He moved his elephant a few steps forward before stopping to face the mother rhino head on. The rhino did not retreat. Instead, she took a few steps toward the elephant and then stood still, staring at the larger beast. Barely separated by fifteen feet, both the pachyderms stared at each other, motionless, with their feet frozen to the ground. The battle of nerves had begun. The rhino eyeballed the elephant in an erect and defiant posture. I watched with tense curiosity to see which one would blink and back off first.

The two animals stared at each other a long time without any movement. The elephant was much larger than the rhino, yet the rhino was more aggressive and was the first to make a move. It sniffed the ground and took two more steps toward the elephant. Rhinos often charge and wound domestic elephants when their drivers take them too close to their calves. The head *shikari*'s elephant's stomach rumbled with uneasiness. The elephant driver whacked it on the head with his stick and barked, *"Agath."* He was commanding his elephant not to retreat but to move forward. The elephant moved three steps forward before stopping only twelve feet from the rhino. The rhino too was stubborn. She did not budge but continued to stare at the elephant. Her daughter kept shoving her gently from behind.

Both the animals were in a stalemate. Each was weighing the opponent's moves. It was neither the rhino nor the elephant but the elephant driver who made the next move. He signaled two more elephants to move forward for reinforcement. Shoulder to shoulder, three elephants marched forward to face the rhino. The elephant drivers knew from experience that the rhino would charge if an elephant turned her back. They forced their elephants to face the rhino head on, compelling her to move under my tree so I could dart her.

One elephant driver threw a stick at the rhinos, hitting the mother on the head. *"Phbrrr,"* growled the mother rhino and turned around. The daughter was jittery. She circled her mother and stood by her neck on her left-hand side. The elephant drivers tried to mimic the rhino's growl, by rubbing their fingers against their lips. Their sounds were in total discord. But it caused the rhinos to move toward my tree. The elephants followed both rhinos, a few steps at a time.

The mother rhino, with her calf tagging behind, stopped at the edge of the forest. She turned around, scanned the elephants, and growled a warning. Perhaps realizing that she was outnumbered, the rhino turned her tail and moved briskly toward my tree. The calf followed the mother. The elephants marching along the flank moved faster than the rhinos and narrowed the gap. Steadily, they steered the rhino toward my tree.

The rhino stopped in a small opening directly under my tree. I was nervous. This was not the first time I had darted a rhino, but I was scared. My pulse quickened, and I could hear my heart beat. My palms were sweating, and I was frozen only ten feet up the tree. It was an easy shot, but I did not move. I shivered with fear that the rhino would spot me. I knew that if I remained motionless and attracted no attention, the rhino would not look up. She had no reason to scan treetops because rhinos have no predators that attack them from trees.

Nonetheless, I remembered the time a big female had tried to knock me out of a tree while I was filming her and her calf. Fortunately, the tree was sturdy, and the elephant drivers were quick to chase the rhinos away. But I was a nervous wreck after that, and the drivers had to lift me out of the tree. Thus, I was not taking any chances by alerting Crooked-Nose-Female to my whereabouts.

I knew it was only a matter of time before the rhino would move away from my tree. The rhino's behavior was normal. Most wild animals stop and pause before crossing forest openings. I waited for her to move. I knew I could sneak a shot on her butt when she took a few steps past my tree.

The elephants approached nearer, forcing the rhinos to move past my tree. I now had a clean view of the mother's butt. I took a deep breath, zeroed the dart gun at her right buttock, and gently squeezed the trigger. "*Phutt.*" The dart hit home. The mother jerked her head as if stung by a bee. I looked at my watch. It was 8:38 in the morning. The rhino continued to move away with her daughter in tow. Man Bahadur, the head *shikari*, then brought his elephant under my tree.

"Badai," I ordered as I climbed down to remount my elephant, "rush six elephants immediately to block the riverbank." We wanted to steer the rhino to a spot easily approachable by the tractor before the rhino collapsed under the influence of the drug. But we had to be extremely careful to avoid chasing the drugged rhino into the river. It would be a disaster if she collapsed in the river and drowned under the heavy influence of the drugs. That was the reason six elephants were dispatched to guard the riverside.

Moments like this made me paranoid. I recalled a report about the wanderlust of drugged rhinos, which indicated that they can easily travel six miles at random. Heavy human population was barely a mile south. My paranoia was totally unfounded. The rhino did not move miles but hardly fifty yards before she stopped. The drug was affecting her quickly. Her head drooped. Her tail became relaxed and stopped moving, even to chase the buzzing insects that were swarming at her hind end. Then she lowered her eyelids and tilted her head until it was almost touching the ground. She was dozing while standing and was finding it hard to keep her balance.

Suddenly, she lifted her head and gave a quick stare at my elephant. I had no idea what would happen next. Swaying like a pendulum, she slowly went down, folding her hind legs first to rest on her sternum. Her eyes were open and bloodshot, and her ears flickered in a steady rhythm.

I looked at my watch. It was exactly 8:45. It had taken seven minutes for the drug to take full effect. I had an hour before the drug would wear off to capture her daughter safely.

The daughter circled her mother several times. She nudged her with her snout as if trying to force her mother to stand up. Seeing that her efforts were futile, the calf joined her mother, lying down to rest. She tucked her snout near her mother's udder and hid her head.

"Let's get on with the calf," said the head game scout. "We don't want to lose time." He did the honors. From his seat on an elephant, he aimed his dart gun and zeroed a dart on the shoulder of the young female calf, using only half the dosage of drugs I had used on her mother. The calf jerked as the dart hit home. She was instantly up on her feet and circled her mother. She stared at the elephants and made a mock charge before backing up and nudging her mother with her nose. But her mother did not budge. The daughter circled her mother again and then went to sleep next to her.

I waited another five minutes for the drug to take full effect. I circled the sleeping rhinos on the back of my elephant. The rhinos were in a different world, totally doped, yet their ears flickered as if they could still hear us. This was a good sign that the rhinos were alive and had not been overdosed to death.

I dismounted from my elephant. Badai, my elephant driver, parked my elephant nearby in a sitting position. I wanted to jump on an elephant quickly if the rhinos got up unexpectedly and we had to dash for our lives. It was far quicker and easier to mount a sitting elephant. I took two steps toward Crooked-Nose-Female and threw a stick at her neck. The rhino did not budge. I threw another stick at her daughter. She too did not stir. I gained confidence and moved closer, one step at a time. I poked the mother's anus gently with a stick, but the rhino did not budge. I moved over and poked the daughter's rear end. She too did not move. The drug had obviously taken full effect, and I now felt safe touching the rhinos. I moved behind the sleeping mother rhino. With my hands on her butt, I shook her a few times. The shake had no effect; she was totally sedated. I moved to the daughter and shook her. She too was unconscious. I looked into her mother's eyes. They were bloodshot and wide open. Her ears were flickering. She was alive but totally immobilized.

I covered her eyes with a black towel to prevent direct light from hitting them and to keep her blind and confused, just in case the effect of the drug wore off too soon. Then I plugged her ears with cotton earplugs that had long tails. As a precaution, I tied the earplug tails to a bush so that they would be pulled out automatically when the rhino stood up, in case we forgot to remove them in haste. The elephants surrounded the rhinos in a tight semicircle.

They left an unobstructed opening in the front, just in case the rhinos regained consciousness and needed an easy way out.

Using pliers, I pulled the darts out of both the mother and the calf. Then I unscrewed the darts' caps, tilted them upside down, and made sure that all the contents had been injected. Man Bahadur, the chief *shikari*, cleaned the tiny wounds caused by the dart's impact with water and applied antiseptic creams. His deputy Vishnu took the rhinos' temperatures by sticking thermometers up their anuses. Sometimes the drug causes body temperatures to increase. We needed to maintain a temperature around 103 degrees Fahrenheit to ensure that the rhinos did not die from overheating. Fortunately, it was normal, and both rhinos were ready for measurement.

Using a long cotton tape, the *shikaris* measured both the rhinos, from nose to tail. They also measured their shoulder heights and the size of the mother's horns and incisor teeth. While they were taking measurements, I attached a big black collar to the mother's neck. This was no ordinary collar, but a thick belt band with a radio transmitter embedded in its center. A tiny magnet was attached to the radio transmitter. The magnet was a switch that when removed turned on the electronic connections causing the radio collar to transmit. Each collar transmitted a different frequency so we could trace individual animals. A special receiver synchronized with the transmitter recorded the signals. Radiotelemetry helped us not only to identify individual rhinos but also to determine their location and movements, without any need for direct visual contact.

I had a set of earphones glued to my ears and a receiver dangling around my neck. I removed the magnet and switched on the radio transmitter. "Radio Crooked-Nose-Female is on the air," I announced with a cheerful voice.

So far, the operation had gone well. Nothing unexpected had happened. We doused the rhinos with water to cool their bodies as we waited for the tractor to arrive and transfer the four- to six-month-old calf back to a taming pit in our camp. The anticipation brought back eerie memories from the past, particularly while I was standing three feet away from a two-ton sleeping animal.

Once, during a previous field operation, a sedated male rhino had awoken while I was busy affixing a radio collar on its neck. With its mouth wide open, the awakened rhino attacked me with its huge head in full swing. Fortunately, the effect of the drug had not worn off completely, and he missed me. I survived that episode having learned three lessons: First, always be prepared for the worst; when in the jungle, expect the unexpected. Second, never approach a wild mammal from the front, even one that is drugged; always approach it from the side or the rear. Third, always cover the animal's eyes; wild animals are usually less aggressive when they cannot see.

I was thinking about this incident again when the tractor finally arrived. Kuber, the mechanic, took command. He loaded the rhino calf using a crew of fifteen men, who noisily disturbed the sounds of the jungle with a chorus of *"haisey hostey haisey hostey"*—a commonly used rhythm to synchronize manpower when loading heavy and delicate objects.

The rhino calf was three feet tall and five feet long and weighed about three hundred pounds. Kuber covered her with a thin, dark blanket heavily doused with water. Vishnu, the deputy head *shikari*, climbed into the back of the trailer, next to the sleeping rhino. Two other helpers rode with him. Waving his right hand, Kuber rode off in his tractor pulling a deeply drugged rhino calf on the trailer.

I had two things to do next. The first was to wake up the mother rhino. The second was to beat Kuber to the camp in order to wake up the calf. I needed to give the rhinos shots of the antidote M:50:50 to ensure that they did not die from the effects of the M:99.

I approached the sleeping mother rhino from her right-hand side holding a glass syringe loaded with M:50:50 antidote. I grabbed her right ear and injected the antidote into a thick vein. The antidote was supposed to work in thirty seconds. I was nervous while I gripped the ear of a two-ton prehistoric beast.

I pulled off the black towel to expose the rhino's huge head and eyes and jerked out the earplugs. Then I dashed to mount Mel Kali, my elephant that was sitting ten feet behind the rhino. I looked at my watch. It took me less than fifteen seconds to inject the antidote and run for the safety of my elephant. Once I was seated, my elephant backed away from the rhino to join the others.

All eyes were glued on the mother rhino as my watch ticked away thirty seconds and she still had not budged. The antidote was supposed to have worked by now. A minute passed, and she still did not move. I hated this waiting time the most. It caused me high anxiety and brought back one particular nightmare. During my ten years of experience in capture operations of large Asian mammals, I had never lost an animal, except one. This single mishap with a young and healthy male elephant haunted me every time I wait for a drugged animal to revive.

That elephant was a beautiful animal with a well-shaped sturdy body and a set of smooth and long tusks. But he was a rogue and had killed three people and destroyed crops and a dozen homes in Jhapa in western Nepal. My plan was to catch this elephant alive and to see if I could break and tame him. The capture operation had proceeded perfectly. I darted the tusker, using the same drug that I routinely used for the rhinos. Like the rhinos, the elephant was sedated in less than ten minutes. After tying his legs tightly to the trees to prevent him from escaping, I gave him a shot of the antidote. I was expecting this handsome jumbo to be on his feet within a minute or so. But he died on me within fifteen minutes. I will never forget this disaster.

"What if the mother rhino, like the Jhapa elephant, never wakes up?" I thought, as I looked at my watch for the hundredth time. Man Bahadur, the head *shikari* read my mind. He had been with me when I caught the rogue elephant.

"It is only sixty seconds since you gave the antidote," he uttered quietly.

"But the drug company's brochure says recovery in thirty seconds," I lamented.

He knew that fear had engulfed my body. "Her ears are flickering," he consoled me. "Anyway, you know these foreign brochures are never right."

"I can see the ears, too," I snapped. "Have you forgotten that the Jhapa elephant died flapping his ears?" He ignored me. He too did not like being reminded of the elephant that we killed by mistake.

The jungle was silent. But I would not have heard a cannon fire. My brain was focused on the rhino. The next thirty seconds were the longest wait in my life. Finally, the rhino moved her head slowly and shook it from right to left. Then she raised her head in an erect posture and swayed it up and down in the air.

"*Uth! Uth!*" we called from our elephant, pleading, "Get up on your feet." The rhino was cooperating. She was up within seconds. "*Namaste,*" I saluted her Nepali style, with both of my palms pressed together.

The rest of the staff clapped in rhythm calling, "Hey, hey, hey." The rhino turned around. She stared at me and jerked her head as if she were responding to my salute. I switched on the receiver. "Beep-beep-beep," it signaled.

"*Agath,*" called my elephant driver and ordered the elephants to move forward and go toward the rhino. "*Hbooyn,*" trumpeted my elephant. Other elephants joined in the hooting while the humans clapped their hands in rhythm and great relief.

"Crooked-Nose-Female is cheerful," uttered my euphoric elephant driver. I doubted his sentiments. Yet the mother rhino seemed to be unaware that we had kidnapped her daughter. She turned her back toward me and quietly disappeared into the bush.

14

TAMING TEXAS RHINOS

I was pleased that Crooked-Nose-Female was back to normal. I rushed to my camp on Mel Kali, my elephant, to wake up and begin the process of taming her daughter before shipping her to Ramona Bass, the chairperson of the Fort Worth Zoological Society in far-away Texas.

I wanted to get there before Kuber, who was carting the baby rhino in a tractor, arrived at our camp. Unlike his tractor, which had to find a shallow river crossing upstream, my elephant had no problem with the terrain near the river, and we reached the camp in twenty minutes. Groups of people were milling around a pit less than ten feet behind my house. We had dug this pit over the last three days. It was fifteen feet deep and seven feet wide. It was to serve as our rhino-taming pit.

My cook, Ram Gurung, handed me a steaming mug of tea as I dismounted from my elephant. A roller—a brilliantly colored bird common to Chitwan—fluttered on the branch of a silk cotton tree above my hut. Bundled under the tree were five children, their eyes sparkling with curiosity. They were anxiously waiting for the rhino calf to reach camp. Two mynah birds played noisily on the roof of my kitchen. I sipped my tea and climbed down a wooden ladder into the pit to see if there were any sharp objects like nails or broken glass. I did not want my baby rhino to be hurt.

Kuber arrived in the next fifteen minutes. He was not alone. A mob of villagers, young and old, male and female, were running behind his tractor. Like the children in our camp, they too were curious about the rhino being towed behind Kuber's tractor. There was nothing we could do but let the villagers assuage their curiosity by watching us unload the rhino calf into the pit.

Kuber backed the tractor cautiously to the pit's edge. We unloaded the rhino by sliding her slowly over planks stretching diagonally down into the pit. Once the calf was securely inside, I climbed down a wooden ladder and gave her a shot of the antidote. Then I scrambled up the ladder. Unlike the way it was with her mother, the drug worked fast, and the calf was on her feet in forty-five seconds. The calf did not like the pit and was hopping mad. In a fury she charged several times at the wall of the pit. For the next hour she would attempt to climb out of the pit. Her feet would slip, and she would fall flat on her nose. She would often stop and stare at the humans squatting around the top of the pit, lose her temper, and charge the mud wall of the pit again and again.

Thinking she might be thirsty, I lowered a red plastic bucket full of water. The rhino charged at the bucket and crushed it to pieces. She did not touch a drop of the water that was spilled on the floor. The bucket made her madder. I picked up another bucket and showered her with water from the top of the pit. It did not cool her off but instead made her angrier. She circled the pit, head-butted the wall, tilted her head upward, and looked straight into my eyes. Her eyes were full of anger. Hidden under the anger, I saw a sense of helplessness. It was a sad sight.

"Leave her alone," snapped Ram Lotan, the chief elephant driver. "This is a wild beast and not a Kathmandu city dog. Let Bala Bahadur Lama do his job." Bala, one of our *shikaris*, was the designated rhino tamer. He had a strong rapport with animals. Over the last few days Ram Lotan had coached him in traditional techniques of taming wild rhinos. I got Ram Lotan's message. He did not want me to interfere with the taming of the rhino. So I resorted to becoming a spectator instead of a supervisor.

The rhino struggled to escape from the pit throughout the day. Later in the afternoon Bala tried to bribe her by throwing her cabbage leaves. She kicked the feed with her leg. The rhino was not ready for human friendship. She circled around and made a few more futile attempts to climb out of the pit. But the walls were muddy, and she slipped. She bellowed three times, "*Yaaii, yaaii, yaaii!*" The pitch of her call expressed panic, pain, and anger.

Later in the afternoon I walked to our elephant stable. Five elephants were tethered to huge poles. They were feeding on rice and molasses that was wrapped in the tender leaves of elephant grass. I asked Badai, my elephant driver, to saddle Mel Kali. Within ten minutes I was on a search for the mother rhino in the riverine forests and tall grasslands. I had a radio receiver with directional antennae in my hand. Hanging on my neck, the receiver was connected to a pair of earphones.

We reached the riverbank. The elephant driver stopped and watered the elephant. I scanned the antennae toward the south, trying to pick up a signal transmitted from the radio collar we had fixed on the mother rhino in the morning. We located her directly in front of us in the grassland. We crossed the river and rode the elephant into the grassland, stopping at brief intervals to scan the antennae. I heard the mother rhino before we saw her. She was wailing, "*Yaaii, yaaii!*" with a loud and coarse pitch. Soon we made visual contact. The mother rhino was restless. She moved a few yards, paused, and bellowed "*Yaaii, yaaii!*" repeatedly. In between the "*Yaaii, yaaii!*" she nibbled a few blades of grass and kept moving. "Searching blindly for her calf," whispered Badai in a pained voice. His words made me feel guilty. I was a hostage taker, stealing young babies from their loving mothers.

It was not the first time I had caught baby rhinos for zoos, yet I did feel like a villainous kidnapper who steals a free and happily roaming child from her mother. In the name of science, conservation, and zoo building, was I becoming a cold-blooded, baby-snatching criminal? I could not take it any longer. I returned to the camp. It was dark when we reached home.

Kerosene lamps glowed around the pit. Two elephants, a tusker and a female, were tied to trees closest to the pit. If the mother rhino ventured into the camp, these elephants would trumpet, not only to chase the mother away but also to wake the camp for reinforcements. Nevertheless, it would be a nightmare if the mother rhino jumped into the pit to join her daughter. I flashed a torch down into the pit for one last look for the night. There were no changes in the calf's behavior. She was still charging around.

I could not sleep. The wailing rhino calf kept me awake. My mind meandered between the mother roaming in the wild and her young daughter imprisoned in a fifteen-foot-deep pit, only ten feet from my bed. How would I feel if my role were reversed with the rhino? I would not dream of being parted with my children, as I loved them dearly. I was haunted by the thoughts of the mother rhino looking for her calf and the pathetic calls of the baby rhino imprisoned in the pit. After sulking alone in the dark for a long while, I consoled myself that my actions were for the long-term survival of the species. I believed a new breeding pool of rhinoceros could be established in the captivity of American zoos. And that we could draw upon this pool to reintroduce the rhinos in Chitwan if they ever disappeared from Nepal, as a part of our agreement with the Americans.

I was back at the rhino pit at dawn. But Bala had beaten me there by several hours. He slept right on the edge of the pit. Fifteen feet down below him, the rhino was finally fast asleep. I could hear her breathing. This sight provided some consolation. I went to the kitchen, drank two cups of tea, and walked around the camp. Still,

I was befuddled about what to do if the calf became edgy when it woke up. Unable to take any action, I went back to bed and did not wake until noon. Furthermore, as Bala was doing his job, there was no point for me to hang around and micromanage his tasks.

When I woke up, I dashed to the rhino pit. There were still a few onlookers. I saw Bala squatting at the edge. He was mimicking the "*Yaaii, yaaii*" call of the baby rhino. I had no idea what he was doing. I thought he must have had a few drinks to kill his stress. I was wrong. He was as sober as the king's priest. He was trying to talk with the rhino, and his talking seemed to work. The rhino was resting in the pit with her wide eyes focused on Bala.

"She is quiet today," said Bala, "but still on hunger strike, refusing to eat or drink."

I nodded at him and went to the kitchen for lunch, and when I returned to the pit, I was surprised to see Bala scratching the rhino's back with a long stick. The rhino jerked and tried to bite off the tip. Bala quickly pulled away the stick, and then poked it back again. He must know what he is doing, I thought as I watched him play his little game. The game went on throughout the afternoon. Then, for the first time, the rhino did not become excited when Bala let her bite off the tip of the stick. Bala tried again with a new stick. The baby rhino let him scratch her back a few times before snapping the stick in half. But the rhino was becoming less aggressive. Bala did not give up. He continued for another hour, during which the rhino allowed him to scratch her back a few more times. Bala lost a few sticks in the process and finally gave up by five in the afternoon.

"Time to try water again," said Bala as he lowered a blue bucket into the pit. The rhino gored the bucket and spilled the water on the floor. To my surprise, she licked the water from the muddy floor. It was the first time I had seen her drink in captivity.

"Maybe she doesn't like the blue bucket," I suggested, not knowing if rhinos were sensitive to any particular color. "Let's try a flat container." We improvised with an aluminum rice plate that was about an inch deep. I was right; it worked. The rhino drank up the water that Bala lowered into the pit. Encouraged by the rhino's behavior, Bala repeated the exercise. Again the rhino finished the second offering of water. She must have been terribly dehydrated. Bala tried for the third time, but the rhino had had enough. She kicked the plate and trampled it into twisted metal.

"What about food?" I asked.

"She has not touched what I gave her," said Bala, pointing at a heap of grass, cabbages, and spinach at the bottom of the pit.

I left Bala to deal with the young rhino in the pit. It was time for me to go back to the jungle to find her mother. I was anxious to see if she was still wandering in search of her calf. Guided by the radio signal, it was easy to find her again. We made visual contact within forty-five minutes. She was foraging in an open grassy patch on the edge of the forest. Yet, unlike yesterday, she was not roaming the jungle restlessly. She was no longer wailing for her calf. I watched her for half an hour and returned to camp, where I had an early dinner and went to bed feeling a bit better.

Day Three turned out to be a good one. I started the day early and immediately went to the jungle to track the mother rhino from my elephant. It took me more than an hour this time to locate her. She had crossed the river into a patch of forest to the west of the site where we had sedated and radio-collared her. I found the scene encouraging as I watched her foraging quietly in a small forest opening with a handsome male nibbling at a bush only a few feet away. Female rhinos average one calf every three to four years after they reach sexual maturity at six to eight years. I hoped that this female could mate with the male in a few days and produce a new calf after a gestation period of fifteen to sixteen months.

"Is that the Pradhan Pancha?" I asked my driver jubilantly, pointing at the good-looking male that was grazing with Crooked-Nose-Female. Pradhan Pancha meant "Village Headman," a name we had given this male rhino because he was the biggest in the area.

"Yes," replied my elephant driver in an equally joyous voice. "I believe Pradhan Pancha also sired the daughter we have in the camp." The elephant driver had good reason to suspect this. Pradhan Pancha was the dominant male in our area. He was easily recognizable by his large head and shapely horn, and he rarely moved beyond a two-mile radius. He had plenty of food around him and enough females to keep him occupied. He also had no challenger that could push him out of his territory. I climbed a tree and watched the rhinos for another hour before returning to camp.

Bala was still working at taming the baby rhino in the pit. He held a long, thin, sturdy bamboo stick in his right hand. A band of white cloth was smoothly wrapped at one end of the bamboo. A stainless-steel bowl filled with a mixture of honey, sugar, and water was next to Bala. They were the ingredients of Bala's "rhino lollipop."

Bala dipped the cloth end of the bamboo into the bowl, lowered the stick, and tried to smear the baby rhino's lips with the juicy syrup. "Bite it," pleaded Bala to the rhino. The rhino ignored him. She moved to the other end of the pit. She turned her back to the stick and went to sleep.

Bala moved to the other end of the pit and tried again. He poked the rhino's snout with the syrupy stick. The rhino turned around to another corner and buried her snout hidden between her shoulder and the wall of the pit. I felt that the baby rhino was not amused with Bala.

"She is not interested," I teased Bala.

"Matter of time," he replied.

Bala did not give up. He was as stubborn as the young rhino. He tried to get the rhino to lick the stick several times, recharging the tip at brief intervals. The rhino behaved as if she had had enough. She nipped at the cloth with anger. But her anger was short-lived. She seemed to like the sweet taste. She looked up at Bala and licked the syrupy end of the stick.

"Got you hooked," murmured Bala. He recharged the stick and dropped it to the rhino again. This time, the rhino did not need any encouragement. She licked the cloth and even tried to eat it, before Bala jerked it away.

"Time to break your hunger strike," said Bala, as he continued seducing the rhino in the pit with the sweet syrup. This time he flashed a piece of cabbage dipped in the syrup, which he had put on the end of the stick in place of the cloth. The rhino chewed the cabbage. Bala offered her more, some dipped in syrup and some without. It did not seem to make any difference to the rhino. She gobbled it all up.

Bala had finally broken the rhino's hunger strike, and I congratulated him. I knew now that this rhino at least would not die of dehydration or starvation. That evening we had a small party to celebrate the initiation of the taming of the rhino. We ate and drank, sang popular Nepali songs, and danced to the beat of a *madal*, a Nepalese drum, played loudly by our Tamang game scouts. Finally, exhausted, I went to sleep around nine, feeling slightly drunk but fully satisfied.

It was past midnight when I awoke to a human voice whispering, "*Yey, nani. Yey, nani*" ("Hello, young lady"). A soft and gentle rhino call followed the human sound. I rushed to the rhino pit. Bala was wrapped up in a blanket, and he was swaying at the edge of the pit.

"What are you doing?" I asked Bala in a loud voice.

"Talking to the rhino," he quietly answered. "Soon we will be friends."

He was right, but it took him two more days of hard work and patience. On Day Five the baby rhino allowed Bala to lower a ladder into the pit and ate out of his hand, while he stayed safely on the ladder. On Day Six the calf allowed Bala to touch and scratch her ears from the ladder. On Day Seven Bala joined the rhino in the pit. He had finally established the rhino-human bond that would make it easier for all of us to interact with her. On Day Eight I too joined

Bala in the pit and fed the tamed rhino. Now we could take her out of the pit and put her in a cage at night, and allow her to roam the camp freely during the day under close watch.

In two weeks' time we found her a mate in the Tikoli forest, a narrow strip of jungle ten miles north of our camp. We tamed this rhino in seven days; he was less temperamental than the female calf. Now we had a breeding pair of rhinos captured and tamed for Fort Worth Zoo. To avoid any inbreeding we caught the male miles away from the site where we caught the female calf, as a precaution to ensure that they were not close blood relatives.

Both the rhinos provided fun and frivolity in our jungle camp. I was very much attached to them. They were like my children, eating out of my hands and often taking afternoon siestas with me in the shade of our camp. We fondly called them the Texas Rhinos. We had not named them, as we did not have that right. Only His Majesty the King had this privilege, since the rhino calves were designated by royal decree as a "State Gift from the King and the people of Nepal to the President and the people of the United States of America." Yet we loved them and did not want them to leave us. However, I knew that I soon would have to ship them away to the Fort Worth Zoo as part of a packaged deal by the World Wildlife Fund, the leading Washington-based wildlife-conservation group.

The World Wildlife Fund had made this deal at the behest of Edward P. Bass, a Fort Worth billionaire and philanthropist. Ed Bass has supported major conservation programs in Nepal, benefiting both nature and cultural heritage preservation. Yet it was not Ed but rather his sister-in-law Ramona Bass who was looking for the newest blood from the Asian rhino gene pool for her Fort Worth Zoo. As the chairperson of the Fort Worth Zoological Society, she wanted her hometown zoo to be in the forefront of American zoos. Ramona had the brains and the funds to accomplish her mission. She knew that no other Asian country but Nepal could provide her with wild rhinos. Thus, she enticed her brother-in-law, Ed Bass, who had strong connections in Nepal and the World Wildlife Fund, to broker a deal.

Fortune magazine had ranked the Bass brothers among America's richest people. Sequestered in Nepal, I did not know that when King Birendra's younger uncle introduced me to Ed in 1979. The king's uncle first met the Bass family when he was traveling with King Mahendra on his state visit to the United States in 1961. King Mahendra and Ed's father, Perry, hit it off at their first meeting during that state visit. Both loved hunting, while Ed did not. He loved daring ventures and liked to create new and controversial projects. One of them was Biosphere 2, the world-famous miniature life-supporting system in a three-acre enclosure.

Despite being preoccupied with Biosphere 2, Ed Bass often visited Chitwan and maintained his interest in saving rhinos in Nepal, where he had also built the Hotel Vajra in the 1970s. An architectural masterpiece, the hotel was designed by top architects and artists from Nepal, America, and Tibet. An unusual Bohemian place in Kathmandu, it soon became a flocking point for artists and scholars from all over the world. While building the Vajra Hotel, Ed was also promoting the Institute of Eco-Techniques, a think tank devoted to balancing human needs with nature conservation.

Then I found out that Ed was years ahead of his time, with a vision of the importance of striking a practical balance between human economic needs and nature preservation. He talked about "sustainable development" in the early seventies, long before it became the mantra of Western environmentalists at the Earth Summit in Rio de Janeiro in 1992. However, at the local level in Nepal, even in the seventies, we had little problem understanding Ed Bass's philosophy. There we struggled daily with the challenge of how to save endangered species such as rhinos and tigers in an island surrounded by a sea of humanity, a sea steeped in poverty and overridden by a mass of humanity hungry for food, fodder, and firewood.

I did not know much about the Fort Worth Zoo in the late 1970s. I did not even know that the city had a zoo. But I had no qualms about providing Fort Worth with two Nepalese rhinos. I had faith in the World Wildlife Fund, particularly its chairman, Russell E. Train, who was a driving force in garnering international support for nature conservation in Nepal. Furthermore, I was given the responsibility of carrying out this task as part of a tripartite deal between the World Wildlife Fund, the government of Nepal, and the Fort Worth Zoological Society. In exchange for the pair of rhinos, Ed Bass would donate $150,000 to the World Wildlife Fund on behalf of the Fort Worth Zoological Society. The World Wildlife Fund would then manage the fund and use it as leverage to generate additional funds from other sources. These funds would be exclusively reserved for saving wild rhinos in Nepal.

I needed funds and international support to implement my first-of-its-kind venture in Asia of providing a second home for the Chitwan rhinos in Bardia, as an insurance against keeping all the rhino eggs in one Chitwan basket. This was the promise I had made to my long-dead friend Tapsi. Thus, keeping my part of the deal, I caught and tamed two rhinos for the Fort Worth Zoo in exchange for the financial resources that I needed to reach my goals. The problem was that I was becoming attached to the rhino calves that I had reared in captivity. These rhinos provided entertainment for our camp. They also provided a source of income for some of the more enterprising children of our staff.

One day I was resting on the big lawn amusing a few children by using the male baby rhino's butt as my pillow. Almost twenty feet away, two boys were playing with the female. One was holding a small bucket and teasing the rhino's rear end with his fingers to make the calf urinate. The other was in front with a bucket persuading the rhino to drink water to recharge her urinary system. Their actions were not new but routine. The boy with the bucket was the son of Vishnu, the deputy head game scout. His partner was the son of Bir Bahadur, one of our elephant drivers. These two kids were working hard to corner the rhino-urine market. The female Texas rhino obliged them. Later they would repeat the process on the male rhino. Vishnu's son collected the rhino urine in another bucket, and the boys would later subdivide the rhino pee into small bottles and sell it as medicine supposed to cure asthma. They would sell each bottle for the equivalent of twenty-five cents—a lot for young children at the time.

Perhaps it seems paradoxical that we adults did not dispel their practice, as it further supported the notion that rhino parts have pharmaceutical properties. Nevertheless, collecting and selling rhino urine was a common practice by rhino keepers in Asian zoos, and it did not involve killing any animals. So if the need for rhino urine kept the species alive, I was happy to allow the boys to collect and sell it.

I often took the rhinos for a walk in the village, to the amusement of tourists. The animals followed me like a pair of friendly dogs, often nudging my legs with their snouts. When the days were hot, I walked them to the river for a bath along with our elephants and the village buffaloes. However, I had to be on guard that they did not get close to an elephant. I did not want to take any chance of their getting hurt. I also never took them into the forest because I did not want to take any chances of an encounter with other rhinos, particularly their mothers.

I lived with these rhinos for three months before we got an order from the Royal Palace in Kathmandu stating that King Birendra had decided to name them. The male calf was named Arun ("Rising Sun") and the female Aarati ("Evening Prayers"). In a small ceremony in our jungle camp, Badai—our camp shaman— whispered these names into each of the rhino's ears after we had performed our usual ritual of worshipping the Goddess of the Forest by sacrificing a goat, a chicken, and a pigeon. It was now the time and our fate to part ways with our beloved rhinos.

I consulted a Nepalese astrologer to choose the appropriate day for the ceremony. He selected May 23, 1991, the birthday of Lord Gautam Buddha, a son of Nepal and the Apostle of Peace. His birthday is an auspicious day to both the Hindus and Buddhists of Nepal.

A quaint handover ceremony was organized at Kathmandu's Tribhuvan International Airport in front of a big yellow Lufthansa German Airline Jet, an aircraft assigned to take the rhinos to Dallas–Fort Worth Airport via Frankfurt, Germany. In a formal procedure, witnessed by Nepalese press, priests, and palace bureaucrats, the American ambassador, Julia Chang-Bloch, formally received the rhinos from the secretary of His Majesty's Government of Nepal, the Ministry of Forests on behalf of the United States of America. The ceremony ended after a few slow speeches and firm handshakes between American and Nepalese officials who had gathered at the airport.

Fate works in strange ways, I thought, as I watched Lufthansa's ground staff load Arun and Aarati, my beloved rhinos, into the cargo hold of the plane. Fate had forced me to snatch the baby rhinos from their mothers, only to nurture and love them before finally putting them on a German aircraft for a journey of no return, across two continents to America.

I could not take my eyes off the airplane as it circled in the clear blue skies of the Kathmandu Valley. My eyes were teary, and my heart ached as I watched the huge yellow plane soar high over the Himalayas and disappear into the clouds. Just below the first-class cabin, in a special compartment of Lufthansa German Airlines Flight 765, were two of my favorite rhinos. They were on their epic journey to a new home in the United States.

A year later I visited the rhinos in the Fort Worth Zoo, where they lived in a large and spacious enclosure. They did not recognize me. However, my feelings were not hurt. They looked good and well cared for. In a gala ceremony hosted by Ramona Bass, the chairperson of the Fort Worth Zoological Society, the mayor of Fort Worth honored me with a title of "Honorary Citizen of the City of Fort Worth" for delivering a pair of rhinos to his town. I felt privileged by this recognition and was encouraged in my efforts to keep rhinos alive, both in the wild and in captivity.

The two Nepalese rhinos proved to be a major attraction to the denizens of America who flocked to the Fort Worth Zoo to see them. But these rhinos were no different from their ancestors, who had also captivated European popes, potentates, royalties, and commoners throughout history.

The face of the greater one-horned rhino. (Courtesy: Masahiro Iijima)

The sharp incisors are the rhino's main weapon of defense.
(Courtesy: Masahiro Iijima)

With armor-like skin, the rhinos resemble modern-day dinosaurs.
(Courtesy: Masahiro Iijima)

A rhino watch post on the edge of Chitwan National Park.
(Courtesy: Fiona Sunquist)

We relied both on shamanism and science for all of our jungle operations, none of which commenced without worshipping Ban Devi, the Goddess of the Forest. (Courtesy: Chris Wemmer)

Population growth and poverty are the root causes of the destruction of rhino habitat. (Courtesy: Sushma Mishra)

A normal day in the life of the people in Chitwan. A Tharu homemaker delicately balances a water pot on her head as she carries a basket full of vegetables. (Courtesy: Tiger Tops, D. B. Basnet)

My heart was broken when I bid farewell to this rhino named Arun ("The Rising Sun") as he boarded a Lufthansa flight to Frankfurt on his one-way trip to the Fort Worth Zoo in Texas. (Courtesy: Sushma Mishra)

Rana Prime minister Juddha (center) is flanked by his
sons and grandsons after a hunt in Chitwan in 1937.
(Courtesy: Kaiser Library)

In the early 1930s, Chitwan was the scene of many rhino massacres.
(Courtesy: Kaiser Library)

Subba Ram Lotan, the Chief Elephant Driver, balances a dart gun on
the head of his elephant. (Courtesy: Brot Coburn)

Mounting an elephant head-on is the most expedient method but
takes a bit of practice. (Courtesy: Sushma Mishra)

The elephants line up before going into the jungle to help catch a rhino. (Courtesy: Brot Coburn)

I always approached the sedated rhinos from behind to make sure that the drug had taken full effect. (Courtesy: Sushma Mishra)

A drugged rhino is loaded on a sledge and hauled to a loading
area. This rhino was on its way to its new home in Royal
Bardia National Park. (Courtesy: Sushma Mishra)

The rhinos return home to Bardia after one hundred years. One of the
rhinos we moved from Chitwan to Bardia gives birth to a calf, indicating
the success of our pioneering endeavors. (Courtesy: Masahiro Iijima)

15

POPES, KINGS, QUEENS, AND THE RHINO

As early as 1500 AD, rhinos have held a mysterious fascination for popes and potentates, royalty and commoners throughout Europe. Pope Leo, who reigned in the Vatican in the fifteenth century, was no exception. Stories about the rhino from his missionaries returning to Rome from their outposts in Africa and Asia heightened his craving for a pet rhino for the papal court. News that the pontiff wanted a rhino triggered a competition among the Christian kings of Europe eager to win political favors. They issued a series of orders to their colonies throughout the world.

Eventually, in 1515, King Manuel I of Portugal presented Pope Leo with an Asian rhino shipped from Goa, the Portuguese outpost in India. The Portuguese monarch believed that the gift would persuade the religious ruler to reserve a large portion of South America for Portugal. Unfortunately for him, the Spanish king, through his ambassador in Rome, had also bribed Pope Leo with an African rhino from his colonies in West Africa. The pope, for reasons not yet discovered, preferred the Spanish-African rhino to the Portuguese-Asian rhino and gave Spain more territory to colonize in the New World.

There is another version of the story of the pope's rhino indicating that many of the stories about the rhinos and European royalty are hearsay or are works of fiction based upon European history. Yet they are compelling and entertaining.

In 1527 the king of Cambay—the modern-day Mumbai in western India—presented a greater one-horned Indian rhinoceros to King Emmanuel of Portugal. The Portuguese king was fascinated by this strange-looking unicorn. He wanted to test the rhino's skills and strengths. He summoned his best elephant to the courtyard of his royal palace in Lisbon and released the rhino with the elephant in a ring to watch a contest between these two huge pachyderms. But there was no contest. The elephant took one look at the rhino and fled in fright from the palace courtyard into the streets of Lisbon. It took a garrison of palace guards to drive the pachyderm back to the royal palace, even though it was a tame Indian elephant. King Emmanuel decided to present the rhino to the pope to win the pontiff's favor. Alas, on the way from Lisbon to Rome, the ship carrying the rhino capsized off the coast of Italy, and the rhino was lost in the Tyrrhenian Sea.

By 1740 the rhino was an object of major curiosity in Europe. An enterprising Dutchman imported a Javan rhinoceros to Vienna from the Dutch colonies of the East Indies—now modern-day Indonesia. He fed the rhino hay, French wine, and Dutch beer. The rhino was a major sensation with the socialites of Europe. Madame Pompadour, the favorite mistress of Emperor Louis XV, was one of the rhino's most ardent admirers. She liked to stroke the rhino's body and feed him orange peels, while singing the praises of his beautiful face.

By the nineteenth century the rhino had become a prized trophy for European colonial rulers in Asia and Africa. However, unlike Madame Pompadour, they did not sing songs praising the rhino's face. They shot them for fun and hung their stuffed heads in their living rooms.

The rulers of South Asia were equally enamored of the rhinos. Babur, the Muslim ruler who established the Mogul dynasty across northern India in 1526, killed a thousand rhinos in the floodplains of the Indus River. Babur hunted rhinos from horseback, often employing as many as three thousand people to help him make his kills. He also played war games with his cavalry during rhino hunts. His cavalry were allowed to feast on rhino meat, but Babur took the heads to decorate his courtyards in Delhi. His knights made walking sticks and shields to protect the human body from swords or arrows out of the rhinos' thick hides.

The Hindu maharajah of Cooch Bihar in India staged one of the most dramatic modern hunts in the early twentieth century. He killed 207 rhinos in northeast India, shooting them from the back of an elephant. The maharajah was also fond of feasting on rhinoceros testicles and believed that they were the source of his virility in keeping his two dozen mistresses amused.

The British imperial rulers of South Asia did their best to compete with the Hindu and Muslim monarchs. The British, who ruled India from 1757 to 1947, referred to the greater one-horned Asian rhinoceros as the Indian rhino, a name that the Nepalese, who never came under the influence of the British or any other imperial power, studiously avoid. However, the British aristocrats also persuaded the rulers of Nepal to invite them for rhino hunts in Chitwan. In 1911 England's King George V bagged eighteen rhinos in Nepal. Three decades later Lord Linlithgow, viceroy of British India, deployed more than one hundred elephants to hunt down thirty-eight rhinos in Chitwan.

By the early twentieth century only a thousand rhinos were left in Chitwan. However, their numbers remained stable until the 1950s, as these hunts were controlled in order to allow the rhinos to recoup. Furthermore, human density in Chitwan was stable, and the rhino habitat remained intact. In addition, Nepal was a closed country, and only a few dared to venture into the sequestered kingdom. Most of the world was not even aware that the rhino existed in this mountainous country.

However, it was not only the Asian and Arab potentates that were fascinated by mythical powers of the rhino horn. Britain's Queen Elizabeth I had a rhino horn hidden in her private chambers. She called it the "unicorn horn" and licked it before going to bed, presumably as an alternative to the sleeping pill. Conversely, many Britons, particularly the cynics and the antimonarchists, believe that her motives were perverse.

The practice of making luxurious handicrafts from rhino horns for noblemen and royalty dates back to the fourteenth century. Chinese craftsmen carved exquisite works of art from rhino horns for the Ming dynasty, from 1368 to 1644 AD. In the 1780s rhino horns were widely used by French royalty to check for poison in food served to them. It was believed that cups made of rhino horn detected certain poisons. The theory was that the keratin and gelatin compounds in the rhino horn reacted to strong alkaloids common in most poisonous substances.

Yemeni noblemen presented daggers, known as *jambiyas*, handcrafted with rhino-horn handles to their young relatives and guests to mark a coming-of-age ceremony. During the oil price boom in the 1970s, even ordinary Yemenis working in the oil fields of Saudi Arabia used their hard-earned wealth to buy rhino-horn daggers, wearing them as status symbols. In the late 1980s one rhino-horn dealer in Sana'a, the capital of Yemen, boasted of importing 36,700 kilograms of rhino horns between 1970 and 1988. This is the equivalent of killing at least 12,750 wild rhinos, mostly African rhinos, whose horns are larger, curvier, and smoother than Asian rhino horns.

However, following pressures from international nongovernment organizations, in 1987 the Grand Mufti of Yemen issued a *fatwa* declaring that the killing of rhinos for making *jambiyas* violated Islamic principles. Combined with the scarcity of rhinos in the wild, the *fatwa* has been instrumental in reducing the importation of rhino horns in Yemen since the 1990s.

Until 1978 I believed the fascination the noblemen and royalty had with rhinos was outdated. I was wrong. Five years after helping establish a sanctuary to save the rhino by creating the Royal Chitwan National Park, I faced my first real dilemma as a conservator and a wildlife scientist in Nepal.

I was at my jungle dwelling in October 1978 when I received a highly confidential letter, marked with the seal of His Majesty's Government of Nepal. King Birendra Bir Bikram Shah Deva, successor to King Mahendra in 1971, had decreed that he was going to perform the Tarpan ceremony in Royal Chitwan National Park. The Tarpan rites required Nepalese kings to hunt and kill a male rhino and then make an offering of the beast's blood to the monarch's ancestors and pray for peace and prosperity in the kingdom. It was expected to be done at least once after a king ascended to the throne of Nepal. I was ordered to be a lead member of a task force to plan the kill.

The order hit me hard. I was not in favor of the monarch's killing a rhino as part of an outdated religious rite. I was a Western-educated scientist and did not believe in these superstitious ceremonies. Furthermore, I was a member of the Species Survival Commission of the International Union for Conservation of Nature and Natural Resources (World Conservation Union)—a Swiss-based global custodian of flora and fauna. Rhinos topped the list of rare and endangered species in the Union's Red Data Book. Saving rhinos, not hunting them, had become my job description and my obsession. Now I, a professional wildlife conservator, was being ordered to help the king of Nepal, who was believed to be an incarnation of the Hindu god Vishnu, the protector of life, to kill a rhino.

Too many questions erupted in my mind. Why did the king have to do it, and why now? Did individual creatures have to be sacrificed for the good of the species? I talked it over first with my wife, Sushma. She belonged to a traditional middle-class Nepalese Brahmin family in Kathmandu. Like most Nepalese women in a society dominated largely by chauvinistic men, she was shy in public, but affirmative and practical in private. I often relied on her judgment. We had been married for six years. She had moved with me to the jungles of Chitwan, giving up the more comfortable life she had known in Kathmandu for a mud-and-thatch hut built on sal tree stilts near the banks of the Dhungre River.

"I am a conservationist, not a hunter," I argued, looking out from the porch of our jungle home as we ate our dinner of *dal, bhat,* and *tarkari* (lentil soup, rice, and curried vegetables) with garlic pickles.

"You are a servant of the king," my wife said. "And as a civil servant, your job is not to ask and reason why." She smiled after quoting Tennyson and then added, "Anyway, what choice do you have in the matter?"

She was right. Did I have a choice? Actually, I had two choices: either resign in contempt of a government order or save my job by staining my hands with rhino blood. Greed for the job won. I also felt that I could do more for the rhinos by staying in my present position. Decades of experience with man and beast in Nepal had taught me to temper my idealism with realism. I also knew that King Birendra was not interested in bagging a huge number of rhinos or in acquiring a trophy for his smoking room. He was participating in a royal ritual, not a massacre. Yet I still had my reservations.

I went to Kathmandu to find Budda Ba, a seventy-five-year-old, wrinkle-faced veteran of a royal rhino hunt during King Birendra's father's era. Born to the Magar community in the mountains of northwest Nepal, Budda Ba had served with a crack battalion of the royal guards and earned a reputation as the enlisted man's enlisted soldier, retiring with the rank of a sergeant. He was not a rich man but had been my father's helping hand for the chores in our own stable. I knew him from my early teenage days.

Budda Ba had traveled with the late King Mahendra and was on active duty when the king performed the Tarpan in Chitwan in

1953. When I went to speak with him, Budda Ba was sitting at a table in his retirement dwelling, an abandoned stable near my home in Kathmandu. I hoped that Budda Ba would help me understand the details of the Tarpan. I also hoped that talking with him would help me resolve my internal conflicts about killing a rhino.

"Some say King Mahendra died in a rhino-hunting accident," I said in order to break the ice, even though I knew that it was not true. I was intentionally trying to provoke him.

"Nonsense. Kathmandu rumors," snorted Budda Ba, who was not only stubborn but also moody. "King Mahendra didn't die in a hunting accident; he died of a massive heart attack."

I shrugged and pretended to be surprised.

"The good king died with a pen in his hand and a smile on his face," he muttered angrily," not a gun in his hand. At his death he was composing poetry on the banks of the Narayani River." Budda Ba started to sing, "*Himalko sunaula chcchura ko chaya muni Chitwanako gainda hathi mujurrako tati,*" muddling together several popular Nepalese songs. "Under the shadows of the golden peaks of the Himalayas march the rhinos, elephants, and flocks of peacocks of Chitwan."

I filled Budda Ba's glass full of *rakshi*, Nepal's country liquor, which I had brought with me to soften him up, as I tried to get him to reveal the details of King Mahendra's Tarpan. Still Budda Ba did not want to talk specifics. All he wanted to do was praise the late King Mahendra and criticize the current monarch, King Birendra.

"Not even fifty elephants in King Birendra's coronation procession," grumbled Budda Ba as he chased his glass of *rakshi* with pickled goat meat. "Too much money and effort spent indulging foreigners and Western-educated brats like you. Little done for his own loyal citizens like me. It has been six years since Birendra ascended the throne, yet he has not performed the holy rhino Tarpan.

Why? Because he lends his ear only to arrogant and Westernized sycophants that have no respect for our culture and civilization."

Budda Ba's words were a consolation to me. It made me feel better that I had compromised my ethics to hold on to my job. I felt that King Birendra was performing the Tarpan only under pressure from religious zealots and that he had stalled the rite as long as he possibly could. Before talking with Budda Ba, I had asked myself, "How could a king who created Nepal's first national park hunt a rhino, the kingdom's rarest endangered species and celebrated symbol of the country?"

But this would not be the only time that I had to live with contradictions in my efforts to save the rhinos. For the time being I felt that Budda Ba was right. The crux of the matter was that King Birendra had not performed the Tarpan, an act he was supposed to do at least once in his reign, immediately after his coronation in 1973.

King Birendra, a bespectacled, cigar-smoking monarch in his thirties, was educated at Eton and Harvard. After Harvard, Birendra studied in Tokyo and took short courses and study tours in Moscow and Beijing. When his education was complete, Birendra returned to Nepal. He followed in his father's footsteps, literally, walking throughout the country to learn about his native land. Birendra naturally hired Western-educated aides, who surrounded him, whether on a trek in the Himalayas or in his palace in Kathmandu.

His aides were more concerned about the new king's image in the Western media than about traditional Nepalese rites and ceremonies. To them most religious traditions were outdated superstitions consuming time and money, with little place in modern Nepal. However, King Birendra came to realize that modern economic models alone could not rule Nepal. Although he was king, he, like everyone else, had obligations and duties, which he could delay but not denounce. King Birendra had delayed the Tarpan long enough. And the Nepalese people, like Budda Ba, were growing impatient.

Neither his aides nor I had any power to delay the ruler's rhino hunt. The constitution of Nepal bestowed King Birendra with absolute power. No one dared or was allowed to question any decisions of this gentle and humble monarch. A few years of Western upbringing were no match for thousands of years of tradition. Traditionalists like Budda Ba linked floods, landslides, and even political mishaps to the monarch's failure to observe the religious rituals such as the Tarpan. They believed that the king's shirking of his religious duties had angered the deities and spirits of his dynasty. Singha Darbar—the Lion Palace—had accidentally burned down in 1973. In addition, there had been a few floods and landslides in some parts of the country over a five-year period, but this was not an unusual phenomenon in a mountain kingdom with heavy seasonal monsoon rains.

Surprisingly, some of the supporters of the rhino hunt were not even Nepalese but a few Western anthropologists who had flocked to Nepal in the seventies. They, too, sided with traditionalists like Budda Ba, arguing that sustaining tradition and preserving culture were paramount to wildlife preservation in Nepal. They openly voiced concerns that young, Western-educated youths like me did not know the significance of our own cultural practices. I resented the opinions of foreign anthropologists who did not have to live within the restrictions of our traditional society. At times I also felt that if these Westerners had their ways, they would convert us into a living museum. I also thought Budda Ba was wrong to criticize the Westernized bureaucrats upon whom King Birendra relied to help him run his government. After all, I was one of them.

Nevertheless, only after talking with Budda Ba did the importance of the Tarpan dawn upon me. Killing one rhino was both a cultural and a political necessity. As Budda Ba believed, it could also help to maintain harmony between religion and modern culture. Moreover, as aptly pointed out by an anthropologist, the

Tarpan elevated the rhino to a royal or sacred status. And in many ways this helped preserve the species.

Yet it was neither Budda Ba nor Western anthropologists but a coterie of courtiers, including me, who would ultimately decide the fate of this one ritual rhino in a meeting at the Royal Palace in Kathmandu, a city full of rumors, deceit, and intrigues.

16

PALACE INTRIGUES

If natural beauty were a measure of its economic wealth, Nepal would rank among the richest nations on earth. Ranging from near sea level to the highest point on earth, this small kingdom displays an ecological spectrum unmatched elsewhere on the globe. The country's natural beauty is equally matched by its cultural patrimony, blending Hinduism with Buddhism. Nepal's rich natural and cultural heritage has attracted thousands of tourists from the West. Once when addressing a travel-trade convention, I joked, "Nepal has three religions: Hinduism, Buddhism, and Tourism."

A colleague, Chandra Gurung, who came from Siklis, a village in the popular tourist-trekking circuit in the Annapurna Himalayas, took my remark seriously. He designed a T-shirt that became one of the hottest selling items to trekkers. It read, "Nepal is here to change you, not for you to change her."

Lord Buddha, the prince of peace, was born in a place called Lumbini in western Nepal. Lumbini was only a few hours away from our Chitwan camp on the East-West Highway. Parallel to the highway, fifty miles north as the crow flies, marched the mighty Himalayas. These mountains, the tallest on earth, buffer the temperate Tibetan plateau from the tropical plains of India, and Nepal stands between Tibet and India.

Before 1950 the Rana prime ministers, a familial oligarchy, ruled Nepal for 104 years. The Ranas practically imprisoned the kings in the palace, and kept the monarchs amused with wine, women, and song. The king had no authority or power over the state's affairs. But in 1950 Nepal witnessed a rare turn of events in politics. The then-reigning monarch, King Tribhuvan, plotted a revolution to overthrow the Ranas. He escaped from his palace to India and joined political forces with commoners operating from across the border. He also forged an alliance with political parties banned in Nepal. This alliance forced the Ranas to abdicate their 104-year rule of Nepal in 1951. King Tribhuvan introduced a parliamentary democracy similar to that of Britain. He introduced democracy and human rights in Nepal. However, he did not live long enough to see whether the multiparty system worked. Unfortunately, it did not.

The king died before an era of political instability set in. The democratic movements splintered into different factions, each hungry for power and money. Politics become centered solely in the capital city of Kathmandu, while life was unstable in the rest of the country. Political uncertainty spelled disaster for the Chitwan rhinos. Poaching and forest encroachment peaked in the 1950s. Deforestation devastated the rhinos' natural habitat, and its population sank to the threshold of extinction.

King Tribuvan's son, King Mahendra, called for a multiparty democratic election in 1956, for the first time in the history of Nepal. Members of the Nepali Congress, the former allies of his father, won the general election with a majority of votes. They formed the government, but their rule was short-lived. Nepotism, corruption, internal bickering, and above all failure to meet the expectations of the people made the Nepali Congress extremely unpopular.

Backed by the military, King Mahendra dissolved the parliament in 1961 and took power in a bloodless coup. He banned the multiparty system and jailed all politicians, including the elected prime minister. Surprisingly, there was little opposition to the king's action. In contrast, the streets of Kathmandu rose in jubilation. Key members of the Nepali Congress Party joined the king to run the country under a nonparty assembly system called the Panchyat Democracy. The system had roots in an old bottom-up approach to governance, where most powers were dispersed at the village and district level. It also gave the king absolute power to "guide" the democracy, with the right to veto decisions at any level of government. No one could or even dared to question or predict how long the king's guided democracy would last. I was no different.

Engrossed in my own world of wild animals and shielded under the "see no evil, hear no evil, speak no evil" environment of the palace, I was unaware that a few years later Chitwan would become the hot spot of a bloody rebellion against the monarchy in Nepal. I had researched and done all my theses on Nepal's wildlife but not on its people and politics. Meanwhile, under the tranquil shadows of the lofty Himalayas, a political turmoil was brewing. Back then, I believed Nepal was too pretty and too peaceful for a revolution as I maneuvered my red government-issued Honda motorcycle through the crowded streets of Kathmandu.

I marveled at how the city reflected my own conflicts between modernism and traditionalism. The medieval brick buildings, some dating back to the sixteenth century, were laced with electric and telephone wires. Rickshaws hauled loads of wood, the most common source of fuel in the Kathmandu Valley. Big, slick German Mercedes Benzes and small Japanese Mazdas honked their horns as they tried to maneuver the narrow streets of Kathmandu. Sophisticated climbing gear, the refuse of expeditions, was hung in store windows next to rugs woven by Tibetan refugees. I drove past Western tourists, backpackers, and climbers; passed groups of Tibetan pilgrims, Nepalese hipsters wearing Led Zeppelin T-shirts, and conservative civil servants in traditional Nepalese dress. Like the rhino-killing holy ceremony of the Tarpan, the streets of Kathmandu reflected conflicting impulses: the drive toward modern life versus the effort to preserve traditional culture. Everyone in Nepal, not just the king and I, was caught between the traditional and the modern world of Nepal.

On the edge of the old city of Kathmandu lay my destination, the Narayanhiti Royal Palace. The palace itself embodied the struggle between the traditional and the modern in Nepalese society. Some of the buildings were old and traditional but not functional. Some were modern, ugly, and functional. I was headed for a meeting in the newer section of the palace, constructed in 1970. It was there that a task force was meeting to plan the royal rhino hunt, for the ancient ceremony of the Tarpan.

A royal guard, outfitted in a neatly pressed khaki uniform, shiny black shoes, and a Gurkha hat emblazoned with a red band, escorted me to the waiting room outside the office of His Royal Highness Prince Gyanendra. Soon other members of the committee, who were senior to me in the pecking order, trickled into the room. The most powerful arrived last.

King Birendra had two brothers and three sisters. Prince Gyanendra, the king's younger brother, was known to be the most powerful of the monarch's siblings. As Budda Ba was fond of saying, sycophancy is a favorite pastime in Nepal. Civil servants and politicians often tried to curry favor with this chain-smoking Nepalese prince, only to be shocked by his no-nonsense business-like behavior. The prince was also a poet, a composer, and a globally recognized environmentalist, the winner of the Golden Ark from the Netherlands and a Member of Honor of the World Wildlife Fund. He was also a staunch traditionalist and the force behind Nepal's nature-conservation program.

As we waited for the arrival of the prince, I recalled how he had helped my career as a wildlife biologist. In 1973 he had sent me to the Mount Everest region to work with Sir Edmund Hillary, who had become the first Westerner to climb the world's tallest mountain in 1953, with Tenzing Sherpa. While Hillary and I did the fieldwork that went into establishing the world's highest region as a national

park, the prince had taken care of the political work back in Kathmandu that made the park a reality. Prince Gyanendra broadened
my educational experience by asking me to accompany him on several foreign trips and sending me for training in Africa, North
America, and New Zealand.

On one occasion, when we were about to meet Queen Juliana
of the Netherlands, I asked the prince, "What am I supposed to
do?" He looked me straight in the eye and said, "Be humble. Be polite. Be yourself. And be a Nepali." I took it to heart and have never
forgotten his words.

Through his personal contacts and royal connections, the
prince had been instrumental in forging Nepal's relationship with
the Smithsonian Institution, the World Wildlife Fund, and the
World Conservation Union. Though he was not popular in many
Nepali political circles, I found him to be a kindhearted intellectual
with a deep commitment to nature conservation. He believed that
poverty was the root cause of environmental woes. He also charted
Nepal's nature-conservation program, not with rhetoric, but with a
pragmatism that encouraged a people-first agenda. He once said,
"What is conservation if not for people?" Prince Gyanendra was
also a staunch supporter of the Tarpan, as he championed the necessity of tradition and cultural preservation.

My thoughts were interrupted when the prince's aide marched
into the royal meeting room. A golden brass sign on the door bore
Nepali script for the word *Dhaulagiri*, indicating the room was
named for a famous Himalayan mountain. The light blue walls of the
room were hung with large black-and-white photos of royal hunts in
Nepal and the head of a moose that King Mahendra had bagged in
the United States. A handwoven, wall-to-wall Nepalese carpet
adorned the floor. In the corner of the room, the angry face of a
stuffed tiger glared at the large rectangular mahogany meeting table.

Prince Gyanendra, the fair-skinned thirty-two-year-old chairman of the committee, entered the room and sat at the head of the

table beneath a portrait of the king and queen of Nepal. He wore a traditional Nepalese dress with a checkered coat and a multicolored *topi*, the traditional Nepalese headgear. It is difficult to describe the *topi* accurately. It somewhat resembles a large, handleless beer mug with a sloping base, cut in half, and turned upside down.

The prince waved his hand and asked the ten committee members to join him at the table. We took our positions, being extra careful to press our hands together and bow our heads before taking our seats. Like committee meetings everywhere, what went on behind the scenes was almost as important as what was said at the meeting. Each of the ten members had his own agenda, and that agenda was how to please the prince.

General Ranga, the oldest member of the committee, sat at the right hand of the prince. A jovial World War II veteran with a wrinkled face, General Ranga had been pulled out of retirement to serve as the chief of His Majesty's Hunting Department. He was also the Queen Mother's maternal uncle; thus, he had easy access to the king and other members of the royal family.

Next to General Ranga sat King Birendra's private secretary, Narayani Prasad Shrestha, a portly former English professor. Since he had been the king's tutor at one time, all the members of the royal family addressed Professor Shrestha in English as "Sir." Next sat Brigadier Sushil, secretary of the Royal Household Department. Members of the Nepalese royal family addressed this stocky fifty-year-old palace veteran as *Sano Mama* or "Little Uncle." He was the younger of the king's two maternal uncles. His Majesty's British-educated press secretary, Chiran Thapa, sat next to Little Uncle. These two men served as the king's eyes and ears in the meeting room. Facing them on the opposite side of the table were staff members from the Ministry of Forests, the Department of National Parks and Wildlife Conservation (DNPWC).

Though they were senior to me, Little Uncle and General Ranga were friends of my father, and they trusted and treated me as a junior partner. All three of us shared a faith in Prince Gyanendra's common sense, an uncommon commodity in Nepal, where courtiers clouded themselves in an aura of omnipotence to influence the Royal Palace. The two men also knew my mother, who had grown up amid the intrigues of the palace, as she was the favorite god-daughter of Rana prime minister Juddha Shamsher.

I realized that once the king had made the decision to proceed with the hunt, there was nothing I could do to stop it. But the way the hunt took place would make a great deal of difference, whether it was beneficial to the cause of saving Nepalese wildlife or a public relations disaster. My goal was to have the rhino hunt conducted in the best possible way. I knew I could rely on the elephant drivers and my game scouts in Chitwan to help me from the bottom up. But I also needed influence from the top down.

The meeting followed the usual pattern of meetings held in the Royal Palace. Each committee member tried to outsmart the others and curry favor with the prince.

"We are not worried about His Majesty's hunt hurting the rhino population," said General Ranga, cutting straight to the point. "The issue here is whether the rhino hunt should be a private or a public affair."

A few members argued for a private function closed to the prying eyes of the public and press. They argued that an open operation could invite criticism in the Western media. It might be looked upon as an act of royal arrogance and create adverse publicity that would hurt foreign aid for nature conservation. They knew that the Royal Nepalese Army, which manned Royal Chitwan National Park, could close the park to the public. Furthermore, they also knew that the palace had power over the media and could censor any news on the ruler's rhino hunt.

I did not like the idea of a closed ceremony and expressed my opinion to the committee. While I was in no position to question His Majesty's decisions on the rhino Tarpan, I was not prepared to lie or hide the event from my peers in the outside world. It was not only wrong but also futile. With hundreds of people and scores of elephants, I could not see how the Tarpan could be anything but a big-time production. I also believed that any attempt to hide the fact would brew rumors and suspicion. Hiding an event of this magnitude would do more harm than good for the cause of rhino conservation in Nepal.

The committee was in a deadlock, and the meeting ended with no decision made. Prince Gyanendra had the habit of making no decisions before building a consensus among committee members. The prince dismissed us with a resolution to meet in a week.

I was determined to get my way in the next committee meeting or outside of it. To do so, I had to maneuver through the jungles of Nepalese government bureaucracy. Akin to bureaucracy everywhere, this required the careful baiting, flattering, stalking, and capturing of fellow bureaucrats. My most important guides were General Ranga and Little Uncle, with whom I met often in private to plot routes through the labyrinth of palace politics.

The place for my political work was Bagh Darbar, Little Uncle's palace, less than a mile from the temple-filled Darbar Square in the heart of Kathmandu. Built by the Rana family in the nineteenth century, Bagh Darbar had its own history of political intrigue. In the early part of the twentieth century, this palace was the scene of a political assassination when a nephew engineered the murder of his uncle and became prime minister of Nepal. Now Little Uncle's home provided us with a neutral zone in which we could talk in a straightforward manner with one another and plan our strategies long before the formal meetings took place.

As other committee members became aware of our meetings, Little Uncle, General Ranga, and I became snidely known as the "Gang of Three" to the other committee members.

"Covering up the hunt makes the king look like a rhino poacher," said General Ranga, a staunch royalist, sipping a Scotch in the sitting room of the Bagh Darbar.

We were in the rear section of the hundred-room palace. Little Uncle could not afford to maintain the entire palace, so he had sold the front portion of his home to the Ministry of Finance, which used it for its offices. Handpainted oil portraits of the kings, queens, and Rana prime ministers of Nepal, alongside Little Uncle's hunting trophies, lined the snow white walls of the room. We sat cross-legged on the floor on *chakatis*—thick cotton cushions—around a low table with bottles of Scotch and beer.

"Kill the snake, but do not break the stick," Ranga continued, quoting a Nepalese proverb to illustrate his belief that the king should hunt the rhino publicly while working to avoid criticism from any antihunting factions. Being the youngest of the three, I was not doing much of the talking. "The country must know and appreciate that our king is fulfilling his duties." He waved his hands and added, "Otherwise, what is the point of the Tarpan?"

"I agree," added Little Uncle, looking at me with his big, black oval eyes. "The whole point of the Tarpan is to demonstrate to traditionalists that the king is doing his duty."

I knew that Little Uncle loved a good hunt. With his brother-in-law, King Mahendra, Little Uncle had hunted polar bears in Alaska and lions in Africa. Little Uncle had been in charge of field operations during King Mahendra's royal tiger hunts in the Terai. "There is absolutely no point in hiding this rhino hunt from the public," he insisted.

"What should we do to make sure the hunt is public?" I asked my two mentors. In the company of Little Uncle and General Ranga, I could speak openly, without any fear of reprisal.

"Avoid hurting the feelings of the arrogant palace aides," General Ranga said to me. "Learn to inflate their egos, and get your job done."

I spent many days trying to do just that. I met privately with members of the committee in order to marshal their support. When the day came, the committee made a unanimous decision that the king's rhino hunt would be no hush-hush affair but rather a transparent event open to the public. Prince Gyanendra even ordered the palace press secretary to publicize the event in the media. The Gang of Three had won the debate.

Little Uncle and I got our instructions from the prince. We were directed to locate an old male rhino in the forests outside the national-park boundary. For public-relations reasons, we had to find a crop-raiding rhino that was foraging the villagers' fields. For biological reasons, we needed to find a rhino who was old and past his breeding prime.

Later in the evening, unbeknownst to the other committee members, I had a private audience with the prince. He directed me to inform my colleagues at the World Conservation Union, the World Wildlife Fund, the National Geographic Society, and the Smithsonian Institution about the king's rhino hunt. Prince Gyanendra, a well-traveled person, understood very well that Westerners, particularly Americans, did not like secondhand information. He also knew that if the Westerners did not get it straight, they would be more inclined to believe the rumors and lies about the king that many antiroyalists were all too ready to feed them. The next day I packed my bags and left for Chitwan.

By royal command I had been transformed from a conservation biologist into a public-relations officer and rookie guide for a royal hunt that would take place in five weeks.

17

ROOKIE AT THE
ROYAL RHINO HUNT

The fog hung over the quietly flowing Rapti River in the Baghmara Forests outside the Royal Chitwan National Park on a chilly December morning in 1979. From a nearby village came the sound of cattle bellowing as villagers attended to their morning chores. A flock of black-headed bulbuls fluttered from tree to tree, singing a metallic *"seet-trr-trippy-wit"* chorus, as if impatiently waiting for the sun to break through the rising fog. The air was laced with the leafy smell of the sano panheli—a common shrub in Chitwan—and the sharp odor of rhino dung.

Crawling on our bellies, Little Uncle and I were close to the rhino dung. We stopped no more than fifteen yards away from a hefty male rhino grazing peacefully at the edge of the forest opening. The rhino stood with its tail toward us. A jungle mynah bird perched on the pachyderm's rump. The bird did not distract the beast from munching the bauhinia shrub that sprouted in the open meadow. Ten feet to our rear, hidden by a thick bush, was a female elephant. Ram Lotan, who became the chief elephant driver after my old friend Tapsi died in January 1975 was mounted on the female's neck, his bare feet hanging down behind her ears. Behind Ram Lotan was another elephant. It was carrying a sergeant wearing the insignia of the

Royal Nepalese Army Signal Corps. He had a portable wireless radio on his back.

Tirtha Man Maskey, the superintendent of the Royal Chitwan National Park, perched nearby on the limb of a sissoo tree. This wiry thirty-year-old held a thick stick to throw at the rhino in the event that the creature decided to charge us. His stick would only distract the rhino for a short time, but it would give us several seconds to rush to our elephants. Our binoculars were focused on the rhino's crotch.

"Do you see them?" whispered Little Uncle, referring to the rhino's testicles.

"Yes," I responded. "It is a male."

Ram Lotan broke into laughter. "If that rhino is a female, then I'm a eunuch born to a whore," he barked. "I can see his balls right from here without any glasses."

Little Uncle and I realized we were belaboring the obvious, but we were too nervous to do otherwise. We had to be sure that the rhino chosen for the royal hunt was a male. Ram Lotan also understood this fact and knew we had been watching this rhino for two weeks. But he could not understand why we were so paranoid about making a mistake and why we felt compelled to identify the sex of the beast repeatedly.

The rhino was old. He had a distinctive scar on his left rump, so we called him *Debre Chak Khate Budo* ("Old Left Butt Scarred Male"). This aging rhino rarely moved beyond half a kilometer from this meadow, and one of the reasons we chose him was because he was old and easy to track. The forest cover around the meadow also ensured an easy approach for the elephants on which the king and his entourage would stalk this old beast.

Our "Do you see them?" dialogue was a routine, a ritual of self-reassurance. For the past three days General Ranga, who was the chief of the Royal Hunting Department, had sent a flurry of messages from Kathmandu, warning that if the rhino turned out to be a female, there would be hell to pay. I would probably lose my job, and Little Uncle would lose any standing he had at the royal palace. Our nerves were even more on edge, knowing that the day designated by the royal astrologer as the most auspicious day for the Tarpan, was drawing closer. On that day, the king had to kill a rhino. And the rhino must be male. The maleness of the rhino was central to the religious ceremony of Tarpan, as it was against Hindu religious edict to use a female for this purpose. Furthermore, no members of the Nepalese royal family would shoot a female, rhinos or members of any other species!

"You have watched this rhino pee, fart, and shit for days," said Ram Lotan, pointing at me with his *lathi*, the wooden rod he used to steer the elephant. "I don't understand why you need to crawl like a crocodile to see if he has balls. There's no jungle wizard here to change his sex into a female." His loud voice caused the mynah bird to flutter off to a nearby tree. The rhino turned around and faced us. "Ssssh," breathed Little Uncle, moving his index finger to his lips.

"Watch out!" barked Tirtha Man Maskey from the treetop. "Get on the elephant."

Ram Lotan ignored them both. "This old boy is going nowhere," he said, pointing at the rhino. "I've seen him graze with cows during the day and steal crops during the night. He is not bothered by humans."

As Ram Lotan predicted, the rhino did not charge. He only stared at us. After a few minutes, he turned his back to us, moved a few steps forward, and continued his foraging. A veteran of innumerable sightseeing tour groups, this rhino was used to humans. Even rhinos that were more skittish than he was usually did not attack humans, unless they were surprised or provoked. And we did not intend to do anything provocative. We did not need to. The rhino was docile and accommodating, as Ram Lotan had predicted. He rarely moved out of his place. Yet we continued to watch him every day for more than two weeks.

Finally the Tarpan arrived, on the twenty-eighth day of the month of Paush in the year 2035 in the Nepalese calendar, which was January 12, 1979. We spotted Old Left Butt Scarred Male at his usual location in an opening in the Baghmara forest, just north of the Royal Chitwan National Park.

As we had done so many times in the past, we crawled on the ground toward the creature to inspect the rhino's testicles with our binoculars. "Do you see them?" asked Little Uncle, hopefully for the last time.

"Yes," I confirmed. "I can clearly see the testicles." Once again Ram Lotan burst out in laughter at our stupidity. We crawled away from the rhino and stood next to Tirtha Maskey some ten yards away from the rhino. "The hunt is going to be easy," I told Little Uncle.

He ignored my comment. "You two!" he barked, pointing his finger at Maskey and me. "Climb trees, and watch the rhino from opposite ends of the meadow. Follow the rhino if he moves into the bush. Do not lose him. I will send a message to Kasra to inform His Majesty that we are ready." Kasra was where the royal party had pitched their extensive camp at the national-park headquarters, twelve miles away.

Little Uncle took out a piece of paper and a pencil from his pocket and scribbled a message. He coded the message "top priority" and ordered a sergeant of the Royal Nepalese Army Signal Corps to send a radio message to His Majesty's aide-de-camp at Kasra. Then Little Uncle left us to meet the royal party at Bodreni on the banks of the Rapti River.

I climbed a tree and watched Little Uncle ride out of the forest on Ram Lotan's elephant. Then I focused my field glasses on Old Left Butt Scarred Male. After nibbling at some shrubs, the rhino moved a few steps diagonally from my position. Then he went to rest in a small depression, below a silk cotton tree, still in full view. Maskey and I had nothing to do but watch the old rhino and wait for the young king to arrive.

"Perfect head shot right through the ear," I muttered to myself, aiming at the rhino with my binoculars. I did not know much about guns and fatal shots. My expertise was limited to shooting drug-laden darts at the rumps of animals to capture them alive, not dead. I squeezed off several imaginary shots at the rhino, partly out of boredom. Crouched on a tree limb, twenty yards from me, Maskey seemed to be equally impatient. I watched him take aim at the rhino with a stick.

A peacock called in the distance. A barking deer responded with an alarm call. A white-bellied drongo bird hovered noisily over the rhino, calling, "*weu-ðül-weu-ðül.*" Yet the rhino did not budge. Fear suddenly crawled over me.

"What if the rhino has died?" I thought. "He is an old beast. He could have had a heart attack. He might be dead before the king arrives."

I climbed to a branch higher up in the tree. I focused my binoculars on the rhino's head. His old leathery ear moved. I breathed a sigh of relief. Old Left Butt Scarred Male was still with us.

Ninety minutes later, I spotted a convoy of elephants meandering toward my tree. Using my binoculars, I counted forty-seven elephants with King Birendra and more than one hundred other people in his entourage packed tightly on the elephants' backs.

"Is it a circus or what?" I shouted loudly to Maskey. "The royal camp commander has brought the whole camp. *Muji!*" I swore, equating the camp commander to the hair around the human anus. He shrugged, indicating that he shared my disgust. The crowd should not have surprised either of us. The king's excursions, whether by plane, automobile, or elephant, always involved a large number of people.

I watched the convoy of elephants as they crossed into an open pasture. Little Uncle's elephant was in the lead. His Majesty's elephant was second, followed by the king's aide-de-camp. Ram Lotan was fourth in line. His passenger was no longer Little Uncle, but Aishwarya, Her Majesty the Queen herself.

Traditionally, the king assigned the best elephant driver to his spouse, although exceptions were made for royal visitors or state guests. It made sense that Ram Lotan, whose cool head had calmed many a panicking elephant, was driving the queen's elephant.

Dressed in a smart khaki safari suit, the queen looked regal on top of the swaying elephant as it moved in steady rhythm toward my tree. The queen's light pink lipstick glistened, contrasting with her big, dark oval eyes and her jet-black hair. She was fair skinned and slender—beautiful but with a reputation as a tough politician who wielded at least as much power as her husband.

The queen's aide-de-camp followed behind her. The ruler's two brothers rode behind the queen. Their spouses, who were also the queen's younger sisters, followed their husbands on their own elephants. Two aides-de-camp of the king's brother rode behind the queen's sisters. A large entourage consisting of the prime minister of Nepal, the minister of forests, the royal physician, the royal secretary, the royal photographer, the royal valet, and a fleet of other high-ranking officials and staff followed them. One of the most important was our friend General Ranga Bikram Shah, head of the Royal Hunting Department, and the man who had made us paranoid about checking repeatedly to be sure the male rhino had testicles.

The king and queen, as well as the king's two brothers and their wives, all rode on crafted leather saddles mounted over sheets of bloodred velvety cloth. The other riders, including the prime minister, did not have that royal privilege. He was crammed like a commoner with three other people in a *howdah*, or wooden pillion. In the past the *howdah* was reserved for children and nannies. Its wooden frame is hard on an elephant's back. Though secure, riding in a *howdah* was considered a sign of weakness. These days *howdahs* were used for tourists but rarely used by field veterans like Little Uncle and me. We rode on a *lampat*—a kind of jute sack packed with straw and covered with a cotton cushion. *Lampats* are easy to saddle on elephants and gentle on their backs.

The royal rhino hunting party approached the clearing. The lead elephants stopped five yards from my tree. No one spoke.

"Where is the rhino?" barked Little Uncle, breaking the silence and demonstrating his authority. All heads turned toward me. From my treetop roost I pointed toward Old Left Butt Scarred Male, resting in his hollow. The elephant riders could not see him, but because I was higher up, I had a clear view of the rhino's deeply wrinkled gray body.

Little Uncle directed all the elephants to form a wide circle around the rhino's location. Then he signaled Bhaggu, His Majesty's personal elephant driver, to move the monarch's elephant directly under my tree. With his well-groomed mustache and close-cropped jet-black hair, King Birendra looked relaxed. His trousers were not fancy but standard khaki-colored military attire. Over his trousers he wore a matching woolen shirt and a sleeveless red down vest. The king's feet rested on either side of the elephant saddle, protected by heavy jungle boots. A tiny pistol tucked in his belt was barely visible beneath his down vest. His hands were gloveless and empty. Bhaggu was holding the king's American Weatherby rifle upright, with the rifle butt resting on the elephant's head.

"Where is the rhino?" asked the monarch in a soft voice as Bhaggu positioned his elephant under my tree.

"At one o'clock, Your Majesty," I responded in nervous English. Western-educated Nepalese like King Birendra used both Nepali and English in conversation.

I felt uneasy. I was positioned at a higher level than the king, a violation of etiquette under normal circumstances. In addition I was balanced on a branch and unable to free my hands to fold them in a praying mode and bow when talking to the monarch, as demanded by Nepalese protocol. Unconcerned about protocol, King Birendra moved his elephant toward the rhino. He stopped at a big grassy knoll overlooking the resting creature. He sat there, looking at Old Left Butt Scarred Male for a long time.

I could feel that the king was reluctant to shoot a sleeping rhino. There was little I could do; I was too nervous to speak out. A Nepali proverb flashed through my head: "Never face a fire or the monarch head on. Both are totally unpredictable." I remained silent and looked back at the ring of elephants in the monarch's entourage. They too were quiet and somber.

Finally the king took the rifle from his elephant driver and aimed at the rhino. I took a long breath and waited for the shot. But the jungle remained silent. The sovereign had not fired the gun. To my surprise, he gave it back to Bhaggu. He rubbed his hands, placed them on his cheeks, and continued to gaze at the rhino.

"Why can't he get on with it?" I thought. Standing in the tree, clutching branches, my arms and legs were about to fall asleep. Having come this far, I wanted the monarch to shoot the darn rhino and get on with his Tarpan.

The silence in the jungle lingered. The eyes of the entourage focused on the monarch, curious to see what he would do next. The king's elephant turned around and returned to my tree.

"Could you please get the rhino up on its feet," the king commanded softly.

Relieved to know what was going on, I clapped my hands, sputtered my lips and called "*haat, haat*" ("move, move"). The rhino did not budge. I waved at Little Uncle and called at the top of my voice, "The rhino is sleeping. His Majesty has commanded us to get the rhino up on its feet."

Little Uncle's elephant moved toward Prince Gyanendra. General Ranga's elephant joined him. I watched them huddle on top of their elephants. Their three elephants slowly began to approach the rhino. When they were about five yards away, Little Uncle's elephant driver threw a thick stick at Old Left Butt Scarred Male and hit him smack on his snout. The rhino jerked his head and stood up in a flash. He stared at the circle of elephants and took three steps toward Prince Gyanendra's elephant.

"Kalu! Do not take His Royal Highness's elephant too close to the rhino," yelled Prince Gyanendra's aide-de-camp at the prince's elephant driver.

Kalu, a red-belted *subba*—a high rank in the elephant camp hierarchy—and a veteran of royal hunts, ignored the order. He moved his elephant a few feet and finally positioned Prince Gyanendra's elephant to face the rhino. Old Left Butt Scarred Male sniffed the ground and charged, not at Prince Gyanendra's elephant but at the line of elephants in the king's entourage. He was trying to break the ring of elephants and dash into the cover of the jungle.

A barrage of sticks and shouts of "Hey, hey, hey" stopped the rhino's charge seven yards short of the elephant ring. The rhino turned around and ran toward King Birendra's elephant. I, too, screamed, "Hey, hey, hey!" The rhino stopped and stared up at me for a long time.

The king calmly watched the scene with his palms resting on his cheeks. His elephant driver was still holding the royal rifle. His Majesty appeared to be more involved with enjoying the show than shooting the rhino. I was getting impatient.

"Your Majesty," I said, gathering courage. "It is time now. We do not want to spook the rhino. If it breaks the ring, we will lose it."

"My Lord, we cannot let this rhino escape. Today is the auspicious day for the Tarpan," added Bhaggu, the king's driver, subtly reminding his passenger that this was a religious act, not a sporting event.

The King flashed a smile and looked at me. I avoided direct eye contact and shifted my gaze toward the rhino. Bhaggu continued to talk. "This big male has destroyed the entire crop of the village of Bodreni," he said in a slow and shaky voice. "The villagers will sing and dance in joy and pray for Your Majesty's long life if Your Majesty chooses to destroy this thief."

The king smiled again. He patted his elephant driver on the back. He asked me in English, "Is it okay?" I bowed my head. Finally the monarch loaded his rifle with shiny, thin copper bullets. Until then I had not known that his gun was unloaded.

"Bhaggu," I called to the king's elephant driver. "Slowly, slowly position His Majesty's elephant for a clean shot." Bhaggu did not need my advice. He knew what to do.

Bhaggu moved the elephant diagonally toward the rhino, stopping ten yards from the beast. The rhino backed up for a few yards, staring into the eyes of the king's elephant. The king shifted his position on the back of his elephant. The rhino moved to the right. The king's elephant moved with the rhino, step by step.

Suddenly the rhino sniffed the ground and charged. Both Bhaggu and I screamed, "Hey! Hey! Hey!" The rhino stopped short, less than five yards from the king's elephant. Bhaggu threw a stick at the rhino but missed. He then moved his elephant two steps forward, challenging Old Left Butt Scarred Male. The rhino turned around and moved about fifteen yards away. He scanned the circle of elephants, moving in a semicircle. Then he turned around and stared at the king's elephant again, eyeball to eyeball.

The scuffle between the king's elephant and the rhino continued for almost fifteen minutes as Bhaggu, the elephant driver, tried to maneuver his elephant to give the king a clean, safe shot. It was Bhaggu's responsibility to make sure the monarch did not shoot toward the village or his entourage, a nearly impossible task as Old Left Butt Scarred Male moved around in circles. Bhaggu was especially cautious. A memory of a royal hunting accident that had shaken Nepal twenty years earlier always haunted him whenever he drove the king on his elephant.

The accident occurred in Sukla Phanta, a game reserve in west Nepal during a hunting safari of the late King Mahendra, King Birendra's father. Prince Dhirendra, Mahendra's youngest son, who was barely in his teens, was on his first tiger hunt. He was riding Bhaggu's elephant. A line of elephants approached him, flushing the tall grasses, trying to drive out the tiger. The nervous prince waited for his shot, clutching his rifle to his shoulder. He saw a bush move. Bang! The prince panicked and fired, almost without looking. A woman screamed. A deer leapt out of the bush. The prince had missed the deer and shot Queen Ratna, the prince's own mother, in the stomach. Fortunately she survived. So did the memory of this horrifying accident in Bhaggu's mind.

Working with extreme care, Bhaggu finally managed to corner Old Left Butt Scarred Male into a safe shooting position. The king aimed his rifle at the rhino's heart. When the king was about to squeeze the trigger, the rhino turned and pointed his butt toward the monarch, as if in defiance. Then the rhino took a few steps and sprinted again at the ring of elephants. A barrage of sticks and shouts kept the rhino from breaking through the line of elephants. Bhaggu tried once again to corner the rhino, but he was unsuccessful. The fleet of elephants carrying the king's entourage blocked the forest escape route. But the rhino had now positioned himself between the king and the village of Bodreni, opposite the forest.

I was getting bored with the cat-and-mouse game that had now gone on for a long forty-five minutes. Suddenly the air was filled with a loud *"Brrr, brrr, brrr,"* the sound of an angry rhino. Old Left Butt Scarred Male sniffed the ground and charged the king's elephant head on. The jungle thundered as the king quickly fired his American rifle. His shot knocked the rhino flat on the ground.

"Sarkar Ki Jai!" (Long live the king!") roared the members of the entourage, inspired by the sound of gunfire and the sight of a two-ton rhino knocked out cold on the ground. The human eruption startled the forty-seven elephants. They hooted thunderously, with a high-pitched *"hbooyn, hbooyn."*

But suddenly, to everyone's surprise, the rhino was back up on its feet. With lightning speed he charged the closest elephant, ridden by General Ranga. Panicked by the raging rhino, the general's elephant bolted. With its tail pointed toward the sky, it ran for its life toward the jungle.

`My mouth gaped. Clutching my treetop branch, I watched as the ferocious, wounded rhino chased the sprinting elephant, with the general hanging precariously on its back. The sound of hooting elephants and human shouts filled the air. As I stared in amazement, three other elephants took off and ran behind the wounded rhino. In all my life in the jungle, I had never experienced such a frightening sight—a wounded wild rhino in hot pursuit of an elephant being chased by three other elephants.

"How long can General Ranga hang on before he falls and is gored to death by the angry rhino?" I worried helplessly. "If he isn't killed by the rhino, he will be crushed by the overhanging branches of the trees." I thought my good friend the general was a dead man.

18

RHINO VERSUS ROYALTY

I climbed down from the tree and walked toward Little Uncle. He was on the ground standing next to a large pool of rhino blood. The king and the royal family sat on their elephants sunk deeply in thought. The air buzzed with anxiety and the sounds of jittery elephants rumbling their bellies. The elephant drivers whacked their animals on their heads to keep them under control. The royal hunting party was in pandemonium. Dismounted from their elephants, a few members of the entourage milled around the king's elephant, talking in loud excited voices.

"Let's find him first and worry about the rhino later," I heard the king say, as I approached the royal party. He was referring to General Ranga, who had now disappeared into the forest.

"I dispatched the three best elephants for rescue immediately after I saw the rhino charge the general's elephant," responded Little Uncle with his hands clasped in a praying mode, and his eyes facing the ground, a normal gesture when talking with the Nepalese monarch. His words cleared up the mystery of why the three elephants had gone off in pursuit of the wounded rhino. Little Uncle briefly glanced at the king, tilted his head down to avoid any eye contact with the ruler, and added, "They should have rescued the general by now. It may be best if we follow the rhino's blood trail. The rhino can't go far before bleeding to death."

After a short consultation, we reorganized the elephants and trailed the blood. I led the way on foot with Little Uncle immediately behind me. Several game scouts followed us, with the elephants behind. The king's elephant was in the lead, followed by Prince Gyanendra and the rest of the royal party all still on their elephants. The trail was not as easy to follow as I had hoped. We crossed the meadow, entered the thick bush, and continued our search. Our progress was slow as we crouched from time to time to search for dribbles of blood.

Thirty minutes later and less than a mile into the forest, I heard voices and ran toward them. To my relief one voice belonged to General Ranga. He was not dead but very much alive. He was squatting on the ground with his back against a big Jamun tree as four elephants and their talkative handlers stood around him. His jacket and trousers were ripped and he had a few cuts on his face, but he seemed to have suffered no major injury.

This was not the first time that the general had survived a ride on a panicking elephant. He was a seasoned veteran of previous tiger hunts, yet he was shaky as he told me what had happened.

"Except for a glimpse of the rhino charging my elephant in the meadow, I have no idea what happened to the beast," said the general, in a high-pitched and shaky voice. "I was dead scared of falling from the elephant. I held tight to the ropes and glued myself flat on the elephant's back. My mind was far from the rhino.

"Bhagor here brought the bolting elephant under control. Three elephants met us soon after. We decided to rest here and catch our breath," he added, gazing at his elephant driver with admiration.

The king's party soon arrived near where the still quivering General Ranga squatted. The elephants were as nervous as the general was. Their bellies rumbled noisily, as if the wounded rhino was still in sight. The general repeated his story to the king.

We took a short break before tracking the blood trail of the wounded rhino. The jungle was dense, and we had to move slowly. Using a *khukuri*—the traditional boomerang-shaped Nepalese knife, we marked our route, chipping at tree trunks to mark the trail.

I worked my way through the jungle for two hours, before I stumbled onto a big pool of blood. The ruffled soil and crushed leaves around the blood indicated that Old Left Butt Scarred Male had rested here before moving on.

"The rhino has lost much blood," I told Little Uncle, pointing at the ground. "He can't be far. Following his blood trail on foot is dangerous; he could be anywhere nearby and attack us."

"Yes," agreed Little Uncle. "We could walk right into his face in this thick bush. An animal as big as a rhino cannot disappear into thin air. Let us line up all the elephants and flush the forest."

We organized the elephants into an arc, spacing them out at a distance of five to ten yards. We kept the king's elephant in the center. Little Uncle and I shared an elephant. The king's elephant was on our left flank, about fifteen elephants away. Moving in a slow and steady march, we swept through the forest in a westerly direction toward the farmland beyond the edge of the forest. The jungle was quiet except for the "*chss, hss*" sound of forty-seven elephants marching through dense bush. After about twenty minutes, I heard a shriek to our right. "*Gainda! Mahiley paayee! Gainda! Mahiley paayee!* (Rhino! I found it! Rhino! I found it!)"

"*Bol sar,*" barked Little Uncle immediately as we rushed toward the sound. "Bring His Majesty to the extreme end of the right flank." *Bol sar* ("Move voice") is the command given to coordinate the movements of a large number of elephants dispersed in a jungle during royal hunts. The exact message is passed from elephant to elephant until the entire group gets the word. Little Uncle's message was relayed from one elephant to the next until it reached the king's elephant driver.

The message proved to be a false alarm. It was a rhino all right but not our wounded male. The spotter, probably with hopes of a handsome reward, had not properly identified the animal before sounding his alarm. He was one of the visitors from the city and did not realize that there were many rhinos in this part of the forest.

"*Jaantha moro*," I cursed the alarmist as "dead pubic hair."

"Watch your language," snapped Little Uncle with a chuckle. "Tongues are chopped off for swearing in the presence of the royal family. Only elephant drivers have the license to use dirty language."

I pretended I had not heard Little Uncle, but his tone eased my tension. We regrouped the elephants and continued our search. There were a few more false alarms as we spotted more than a dozen rhinos. We were deep into rhino country.

After three hours and some ten miles of meandering through the thick jungle, we found our rhino. He was crouched in a small wallow in the middle of the jungle. His ears were flickering, driving away the insects hovering around his head. Blood oozed out of the wound in his left chest. But his eyes were wide open. Old Left Butt Scarred Male was wounded but alert and alive.

We circled the rhino from a distance. The king's elephant approached the rhino step by step. The rhino heard the elephant and stood straight up. He jerked his head down toward the ground. Then he charged the king's elephant at full speed. I held my breath.

Fortunately the king was well prepared for action. "*Bang!*" thundered the monarch's rifle. The shot stopped the rhino momentarily but did not knock it off his feet. He took a step back and charged again, straight at the king's elephant.

The king fired again. The second shot knocked the rhino down. But he was back up on his feet in an instant. He backed off a few paces. Then he turned his tail toward the king and surveyed the circle of elephants in front of him. Abruptly he turned around and in a flash attacked the king's elephant again.

More rifle shots boomed through the jungle. These shots knocked the rhino cold to the ground. The thunderous sound of gunfire was followed by a hushed silence that lasted for almost fifteen seconds. Then the royal entourage cheered, "Long live the king!" A few elephants hooted. The cheering sounded more like a collective sigh of relief than an outburst of joy.

I watched the rhino for three minutes, and then I moved my elephant in front of the rhino and hit him with several sticks. There was no movement. I dismounted and cautiously approached the rhino from behind. I tugged his tail. Still no movement. The rhino was dead. I moved to the front end of the bleeding pachyderm and looked in his eyes. The big black ovals were bloodshot with anger, even in death.

Guilt rushed through me at the loss of this magnificent creature. Old Left Butt Scarred Male was a tough old rhino. He had gone down not as a coward but as a fighter, single-handedly battling a young Nepalese monarch equipped with a high-powered American rifle and forty-seven royal elephants.

"Your Majesty, the rhino is dead," I announced, folding my hands and bowing to the monarch. I faked a smile to hide the sadness in my voice. The king dismounted, followed by Queen Aishwarya, Prince Gyanendra, Little Uncle, and General Ranga. Soon most of the members of the entourage were also on the ground, forming a big circle around the rhino. No one talked. Everyone glanced nervously from the rhino to the king. Prince Gyanendra fished out a 555, a slim, aromatic English cigarette, and lit it with a gold lighter. I looked at him greedily; I was dying for a cigarette. Being a rookie on a royal rhino hunt, however, I had no idea if it was proper to smoke in front of the ruler. The elephant drivers were less concerned about protocol. Some lit cigarettes, while others puffed on the inexpensive locally made smokes known as bidis. A few members of the entourage dashed into the bush to relieve themselves. They had been riding the elephants for a long time—almost six hours.

Using their *khukuri*, the elephant drivers cleared away the bush around the dead rhino. Then the king knelt in front of the rhino and posed for a photograph. The royal photographer, a short, pudgy fellow with big eyes bulging out from a slightly crooked but smiling face, clicked his Nikon camera and captured the moment for the royal records. Soon after the king and members of the royal family left the scene. A few members of the party, including the royal photographer, stayed behind.

The royal family had hardly disappeared when General Ranga took charge. He ordered a member of the Royal Nepalese Army Signal Corps to dispatch a radio message requesting vehicles to transport the dead rhino out of the jungle and back to the king's camp.

The wrinkled general was now in a cheerful mood. He patted my back and the backs of many onlookers with a flourish of self-congratulations. The hunt we had worked on for so long had gone well. The king had bagged his rhino. Now the Tarpan would proceed as planned.

General Ranga asked all of us to help turn the rhino sideways so that the rhino's genitals would be clearly visible. I had no idea why he wanted us to do that. Nevertheless, I joined more than two dozen men in shifting the two-ton rhino's position to expose its genitals. Then the general walked to the rear end of the animal and held the rhino's testicles in his hand.

"Take pictures here," said General Ranga, beckoning the royal photographer. The camera clicked as the onlookers laughed. Even then the general was not finished playing with the rhino's genitals.

"Bhagor!" shouted the General to his elephant driver. "Pull the penis out." With no signs of embarrassment, Bhagor slowly pulled the rhino's penis out of its socket. It seemed to be a never-ending process. He finally stopped. A shaft of flesh almost a yard long and three inches in diameter dangled out from between the rear legs of the rhino. The royal photographer flashed his camera, taking pictures of the rhino's penis from several different angles.

"Wow! That's big," someone called.

"What did you expect?" snapped the general. "Your size?"

The jungle burst with laughter. Fortunately the members of the royal family were long gone. They would not have been amused by General Ranga's crude display. Later I found out that the general's act was neither crude nor simply humorous. It was well calculated and planned. The general wanted all the members of the royal entourage to witness that the king's kill was indeed a male rhino, beyond any doubt. His actions, including the photographs, were designed to quash any gossip once the entourage returned to Kathmandu. It was his job to ensure that no one expressed any uncertainty about the rhino's sex, now or in the future.

As we waited for the transport vehicles to arrive, the elephant drivers and curious bystanders swarmed around the dead rhino. Soon the jungle rattled with the sound of vehicles, and a tractor, a jeep, and a few other trucks emerged, accompanied by the fleet of people who had cleared a path for them through the jungle.

General Ranga and Little Uncle roared off in a sturdy Russian jeep and left me in charge of transporting the carcass of Old Left Butt Scarred Male to Kasra, the king's camp at the national-park headquarters.

In the days before there were roads or motor vehicles, the rulers of Nepal performed Tarpan at the site where they killed their rhinos. However, in 1979 it was logistically easier to move the rhino to the ritual ground than to move the ritual ground to the rhino.

I was prepared for the task of rhino transport. In the late 1960s the World Wildlife Fund had presented the Nepalese Ministry of Forests with a motorboat and trailer. The foreign experts believed that the boat would be useful in patrolling the rivers of the Royal Chitwan National Park for rhino poachers. The boat proved to be a useless gas guzzler, totally unsuited for the shallow waters of the region's rivers. It was rarely used.

As it turned out, the trailer was much more useful than the boat. Kuber Gurung, the mechanic of the national park, was a wizard of mechanical improvisation. Kuber was able to adapt all sorts of equipment for use in the jungle and to keep our much-abused vehicles in running order. I relied on Kuber for much of my work over nine years in the jungles of Chitwan. Kuber made a few minor modifications to the trailer and turned it into a rhino-transport machine.

With the help of a squad of *pipas*—laborers and handymen of the Nepalese army, we rolled the rhino onto the trailer using little more than brute force. The process took an hour. The trailer was hooked to the back of a four-wheel-drive Toyota truck. In keeping with the orders of General Ranga, we made sure that the dead rhino's penis was prominently displayed so that everyone who saw the king's rhino could attest to its sex.

We rode out of the jungle through villages and towns in a convoy of elephants and motor vehicles. A three-man team of palace security officers rode in the front in the Toyota truck that was towing the dead rhino. They were in civilian clothes and carried concealed handguns, except for one who openly displayed his Israeli Uzi machine gun. Tirtha Maskey, the park superintendent, and I rode on the front end of a tractor. Kuber drove the Toyota truck towing the dead pachyderm. A *pipa* sat precariously on the rhino, holding the protruding penis. Five elephants marched on either side of the rhino. A brand-new Land Rover carried soldiers from the Royal Nepalese Army Military Transport Unit. They wore smart uniforms but were unarmed. The guards of the Rhino Patrol Unit, armed with antiquated British 303 rifles, followed close behind in an old Russian jeep. The chief district officer, accompanied by the district's chief of police, rode behind in another jeep.

I am not sure how my Western anthropologist friends would have reacted to this ritual and procession. To me it was feudalistic and pagan, violent and bloody, comic and chivalrous. But my mind had been "culturally polluted by Western education," according to some of the traditionalists of my culture. Yet at the same time I felt honored to have participated in this unique Hindu ritual that some Nepali priests say dates back to the Rajput kings of India of the ninth and tenth centuries, the ancestors of my king. It was after all part of my patrimony.

A crowd of men, women, and children chased our convoy. They often shouted, *"raja ko gainda"* ("king's rhino") as we moved along through several villages. When the crowd came closer, the *pipa* waved the rhino's penis, triggering blushes and bursts of laughter, as we rolled slowly toward our destination, the royal campgrounds at Kasra.

19

PRAYERS IN THE DUSK

It was dusk when we reached Kasra with the king's rhino. The camp was divided into three areas. King Birendra and his entourage inhabited an enclave on the banks of the Rapti River, an area cordoned off by a ten-foot-high canvas wall protected by the Royal Guards, who were armed with semiautomatic rifles. The king and his two brothers were in large white tents, complete with a separate bath tent with running water. Near the king's tent was another large tent used as an office by the king and his aide-de-camp.

A few yards away was a circular thatched gazebo that served as the royal dining hall. On one side of the gazebo was a small but well-stocked bar. On the other side was an open-pit fire. A good twenty yards from this cluster were the tents set aside for the high-ranking officials and noncommissioned officers. A noisy diesel generator provided power for the entire camp. In the far north the snowcapped Himalayas loomed high, peacefully in the distance.

A large reception greeted us as we towed the rhino across the Rapti River and laid it on an embankment near the king's tent. After delivering the rhino, my official duties were over. Like others in the Royal Camp, I stood patiently leaning against a huge sal tree to watch the proceedings of the ancient rites of the king's Tarpan.

A group of soldiers serving in the Royal Nepalese Army un-loaded the carcass and aligned it in a north-south direction on the ground outside the royal encampment. Then Shakti, the royal taxi-dermist, took over the ceremony.

For several generations Shakti's family had skinned game and mounted hunting trophies for the Nepalese royal family. Shakti was a Sarki, the lowest caste of cobblers, who were permitted to eat cow meat, in the Nepalese Hindu hierarchy. However, as a key member of the royal household, Shakti had more prestige than many upper-caste Brahmins in the social pecking order of Nepal. All members of the royal entourage treated this gentle, gray-haired, sixty-year-old untouchable with unaccustomed respect and dignity.

We watched entranced as Shakti, with the help of the *pipas*, skillfully cut open the rhino and disemboweled the two-ton animal. He carefully stored each and every bloody bit in large buckets. He would eventually profit by selling the guts of the rhino as medicine. Tradition provided him this once-in-a-lifetime perk.

With the help of the soldiers' pushing, pulling, and jostling the rhino's huge carcass, Shakti positioned the dead pachyderm belly up and anchored the rhino's legs to nearby trees. The rhino's head was pointed south toward Varanasi in India, the holiest Hindu city. The rhino's penis was pointed north toward the Himalayas, the abode of Shiva, the Hindu god often represented by a lingam, or stone shaft that scholars consider a phallic symbol of fertility.

Using buckets of water, Shakti cleaned the rhino's body from head to tail. By the time he had finished, even the ground around the rhino was spotless. Finally, he jerked the body of the rhino a few times. Satisfied that it was firmly anchored to the trees, the royal taxi-dermist saluted the head priest and backed off to stand beside me.

The head priest was a saffron-robed Brahmin, with sunken eyes and a slender body. A long pigtail dangled from the back of his glistening, shaved head. Six other priests, their hair cut in the same fashion, stood behind him.

After taking charge of the king's rhino from the untouchable, the head priest doused the beast with water from the Rapti River, scrubbed it, and applied mustard oil to the skin to purify it after its cleansing by an untouchable. Another priest painted the ground around the rhino with a mixture of cow dung and rust-colored soil. Both cow dung and cow urine is considered holy in Nepal. A third priest drew two parallel lines on each side of the rhino using blood red vermilion powder. Other priests drew a variety of sacred symbols on each side of the rhino. The symbol on the left side was the Hindu swastik, an ancient Hindu symbol or holy icon that means "to be good," which was hijacked by the Nazis in the twentieth century.

The head priest also drew the Sanskrit letter *om* on the ground. It is a sacred letter to both Hindus and Buddhists. Though in written form it is represented by a single letter in Devanagari script (a derivative of Sanskrit), it is pronounced in three "words," "A, U, M," in the oral form. Each word is used as a syllable and chanted with a long draw. The first syllable represents the physical states of the body in relation to the universe, the second the mental state, while the third represents the unconsciousness states of the mind and the body.

After drawing the *om* on the ground, the priest drew a star that resembled Israel's Star of David. This is a symbol of Saraswati, the Hindu goddess of wisdom. A trident, another symbol of God Shiva, was drawn at the tail end, facing the Himalayan mountains to the north. Then the priests placed a low wooden platform on the right side of the rhino. They circled the platform with saffron-colored powder, and then placed palm-sized sesame-oil lamps and leaf plates full of fruits, vegetables, rice, yogurt, milk, honey, and other offerings around the rhino.

As the priests finished decorating the Tarpan site, I looked at my watch. It was just after seven in the evening, almost twelve hours since the king fired his first shot. The evening was chilly, the surroundings damp with dew. Save for the steady sound of the River Rapti flowing quietly in the twilight, there was an eerie silence.

The setting, lit with oil lamps, was serene, despite the background of an eviscerated rhino lying belly up. The situation echoed the miraculously mixed traditions of Nepal. Lord Buddha, the apostle of peace, had been born in the Terai, in 563 BC at Lumbini, just a hundred miles west of where we were standing. Like King Birendra, Lord Buddha was born to a Hindu royal family. He may have searched through these very woods in his religious quest to end "*dukkha*," the Buddha's term for suffering. Now, more than twenty-five hundred years later, my people, the people of Buddha's native land, had woven Buddhist and Hindu traditions into a seamless but seemingly contradictory ritual web. Our king is believed to be the incarnation of the Hindu god Vishnu, the creator and the savior. Yet he had to kill a rhino in order to achieve peace and harmony in his kingdom.

King Birendra arrived for the Tarpan ceremony at exactly 7:15 P.M. He was dressed in the traditional Nepali white *daura-surual*, a loose-fitting shirt buttoned across the chest, and trousers that resembled homespun jodhpurs. He took off his red cotton slippers outside the saffron circle and sat in the lotus position on the wooden platform next to the rhino's chest. The evening buzzed with the sounds of priests chanting Sanskrit verses.

The king lit an oil lamp and incense sticks. Then a priest lit the rest of the oil lamps and the incense sticks surrounding the rhino. Another priest walked to the rhino with a handful of incense sticks and waved his hand inside the animal. The king sprinkled water several times on the rhino's head. Then he threw water on his own feet, an act of purification, and stepped out of the saffron circle. A priest squatted at the head of the rhino. He lifted the animal's ears, blew into each ear three times, and whispered into the animal's ears. I could not hear what the priest was saying, but later I was told that the priest was asking the rhino to allow the king to step into his body. The body of the rhino might have been dead but not his soul. Even His Majesty the King needed permission from the dead unicorn's soul to enter its body.

The king sprinkled flower petals and rice on all the leaf plates that were laden with offerings around the rhino's body. He then moved toward the rhino. At exactly 7:33 P.M., the auspicious moment decreed by the royal astrologer, the king climbed into the rhino's body. The Royal Nepalese Army Band played the national anthem of Nepal. Unlike at other occasions, the priests did not freeze to attention. They continued muttering their mantras in Sanskrit. The air was filled with an atonal mix of brass and sonorous mantras.

Half of the king's body was hidden as he knelt down inside the rhino. The head priest stood beside the rhino reciting prayers with folded hands. Slowly the king disappeared inside the rhino. Soon his head emerged, followed by the top half of his body. He lifted up his cupped hands filled with rhino blood in supplication. His eyes were closed. Then, standing upright from the belly of the rhino, he prayed for the soul of his dead father and the rest of his departed ancestors. He appeared to be in a trance as he prayed for his country's peace, prosperity, and harmony. The royal priests circled the rhino, continuing to chant mantras.

After he finished his prayers, the king climbed out of the rhino and sat with his legs crossed in the lotus position on the wooden platform, his white clothes drenched in blood. His posture was relaxed, and a faint smile was etched on his face in the yellow glow of the kerosene lamps.

Seven priests lined up and marked the king's forehead, not with the rhino's blood but with a mixture of rice, vermilion powder, and saffron. In return the king gave each of them a gold coin as an offering, not a fee for services. However, the priests could keep the money on behalf of the deities. The coin-giving ceremony ended the Tarpan. The king walked back to his tent, nodding to acknowledge the greetings of onlookers with a regal smile on his face.

The sights and sounds of the ritual overwhelmed me. I was thrilled and repelled by the sight of a gracious monarch disappearing into the darkness of the rhino and emerging with bloody hands and clothes. I walked up to Little Uncle, my partner in organizing the king's rhino kill, and muttered, "It is hard to be king of Nepal. I feel sorry that His Majesty must go through these macabre rituals."

"What is macabre about it?" snapped Little Uncle. The irate look in his bulging eyes shut me up.

Little Uncle was right. I had decided to help kill the rhino, and I had done my duty, just like the king. It was not a time for questions. It was a time for acceptance. I waited for further orders. They arrived in the form of the king's military secretary, still dressed in the military regalia that he had worn for the hunt.

"By command of His Majesty," barked the military secretary, "anyone who wishes to pay homage to his departed ancestors is permitted to enter the rhino's stomach. They can make any offerings befitting their caste and religion. The camp commander will ensure that this takes place in an orderly sequence. Priests will be on duty on a rotation basis. The proceedings will be in accordance with the ranks and profiles of the Home Ministry."

I was surprised at how delighted I was by this unexpected royal decree. It relieved all my tensions. My misgivings about the rhino hunt disappeared once I realized I too had the chance to be an active participant in the Tarpan. The rest of the crowd shared my enthusiasm. We all rushed about, preparing ourselves to make our offerings. Little Uncle and I went with a few others to purify our bodies first with a dip in the Rapti River. My karma was right.

Karma is a word that is often confused with fate or coincidence. However, for strict followers of Hinduism and Buddhism, everything in the universe happens for a reason. There are no accidents; there are only causes and consequences for all actions and reactions. It was in my karma that I had been fasting for almost twenty-four hours, a prerequisite for performing the Tarpan. I simply had had no time to eat.

I took my place in line and waited in eager anticipation. Though I was a Western-educated scientist, I welcomed the opportunity to honor my ancestors in the belly of the rhino. My father had died in 1969, and my mother passed away in 1972. I knew that my mother especially would appreciate my taking this rare opportunity to honor her spirit. I was hoping that my performance of the Tarpan would help benefit my parents' otherworldly existence as well as the path of the life I had chosen as a wildlife biologist.

"Come on, move on," said the priest, breaking me out of my trance. "It's your turn."

Wrapped in a white towel, I sprinkled water on my feet and head as a final act of purification and approached the carcass of the rhino. The rhino's belly came up to my knee. I lifted up my right foot and placed it inside the rhino. My foot felt the warm flesh of the pachyderm. I grabbed onto the tough hide of the rhino and brought my other foot inside. I was standing inside the rhino's stomach. It was dark, warm, and smelled of incense. As the king had done before me, I knelt down and scraped blood and pieces of meat from the inside of the rhino's body.

I was surprised that I did not find the experience gruesome. On the contrary, I was light-headed with joy. I lifted my bloody palms to the sky. I closed my eyes and started to pray, paying homage to my dead ancestors. Images of my parents flashed before me. I was in a spell—a magic moment of peace.

A priest broke the peaceful reverie. "Hey!" he said. "There is a long line. Time to get out."

His sharp voice shocked me back to reality. I climbed out and walked to my tent, without speaking a word. After months of suffering political, physical, and mental stress, I was finally at peace.

I had found my soul in the body of a rhino.

20

MOVING RHINOS

The Babai River flowed gently beneath the dew-dripping acacia trees.
It was a typical January night in Nepal's western Terai. A full moon
flooded our cargo of huge wooden crates draped with sheets of
black cloth. Our convoy resembled a mobile military unit on its way
to the next campsite as we drove quietly through the Royal Bardia
National Park, some 480 kilometers west of the site where we had
completed the holy ceremony of the Tarpan.

Hidden under the black cloth were two two-ton adult rhinos,
one male and one female. They were on the last leg of their trip-of-
no-return. But for me it was the beginning of the end of a dream, a
dream that had been a twenty-year obsession: to provide a second
home for the first time in Nepal for the greater one-horned Asian
rhinoceros. So here I was, twenty years later, keeping the promise I
had made to Tapsi when I wallowed with his elephants in the Rapti
River on a hot July afternoon in 1968 in the Royal Chitwan National Park. Kuber, my trusted lieutenant and the mechanic of the
Royal Chitwan National Park, was driving me in an Isuzu pickup
truck. Two red Hino trucks that contained the rhinos and a Toyota
pickup truck followed us.

"We have come a long way," I told Kuber, "since we entered
the body of the rhino at the Tarpan in Kasra." It was also exactly

eight years since King Birendra's Tarpan. I felt nostalgic and re-membered the day I had found my own soul. Kuber lit a Rhino brand Nepalese cigarette but kept quiet.

Following his rhino hunt for the holy ceremony of Tarpan in 1979, King Birendra had issued a new decree that doubled the size of the Royal Chitwan National Park to cover over a thousand square kilometers of pristine forests and grasslands. The rhino pop-ulation, estimated to be less than a hundred in the 1960s, had re-bounded to more than 350 in the 1980s. In addition King Birendra had created the Parsa Wildlife Reserve as an unbroken band of pristine forests on Chitwan's eastern flank. Tourism boomed, pro-viding jobs and opportunities to the local communities and extra foreign exchange to the government treasury. Poaching and habitat destruction were firmly brought under control. The grasslands re-generated, and local villagers harvested them on a sustainable-yield basis once a year.

My fame had also peaked since I entered the rhino's body at the king's Tarpan ceremony. Despite heavy competition, in 1982 I was appointed the executive director of the King Mahendra Trust for Nature Conservation, a new nongovernmental organization cre-ated by the legislative assembly of Nepal. American, German, Japanese, and Nepalese television made films about my work in Chitwan. In addition an international jury awarded me the J. Paul Getty Conservation Prize, often called the "Nobel Prize" of wildlife conservation, in 1987. The rhino's soul had blessed me.

My goal to pioneer a new and daring venture, to provide new homes for rhinos, was becoming a reality as we reached the banks of the Babai River after a grueling fifteen-hour journey through the ravines and dusty roads of southern Nepal. Finding new homes for the rhinos had been a fixation of mine for a long time, ever since my old friend Tapsi had planted the idea into my head twenty years ago. However, largely due to lack of funds, the idea had remained dor-mant for two decades. Chris Wemmer, the chief curator of the

Smithsonian Institution's Conservation and Research Center in Front Royal, Virginia, provided the capture equipment and drugs I needed to find new homes for the rhinos. Chris, a veteran of many rhino-, tiger-, leopard-, bear-, and deer-capture operations in Chitwan, knew precisely what we wanted and how to get them to us using the diplomatic pouch of the State Department.

Earlier, we had expressed our gratitude to the Americans and provided two more pairs of Nepalese rhinos to the zoos in San Francisco and Washington, D.C., to enable them to advance their captive-breeding programs. Our program had the full support of the US government and the American embassy in Kathmandu.

After all this international activity, I turned my focus back to my homeland. The two rhinos that I had caught and caged would be the first rhinos to walk the jungles of Bardia for more than a century. This transfer had started almost twenty-four hours earlier in Chitwan, with Badai, our camp shaman, sacrificing a black goat, a red rooster, and two white pigeons to Ban Devi, the Goddess of the Forest. We could not, and we would not, do anything without first pleasing our protector of the jungle.

This morning the goddess was not pleased. The heavy-duty tractor, without which we could not load the two-ton rhinos, did not start, even after Badai blessed it with goat, chicken, and pigeon blood. By ten in the morning, my trusted lieutenant and friend Kuber Gurung, who handled transportation logistics, gave up in frustration. He jumped into a pickup truck and drove north to the town of Bharatpur to get a new set of batteries for the tractor.

I climbed onto the back of my elephant and headed west toward Baghmara to meet another colleague, Anup Joshi. Anup had been up since dawn with thirty elephants and ninety men. This team had scouted and encircled seven rhinos for me to catch, crate, and transfer to Bardia.

"Not a good start," I explained to Anup when I reached him after a forty-minute elephant ride along the banks of the Rapti

River. "The tractor has gone kaput, and we need to wait for Kuber to get new batteries from town."

"Perhaps the goddess of the Chitwan does not want us to snatch her rhinos today," Anup responded. "But we have cornered seven rhinos within a radius of less than a kilometer. Do you want to check them out?"

I certainly did. With Anup's elephant leading the way, I went on an inspection tour of the rhinos. I often had to climb from elephant back to higher treetops to see the rhinos. The first two in one ring were a young male and a female. In another ring was a female with a bulging belly that looked pregnant. In the third ring was an adult female with a mature calf about to finish weaning and separate from its mother. In the last ring was a pair of handsome young rhinos, a male and a female. The male had a short stout horn, while the female's horn was smooth and curvaceous. I liked this pair, whose age I estimated to be around ten years. I named them *Ramro Jodi* or the "Handsome Couple."

"Forget the pregnant-looking female," I told Anup. "We will catch the Handsome Couple first, and go for three more, if we have time."

I killed time shuttling between the different lots of rhinos held at bay by our elephants. It was noon when I heard Kuber's tractor approaching the jungle. I had less than five hours before dark and five rhinos to catch. It would be an uphill battle. The goddess was still not appeased. The female with the calf broke loose and escaped from the ring. Fear of elephants was no match for the rhino's thirst and her anger at being cornered for more than six hours.

"Let's catch the Handsome Couple first," I told Ram Lotan, the chief elephant driver, once again, and he took charge. "Use the elephants to reinforce the ring around them."

From the back of my elephant, I climbed with my dart gun up a small tree at the northeast edge of the ring of elephants that had encircled this handsome rhino couple and watched Ram Lotan cornering them. From the back of his elephant, Ram Lotan waved his hands and signaled me to be ready. Using his elephants, he forced the rhinos to move slowly toward my tree. Except for the sound of rustling bushes, the jungle was quiet. The male moved about ten yards ahead of the elephants and paused beneath my tree. The female tailed about six feet behind.

"What if the beast spots me and knocks the tree down?" I wondered. No matter how many times I had done this before, my heart pounded fast and my palms were sweaty. I squeezed the trigger and shot the drug-loaded dart into the male rhino's neck to put it to sleep. The rhino jerked his head and moved into the thick bush behind my tree. Then he stood still and gently swayed his drooping head. The drug was taking effect.

The female moved away toward the edge of the jungle. Two elephants followed her at a distance. The male rhino's body rocked gently as he tried to keep his balance. I waved at Ram Lotan to warn him to stop the elephants, as I needed time for the drug to take full effect.

The male rhino went down in a long five minutes, but I gave it another three minutes before signaling Ram Lotan to bring his elephant to my tree. I climbed on top of Ram Lotan's elephant and approached the sleeping rhino. I threw a stick at the rhino. It had no effect. I dismounted from my elephant and hurled a bucket of water at the rhino. He still did not budge. I went through the routine precaution of ensuring that the rhino was deeply sedated. I poked a stick at his anus and pulled his tail. No effect. Though his ears were flickering, the rhino was in a different world—asleep under the influence of the drug atrophine, a morphine derivative.

I covered the rhino's eyes and plugged his ears with cotton pads. Top Khatri, a Nepalese field biologist, took the rhino's temperature from the anus and measured his body. Shanta Raj, another biologist, fixed a radio collar around his neck. We needed this collar not only to monitor the rhino's movements in his new home but also to find him, just in case the rhino escaped during the fifteen-hour journey along the rough road to Bardia.

By the time we finished all the measurements, Kuber had maneuvered our big old Mitsubishi tractor, fitted with new batteries, through the thick bush. A long torsion cable hooked to the tractor dragged a five-by-twelve-foot sledge made of sal wood. The top of the sledge was heavily padded with jute, and its base was reinforced with thick steel plates.

Kuber maneuvered the sledge parallel to the sedated rhino. Using more than two dozen men, he jostled the rhino on top of the sledge. Then he cautiously hauled the rhino toward a loading bay, about a mile outside the jungle.

I stood at the rear end of the sledge, balancing my bottom on the butt of the rhino and holding a dart gun in my right hand. The dart gun was loaded with an extra dose of drug, just in case the rhino woke suddenly. A row of elephants with their drivers marched alongside the sledge.

It took us almost thirty minutes to haul the sedated rhino to the loading area. The loading area was a large rectangular hole dug into the ground, six feet deep, ten feet wide, and fifteen feet long. The mouth of the hole sloped gently down into the pit to enable a big truck to move in and out of it. A bright red Hino truck was parked inside the pit.

An empty six-by-ten-foot wooden crate stood outside the pit. The crate had two doors, one in the front and one in the back. Both the doors slid vertically from the top to the bottom of the crate, and it could be bolted from the outside. Kuber parked the drugged rhino in front of the crate.

Using the power of the tractor and its torsion cable, Kuber dragged the sledge with the sleeping rhino into the crate. He was lying in an awkward position, with his huge body resting on its side. It took some effort for us to bend and push the legs inside the cage. The huge cage looked too small for the rhino. I was concerned as to whether he would be able to stand on his legs, as there was little room to move within the narrowly packed cage.

Half a dozen men climbed on top of the crate and lowered the doors, leaving a small gap. Through this gap, I entered the cage, jerked off the earplugs and the eye cover, and quickly got out. It was an eerie feeling. I had handled many drugged rhinos and even entered the stomach of a dead one. But I had never felt so scared and claustrophobic as in the few seconds I was inside the cage with a sleeping rhino.

Next, I had to go inside the crate, search for a thick vein behind one of the rhino's ears, inject the antidote, and get out of the cage within thirty seconds. The margin for error was very small, and the risk of being trapped inside the cage with a wild rhino was very big. "Anup, double the dose for me," I asked one of our field biologists, who was toying with a syringe and the antidote M:50:50 used for reviving sedated rhinos. "I can't take the risk of being trapped inside the cage with a two-ton wild rhino. We will do an intramuscular and not intravenous injection."

I decided to inject the antidote thorough the rhino's muscle rather than through his vein, even though the latter worked faster. It was slow and risky for the rhino but safe for me. But I was worried about the rhino. A literature review had indicated that a drugged rhino should be resting at ease on its thorax in its natural resting position, with its legs neatly folded on the sides. Our rhino was lying sideways in an awkward position, with his forelegs dangling in the air and his hind legs on his belly. Nevertheless, I could not take any chances. Anup, an excellent field technician, was prepared to go inside the cage and give the rhino an intravenous shot. But I overruled him. It would be not only cowardly but also unethical for me to risk his life and not mine.

While Anup was loading the antidote in a thick syringe, we lowered the front door and secured it tightly with iron bolts. The back door was wide open, exposing the rhino's large rump. I checked the radio signal; all systems were in place. It was time to wake up the rhino.

Anup handed me a glass syringe with three cubic centimeters of M:50:50. I crawled in from the back door until half of my body was in the cage. I felt creepy sharing a tight cage with a belly-up two-ton prehistoric beast. Because of the awkward position of the rhino with his four legs in the air, I had to struggle to find the right place to inject the antidote. My hands were shaking. My nightmare was that the men on top of the crate would slip, causing the heavy door to fall and lock me inside the crate with a wild rhino recovering from the effects of a drug.

Finally I injected the antidote into a soft, pink muscle in the rhino's groin and took a deep breath as I wriggled out of the crate. The men on top of the crate lowered the second door, leaving a gap of about a foot, to pull out the sledge. The noisy surroundings gave way to a solemn quietness. All eyes were glued to the crate with the same questions haunting our minds. Would the antidote work? Would the rhino wake up? I had never lost a rhino. But there could always be a first. I thought back once again to the elephant that died on me after I had given it a shot of antidote.

It took ten long minutes before we heard a grunt. Instantaneously the cage shook and rumbled with a hammering sound of "Thwack, thwack" as the rhino kicked the crate's sidebars. Hundreds of human howls of *Gainda uthyo!* suddenly breached the solemn scene. The humans were cheering, "The rhino is awake!"

I exhaled a long breath of relief. The rhino was alive. But he still had to get on his feet. The rhino shook and rattled the well-built cage.

"Could it topple the cage on its side?" I asked Ram Lotan, the chief elephant driver.

"No," he replied, from the top of his elephant. "It is a very agile animal that will be on its feet in no time."

He was right. The caged rhino twisted, turned, and was up on his feet in less than two minutes. "*Thwack, thwack!*"—the rhino head butted the front end of the crate. Then he backed up and pressed his butt against the rear end to force the cage door to break. Fortunately the cage was too sturdy. It was made of solid sal-wood planks and reinforced by thick steel anchors.

The rhino gave up and splashed the cage with his urine. I climbed on top of the cage and poured a bucket of water through the narrow openings of the wooden planks. The rhino rammed his head upward, almost cracking the roof of the crate. I jumped from the top of the cage to watch the rhino safely from the ground.

Kuber moved his tractor to the other end of the crate and winched the sledge out with a clever pull-stop-pull maneuver. Each pull caused the rhino to move a step forward, lessening his weight on the sledge. As the rhino moved forward, Kuber waited a few seconds before jerking the sledge out, little by little. Once the sledge was pulled out, we bolted the second door and covered the cage with a thick black cotton sheet.

The rhino became quiet when he could not see outside. He was ready to be loaded into the Hino truck inside the loading pit. Using the strong torsion cable and his powerful Mitsubishi tractor, Kuber winched the crate onto the truck. Then he drove the truck out of the loading pit and parked it under a big Semal tree. Our first rhino was ready for his long journey to a new home. And I was ready to catch his mate, the female half of the Handsome Couple.

I moved back to the jungle, followed by a string of elephants. The female rhino was exactly where we had left her. Encircled by our team of skilled elephants and their drivers, she had nowhere to go but stayed calm under the cover of the bush. Within the next hour we had her on the back of another truck. The bright red sun was dipping over the horizon. We had no time to catch any more rhinos; I had to be satisfied that I had two rhinos for our maiden voyage to Bardia, ready to find them a new home in Nepal.

☼

24

A NEW HOME FOR
THE RHINOS

*I*t was January 20, 1987, a historic day in the life of the rhinos of Nepal and a memorial day that remains cemented in my mind. Our journey was bumpy, dusty, and arduous and lasted all night long.

To reach the release site, my crew crossed three rivers, bypassed two overturned trucks, and braked for several bullock carts and numerous stray herds of cows along the rugged, dusty road and the forest trail that connected Chitwan with Bardia. The journey took more than fifteen hours to reach the Royal Bardia National Park, the new home for the Chitwan rhinos. It was almost noon before we reached the release site on the banks of the Geruwa River valley on the western flank of the Royal Bardia National Park.

We backed the truck with the male rhino into the unloading pit, which was similar to the loading pit in Chitwan. Six elephants, recently procured from India, surrounded the unloading pit in a semicircle. Kuber climbed on top of the crate and unlocked the door. I got on top of an elephant directly in front of the cage. Our strategy was to use the elephants to drive the rhino toward the river so that he could quench his thirst. From the top of an elephant, I watched Kuber use a pulley. He hooked it to an overhanging branch in order to lift the heavy door open.

I assumed that after being confined for more than fifteen hours in such tight quarters the rhino would be ready to burst out of the crate like a running bull in the Spanish city of Pamplona. He did not. With his butt end first, the rhino slowly strolled out of the cage. Then he turned around and stood majestically to face the elephants, eyeball to eyeball.

We were unprepared for what happened next. It was not the rhino but rather the elephants that took off—the sight of the rhino scared the elephants. First, the young female elephant on my right took off toward the trees, emitting peculiar calls that sounded like *"Eiünng, eiünng."* This triggered my elephant to follow her. Then the rest of our elephants bolted, hooting and trumpeting in panic and filling the air with the confused sounds of *"Eiünng, eiünng, eiünng."*

The release of our first rhino was total chaos. I held tightly to my elephant, as I was afraid of falling off. Fortunately, the elephant driver brought it under control in the Phanta, a huge patch of open grassland almost a mile from the rhino-release site. It was an hour before we could reorganize and resolve the mystery of the bolting elephants.

Unlike our Chitwan elephants, these Bardia elephants, which had only recently been imported from India, had never seen a rhino. This was their first encounter with a prehistoric beast. Consequently, they galloped off to save their lives from the wrath of a strange-looking unicorn that had coolly walked out of a wooden crate to stare them down in the majestic projection of its power.

Meanwhile, our first transported rhino had disappeared into the bush. I was not too worried because we could easily locate it with the radio collar dangling from its neck. I was more anxious to release the second rhino.

The first truck pulled out of the unloading pit and a second truck took its place. Kuber unscrewed the bolts of the crate and opened one door. This time the elephants were kept out of sight. I was standing on top of the crate. To my surprise, the female rhino refused to move out of the cage. We yelled and pounded the cage with our feet. The rhino stayed put. We decided to give her a rest and let time take its course. Nothing happened for the next ten minutes.

"I am impatient, hungry, and sleepy," said Kuber. "I will have to tickle her hind end to get her out of the cage."

From the top of the crate, Kuber bent over the door and poked an iron rod at the rhino's rump. The rhino banged the side of the crate with her head. The cage shook. I got worried, as eight of us were packed tightly on top of the cage, which was within the reach of the wild rhino. She could shake us down. Kuber was unconcerned. He continued poking the rhino until it worked. Finally, the rhino splashed the cage with her urine and walked out of the cage. With her nostrils flared, she sniffed the fresh air of her new home. She gave Kuber one last look and calmly trotted toward the river, disappearing into the tall grasses in freedom.

I walked to my pickup truck and switched on the radio receiver. The signals indicated that the radio collars on both the rhinos were working. Using the signal, we were able to locate both rhinos grazing on the bank of the river.

I left the task of monitoring the rhinos to Gagan Singh. He was a native of the area and a game scout whom I had poached from the Forest Department. Gagan knew the reserve like the back of his hand. He had no formal education beyond the third grade, yet Gagan was worth more than a dozen PhDs for his knowledge of the wildlife of Bardia. He could track any wild animal, be it a tiger, a leopard, or a wild elephant, on foot. Now he would spend the rest of his days tracking rhinos with a radio receiver.

Contented with a job well done, I drove off to Thakurdwara, the Bardia Park headquarters, to sleep for the next twenty hours. The next day I returned east to Chitwan. I still had eleven rhinos to move. My target was to move thirteen rhinos and study them in their new home for about three years. Based on the outcome of the study, I planned to move more rhinos after that.

Over the next three days, I caught and moved four rhinos. This time the Goddess of the Forest seemed happy; the tractor was not a problem in our second round. But people were. The story of the "*sutni gainda*" or "sleeping rhinos" spread like a bushfire throughout southern Nepal. Large crowds gathered at our capture site vying for a chance to touch the immobilized beasts. Hundreds of villagers perched like monkeys on treetops and watched us catch wild rhinos. Once a rhino was on the sledge, the villagers ran behind it trying to touch the sleeping pachyderm. After laying their hands on the rhino, as if it were a holy symbol, they touched their foreheads as a blessing. We mimicked their behavior to seek the rhino's blessing to enable us to complete our operations safely, both for rhinos and humans. It seemed to work; in two weeks' time, I reached my target and had moved thirteen rhinos to Bardia.

Helping me in this operation was Dr. Eric Dinerstein, a brilliant scientist from the Smithsonian Institution. He was a former American Peace Corp volunteer in Nepal who had studied the wildlife habitat in Bardia. Eric, who spoke fluent Nepali, was an American from New Jersey. However, with his soft-spoken voice and in-depth knowledge of the language and culture, he could easily be mistaken for an upper-class Nepali. In addition to assisting with the capture operation, Eric helped us identify the release sites in the Royal Bardia National Park.

Over the next three years five new calves were born in Bardia, indicating the biological success of our pilot operation. But I doubted that only thirteen rhinos provided a good breeding base to expand the rhino population in their new home. I reckoned that I needed at least thirty-five to start building a viable second home for rhinos in Nepal.

Ed Bass, the Texan, visited Nepal and surveyed the Babai Valley with a team of our experts. This team recommended that two dozen rhinos be moved from Chitwan to Bardia over a period of two years. Their findings were consistent with my own intentions. How-

ever, multiples of eight and twelve are regarded to be unlucky numbers in Nepal. In times like these I too was superstitious. Therefore,
I decided to move twenty-five rhinos—ten males and fifteen females.
I also did not want to wait two years but decided to move all the rhinos within two months. The political dynamics of Nepal were changing fast. Two years was too long to wait in Nepal. The crucial factor
was time and not funds, as the revolution against the king was gaining momentum. Riots, roadblocks, and other political agitations
were becoming more frequent in the district of Chitwan.

I identified three special sites to catch our rhinos. They were
five miles apart. I was not too fussy about where I caught the rhinos, but I was very fussy about which rhinos I caught. My primary
objective was to kill two birds with one stone. Though my key objective was to provide a new home for Chitwan rhinos, I also
wanted to move those that were crop raiders living near farmlands
and harassing farmers.

Most rhinos in Chitwan congregated in the riverine forests and
grasslands. Prime rhino habitat covered only about 20 percent of
the thousand-square-kilometer sanctuary. A few rhinos found that
food was more palatable and available in large quantities beyond
the park boundary. They raided crops and were becoming a nui-
sance to the villagers. In some parts of Chitwan, almost 90 percent
of the crop was lost to rhinos. Thus my primary targets for resettlement were the crop raiders. We used distinctive body markings
such as scars, horns, and other signs to track our animals.

I caught the first lot of five rhinos near the site of King Birendra's rhino hunt. It was a nice, easy operation. NHK, the biggest
Japanese television station in Tokyo, filmed that operation. I also invited a friend, Jim Jabara, an American filmmaker from Michigan,
to make a documentary on the life of rhinos and include our efforts
to find them new homes. The film included an amusing anecdote
about God Brahma's creation of the rhinos and the life of rhinos in
Chitwan. It also included some hard science and proved to be of high

educational and scientific value, as it was the only film that recorded the life cycle of the Chitwan rhinos that we moved to Bardia.

I got the second lot of rhinos in Tikoli, a patch of forest outside the park, and the third lot from Kathar at the far eastern end of the park. I had the full cooperation of the local villagers during my capture operation. In many villages I was treated like a hero because I was removing rhinos that had been pests to their crops. But to me rhinos were not pests; they were sacred beings.

The preservation of Nepal's ancient temples and monasteries had won international support and popular enthusiasm from the country's devout Hindu and Buddhist believers. Some of these had been destroyed, but with an infusion of cash and technology, they were restored or rebuilt, as has been done over time throughout our history. But no amount of money, motivation, or manpower could restore the rhinos once they became extinct. This would be a tragedy, not only for Nepal but also for all of humankind.

During many of our important festivals, it was a habit of mine to move religious objects or offerings, such as rocks or flowers, from temple to temple. My transplantation of rhinos from Chitwan to Bardia was a similar exercise. Here I was also moving a sacred object from one holy site to another.

Since I had entered the body of the rhino that King Birendra had sacrificed, its soul had engulfed me. I felt like a rhino myself, an ungainly creature put together from different parts. Part Eastern and part Western. Part city slicker and part jungle dweller. Part scientist and part drunken singer of bawdy songs. Part hunting guide and part preservationist.

Despite the unlikely parts, we humans are capable of grace and beauty and of love and kindness, not only for our own species, but also for other animals and plant life. The Hindu and Buddhist respect for nature that was ingrained in my upbringing had been revived after I found my own soul inside a rhino's body. I do not believe that only we Nepalese are best equipped to practice this respect. Our collective human consciousness tells us that we should not destroy what we love.

The rhinos are a special part of our world. We are also a part of their world. They go. We go. But if we maintain a ritual mindfulness, like the king of Nepal, we may even be able to preserve what we are forced sometimes to kill.

Years ago I had promised Tapsi, the craggy elephant driver with a rotten tooth and a talent for cursing with the choicest of invectives, that I would take his sermon seriously. That sermon — "Don't keep all your eggs in one basket" — is old and universal in application. My work has ensured that the rhinos are not restricted only to Chitwan but have been allowed to flourish in Bardia.

Tapsi has long been dead. But I kept my promise. My effort to bring back the greater one-horned Asian rhinoceros from the brink of extinction was like traveling the bumpy highway from the Royal Chitwan National Park to the Royal Bardia National Park. Slow. Tortuous. Engulfed with uncertainty, yet ultimately resulting in success.

The thirty-eighth rhino that I moved from its natal area in Chitwan to Bardia was a huge, well-groomed male with a nice curvy horn. I named him *Tapsi Mukhi* ("Tapsi Face"), even though the rhino had no resemblance to my long-dead mentor, the master of the jungle.

My mission was complete, as Tapsi Mukhi walked out of his cage and melted into the rolling grasslands of his new home in the Babai Valley of Royal Bardia National Park. It was my tryst with destiny to restore rhinos to the forests and grasslands of Bardia, where they once roamed, freely and fearlessly, a century ago.

A coldhearted colonial officer of the British Empire shot the last free-ranging rhino in this region in 1878. But he only destroyed the body, not the soul, of the rhino.

The rhinos had returned home after a hundred years.

☀

EPILOGUE:
Hope or Uncertainty on a Himalayan Scale

*B*ack in *1968, when my friend Graeme Caughley and I took the first* systematic census of rhinos, we estimated the population of rhinos in Nepal to be somewhere between 90 and 108 individuals in the Chitwan region. Fortunately, the government of King Mahendra implemented our recommendations. They took strong actions against poaching and habitat destruction and established Nepal's first internationally recognized national park in 1973. Since the establishment of the Royal Chitwan National Park, the rhino population had increased incrementally. By 1980 their numbers had reached over three hundred.

The rhinos continued their remarkable comeback, and by the early 1990s the number of rhinos in Nepal had grown to more than 450. Moreover, by the beginning of the new millennium, the number of rhinos in Nepal peaked at nearly 550. But after his son Crown Prince Dipendra butchered King Birendra on June 1, 2001, rhino numbers began to tumble, indicating that the fate of the rhinos was very much linked to the fate of the king.

King Birendra had sacrificed a rhino and performed the religious ceremony of the Tarpan for peace and prosperity in the Himalayan Kingdom of Nepal. He had strictly observed the rituals mandated by the ancient scriptures in the holy books and had prayed to the rhino's soul. Yet peace and prosperity evaded Nepal after his death.

Taking advantage of King Birendra's murder, the Maoist rebels stepped up their campaign of terror. Peace talks initiated by the government with the Maoists failed. A truce was nowhere in sight. The rhinos topped the list of Nepal's endangered species that suffered from the brutal armed conflict as law and order broke down. The Royal Nepalese Army soldiers that guarded the parks and reserves were deployed elsewhere to fight the rebels or remained confined to their barracks, creating an open season for the poachers. More than a dozen national-park staff members were murdered by the Maoists. Guard posts were blown up. The insurgents also seized vehicles belonging to the antipoaching team. The numbers of rhino guard posts in the Royal Chitwan National Park were reduced from thirty-three to eleven. Frequent attacks and killings made it impossible to operate these strategically located antipoaching centers.

Taking advantage of the vacuum created in Chitwan, new poachers, belonging to organized-crime syndicates in India, muscled into Nepal. They taught Nepalese poachers new techniques. These included placing poison around rhino wallows and saltlicks and electrocuting rhinos by hooking live wires to the overhanging high-voltage transmission lines in rhino country. The modern high-powered rifle replaced the old muzzleloader as the poacher's new weapon of choice.

By 2005 Nepal was in total chaos and under siege by a ruthless rebel movement spearheaded by the Communist (or Maoist) Party of Nepal. Modeled after the Shining Path movement in Peru, the Maoists' goal was to establish a new regime in Nepal—a replica of the Khmer Rouge that ruled Cambodia from 1975 to 1979. Like Pol Pot, Prachanda (the "Feared One" and the "Supreme Leader" of the Nepal Communist Party) was on a mission to transform Nepal into a communist agrarian society ruled by the proletariat. Large parts of the country, particularly the rural areas, fell under Maoist control. These included areas that are the refuge of the rhino population in Nepal. Consequently, the rhinos also became victims of the harrowing conflict in Nepal. The number of rhinos in Chitwan declined from nearly 550 to about 370, the lowest in three decades. Chitwan rhinos were not the only ones being slaughtered. The rhinos that I had found a new home for in the Bardia National Park were also ruthlessly decimated.

In addition to the thirty-eight rhinos I had moved from Chitwan to Bardia in 1987, my colleagues, Chandra Gurung and Tirtha Man Maskey, who followed my example, relocated another forty-six rhinos to Bardia in the 1990s. The population of rhinos in Bardia was estimated to be more than 115 by 2000, with the addition of at least thirty calves born in that decade. At least seventy-two of these rhinos freely roamed the Babai Valley on the eastern flank of the Royal Bardia National Park.

Anxious to find out what had happened to these rhinos, a forty-member international team from the World Wildlife Fund, the World Conservation Union, and the Nepalese government ventured into the Babai Valley in May 2006, following a cease-fire agreement between the government and the Maoists. Regretfully, I was not on that team. But the team did its job and made a field assessment of the status of rhinos introduced in Bardia by my colleagues and me.

This team of experts was shocked to discover that only three of the original seventy-two rhinos were left in the Babai Valley. The rest were victims of wide-scale poaching. Though there is no proof that the Maoists were involved in the poaching, international experts blame the insurgency as the key contributor to the rapid decline of living rhinos. The experts predicted that if the civil conflict that peaked after the palace massacre was not resolved and the poaching brought under firm control, the rhino would be extinct in Nepal within the next ten years.

Clearly, neither the soul of the rhino nor King Birendra's own soul was resting in peace. The future of Nepal, and with it the future of the Chitwan and Bardia rhinos, appeared to be doomed.

By the end of 2006, the situation in Nepal had taken unprecedented twists and turns. These fast-paced political events would be either a bane or a boon for the rhinos of this rapidly changing country. King Gyanendra, the next in line to the late King Birendra, and a royal who had played a central role in saving rhinos, dissolved the Parliament in May 2002, on the recommendation of Prime Minister Deuba. Deuba was trying to wrest the leadership of the Nepal Congress Party from his rival Girja Prasad Koirala. Subsequently, King Gyanendra's popularity began to tumble, indicating his failure to grasp the intricacies of the warring tribes of Nepalese multiparty politics.

Political pettiness had produced eleven governments in eleven years since Western-style democracy was introduced in Nepal in 1991. Yet the politicians of Nepal continued to play musical chairs, even after Parliament was dissolved. King Gyanendra hired and fired Deuba twice and changed government leadership five times between 2002 and 2005. Furthermore, on the first of February 2005, heeding the recommendation of a coterie of uninformed and inexperienced advisers, King Gyanendra declared a state of emergency. He assumed direct power, citing the need to defeat the Maoist rebels.

The king's action did not have the desired effect. It neither restored peace to Nepal nor stopped the carnage in rhino poaching, which reached dangerous levels, with at least thirty-seven rhinos poached in the year 2005. The king became a pariah in the eyes of the Western world. The media, both international and national, began to vilify him. By the beginning of 2006, he had lost the support of the few educated elites who had once praised him for his professionalism, leadership, and vision, particularly in making Nepal's national parks and wildlife-conservation programs exemplary in the global community, when he was a mere prince.

The king's state of emergency had the opposite effect to the one he had anticipated, endangering the very existence of monarchy in Nepal. It galvanized a previously unimaginable strategic alliance between two archrivals, a seven-party consortium of democratic forces in Nepal and the Maoist insurgents. This alliance was forged discreetly in New Delhi, the capital of India, Nepal's powerful southern neighbor. It also had the tacit support of the government and political parties of India, particularly the ruling Congress Party and its ally, the Communist Party of India.

On April 4, 2006, the alliance of seven Nepalese political parties and the Maoists jointly launched an aggressive mass uprising against King Gyanendra. Over the following nineteen days, the face of Nepal changed drastically. His Majesty's government tried to quell the uprising. But thousands of agitated youths in the streets of Kathmandu burned cars, destroyed government buildings, and pelted police officers with Molotov cocktails. Transportation came to a standstill as the Maoists blockaded the roads and the highways, causing food shortages and other hardships. All sides, particularly the security forces and the Maoists, reacted brutally. Violence begat violence, and twenty-one people were killed in the nineteen days of the uprising against King Gyanendra.

In the final days, foreign pressure from the United States and the European Union was heavily exerted on King Gyanendra to surrender his powers and restore the parliamentarian system of democracy. Finally, wisdom prevailed. Unable to withstand both external and internal pressures, the king finally conceded. At midnight on April 24, 2006, the history of Nepal took a dramatic turn. In a televised address to the nation, the king restored the Parliament and surrendered all his powers back to the alliance of Nepal's seven political parties and the Maoist rebels.

Over the next few days, the Parliament convened and stripped all the powers and privileges from the king. This included his command of the ninety-thousand-member Nepalese army as its commander-in-chief. His status as the "God-King" was rescinded. The parliament declared that Nepal was no longer a "Hindu kingdom" but a secular state. They even removed the word "Royal" from the name of Royal Chitwan National Park. Yet the new masters of Nepal did not go so far as to banish monarchy from the country. Even after days of haggling, the Maoists and the seven-party alliance could not reach a consensus to abolish the monarchy. Finally they decided to leave that decision to a Constituent Assembly scheduled to be elected in November 2007.

As of September 2007 the future of Nepal's 248-year-old Shah Dynasty hangs in the balance. Assuming that the November 2007 Constituent Assembly elections will be free, fair, and transparent, it will not be the guns of the Maoists or the Nepalese army but the elected political power brokers who will decide the fate of King Gyanendra and the Shah Dynasty that have reigned in Nepal since 1789. Likewise, the destiny of rhinos in Nepal might not be decided by wildlife biologists like me but by the new emerging political actors.

Even when they could not agree on the future of monarchy in Nepal, in a positive and surprising move the Maoists and the seven political parties did forge an understanding for the conservation of Nepal's rhinoceros. Three of my long-standing partners in conservation engineered this unusual deal in Chitwan. They were Mingma Norbu Sherpa, director of Himalayan Programs for the World Wildlife Fund; Tirtha Man Maskey, vice-chairman of the Asian Rhino Specialists Group; and Chandra Prasad Gurung, program director of the World Wildlife Fund in Nepal. Another colleague, Narayan Poudal, director general of Nepal's Department of National Parks and Wildlife Conservation, played a behind-the-scenes role in organizing this first-of-its-kind meeting of the minds among all the different rival factions in Nepal.

On August 28, 2006, national-park staff and the Maoist rebels met openly in the Royal Chitwan National Park with representatives from the major political parties, governmental and nongovernmental organizations, community leaders, and youth groups. In this unprecedented gathering, the Maoists agreed to join conservationists to save the rhinos. Along with representatives of nineteen organizations, they signed a twenty-point resolution, aptly titled "The Rhino Conservation Chitwan Declaration — 2006."

This declaration set a goal of saving the rhinoceros in Chitwan by launching proactive conservation programs, with coordination and cooperation among all the parties represented at this meeting. They also vowed to help park authorities to implement innovative security techniques by involving local residents in protecting the rhino and its habitat. Furthermore, the declaration prescribed a reward-and-punishment scheme to halt poaching.

Akash, a Maoist commander of the region, declared his cadre's commitments to protect rhinos from poachers. Besides agreeing to sensitize his fellow Communist guerillas to the importance of conservation in Nepal, he declared that the Maoists would take "severe actions" against those who sought to kill rhinos or destroy their habitat. Many observers present at the meeting have interpreted "severe actions" as a Maoist euphemism for brutal beatings, breaking of limbs, and even killing of those who violate their order. Time will tell if such threats are empty or if they will discourage poaching.

The most significant and historical development happened on November 21, 2006. Setting aside the fundamental differences of their political mandates, the warring factions of Nepal, including the Maoists, demonstrated that their search for peace is genuine. To an ecstatic sigh of relief throughout Nepal, the Maoists signed a peace deal with the government, ending an eleven-year-old civil war in Nepal that has claimed thirteen thousand human lives. Peace is fundamental to the preservation of rhinos and other endangered species of Nepal. Thus the peace pact in which the Maoists agreed to lay down their arms is a boon for the rhinos.

Another development that sheds a ray of hope on the future of rhinos stems from an unusual decision taken by the Supreme Court of Nepal. On December 4, 2006, this highest judicial body made an extraordinary ruling by ordering the government to set up adequate guard posts and increase security in the Royal Chitwan National Park.

The recent peaceful developments in Nepal are indeed encouraging, particularly the agreement to end the civil war. But does this imply that the future of rhinos in Nepal is assured?

I was in Nepal in September and October 2006, when I met with old colleagues, both in the government and in the nongovernment sectors. A few were candid and outspoken. Some asserted that the political situation in Nepal is still too unsettled to assume lasting peace—a prerequisite for the survival of rhinos in perpetuity. Others cautioned me not to be blinded by optimism. They also warned me that by living in America I might have lost myself to a separate reality. Three events that occurred in Nepal between June and October 2006 may justify their reservations.

First, in a very unusual move, the new coalition government of Nepal jailed three of its own Chitwan Park staff. This action was taken following a complaint that an accused poacher died in their custody. Yet conservationists claim the trio are among the best of Nepal's civil-service corps. Their valor in poaching control and safeguarding the rhino's habitat was outstanding, despite threats to their lives and intimidation from the rebels. A Kathmandu rumor claims that these park staff members were arrested at the behest of an organized-crime syndicate that had bribed senior officials of the ruling parties. Though the three staff members were eventually released, the government's action has demoralized most of the staff of the national park and wildlife conservation service in Nepal. One staff member went into hiding. A few took extended leaves of absence. Many of those stationed inside the national parks did not venture beyond the confines of their office.

Second, radical changes to the political structures seem to have had little effect on rhino poaching. According to a news report from *Kantipur* and the *Nepali Times*, two of Nepal's largest and most credible media groups, poaching in Chitwan continues unabated. At least thirty-seven rhinos were poached between February 2005 and April 2006.

Furthermore, at least a dozen rhinos have been killed since the Maoists and the seven-party alliance snatched power from the king and formed a new government in April 2006. Tourists returning from Chitwan say that rhino sightings, once frequent, are becoming rare. Some believe that the Maoists are in cahoots with poachers, as a means of fund-raising for their cause. Their participation in signing the "Rhino Conservation Chitwan Declaration—2006" may have been largely rhetorical to appease Western conservation watchdogs. Furthermore, Bardia, the second home of the rhinos in Nepal, is still unruly. Threats, extortion, and poaching have not been stopped, even if it is not clear whether these bad actors are real Maoists or criminals masquerading as Maoist cadres.

The third event is devastating for the cause of conservation in Nepal. In a tragic helicopter crash on September 23, 2006, Nepal and the world lost a host of the world's most accomplished leaders in conservation. For me the loss of these heroes and builders of the conservation movement was deeply personal and heartwrenching.

Three of those who died in the catastrophic crash included Tirtha Man Maskey, Chandra Prasad Gurung, and Mingma Norbu Sherpa. These three were my friends and band of brothers for more than three decades in Nepal's conservation movement. For thirty years we shared dust and sweat, tears and joy, food and drink, elephants and motorized vehicles, as we jointly created national parks and protected areas throughout Nepal and saved many endangered species such as the rhino from becoming extinct. They were my partners, who helped me find new homes for rhinos. They helped me organize the holy ceremony of the rhino Tarpan for the king of Nepal. Together we wandered through the steaming jungles and trekked in the cool mountains of Nepal on foot. Together we visited many countries in all the continents of the world, to listen and learn from foreign experts and to promote and raise funds for saving Nepal's wildlife.

I spent a joyous evening with them in Kathmandu on the eve of their ill-fated helicopter journey in the Kanchenjunga Conservation

Area of Nepal, where the helicopter crashed. I shudder with agony when I recall that my friend Chandra Gurung had insisted that I join him, Mingma, and Tirtha, on this fateful trip to celebrate the success of conservation in the Kanchenjunga mountain region of eastern Nepal. A scheduled royal audience with Her Majesty Queen Ashi Sangay Choden Wangchuck of Bhutan in Thimpu prevented me from taking this fatal trip.

Jim Ottaway Jr., our mutual friend and an editor for this book, was also invited to join the trip. But his business in New York prevented him from going. Jim had been to the area eight years before because he had supported the beginning of the Kanchenjunga Conservation Project in Nepal. Another friend, Karna Shakya, a conservationist, writer, and hotelier, cancelled his trip only an hour before boarding the helicopter that crashed. An unexpected union problem instigated by the Maoists in his hotel forced him to stay back.

My eyes drain with tears and my body quakes with fear when I ponder how fate acts impulsively, with all its cruelty, unpredictability, and spontaneity. I tremble with pain when I wonder why Yama—the Hindu God of Death—chose Chandra, Mingma, and Tirtha and twenty-one other good people but not Jim, Karna, and me—the elderly men in our band of conservation soldiers.

The helicopter crash was especially disastrous for Nepal. It lost all the key members of its core parks and forestry leadership, with a combined expertise and experience of two hundred years in conservation. In addition to my Nepalese brethren, Nepal lost many true friends from the international community that had ardently supported Nepal's conservation efforts despite the eleven years of civil war in Nepal. They included Nepal's core friends from the World Wide Fund for Nature in the United Kingdom, the government of the United States, the government of Finland, the World Wildlife Fund–U.S., and others in the media and the private sector.

What will be the fate of rhinos and other endangered species in Nepal with this tragic loss of some of the world's most accomplished conservationists? Who will ensure that the Maoists or any un-scrupulous members of the ruling party will not be co-opted, ca-joled, or bribed by a gang of rhino poachers?

Like many Nepalese, I was hopeful when the Maoists signed the peace agreement. Once inside the government, however, the Maoists resorted to violence largely through the actions of their po-litical wing, the Young Communist League.

The land of the rhinos soon erupted in unprecedented murder and mayhem, caused by the failure of the government and the Maoists to acknowledge the legitimate demands of the Terai people in the in-terim constitution. Consequently, the Terai Jantantrik Liberation Front (TJLF)—a splinter Maoist group—emerged as a new political force in Southern Nepal. Their clarion call was to snatch full sover-eignty and independence of the Terai belt from the central government in Kathmandu. In addition to the TJLF, many other reactionary groups joined in the violence. By the end of September 2007, diverse ethnic, tribal, caste, and regional groups emerged to assert their own demands for autonomy, and law and order eroded in the Terai as a re-sult. To add to the pandemonium, on September 18, 2007 the Maoists walked out of the coalition government they had joined on April 1, 2007 and threatened to go underground and start a civil war.

As this book goes to press, the future of Nepal and with it the fate of the rhinos is at best uncertain.

I am programmed to be an optimist after working in conserva-tion in developing countries for more than three decades. I believe that the year 2008 will be good for the rhinos. My optimism seems to be justified by astounding news that broke on March 14, 2007. In a daring move, a team led by Ana Nath Baral, assistant protection officer of Chitwan National Park, arrested Ramesh Chandra Pokhrel, a well-educated, well-traveled former airline pilot of Royal Nepal Airlines on charges of masterminding a clandestine rhino-poaching operation. Acting on a tip, the park authorities had caught the poacher red-handed in a secretive raid a month earlier in his expensive home in Kathmandu. They also recovered the evidence hidden in his car, consisting of one rhino horn, an automatic rifle used for killing rhinos, and several rounds of ammunition.

The arrest of seventy-six-year-old Pokhrel, a member of a well-connected, wealthy, upper-middle-class family, created a sensation in Nepal. The news also revealed that Madhav Bahadur Budhathoki, a sergeant and a veteran of the Nepalese Army's jungle-warfare unit, illicitly supplied Pokhrel with the ammunition. Pokhrel confessed that he had himself shot nine rhinos in the past five years, but he did not disclose his patrons or how the rhino horns were smuggled out of Nepal. Nevertheless, this arrest exposed the existence of an active ring of sophisticated poachers who know how to take advantage of the political turmoil in Nepal. After nabbing Pokhrel, the park authorities jailed eight other alleged rhino poachers. If there is no miscarriage of justice, all these poachers, including Pokhrel, could face a jail sentence of five to fifteen years or a fine the equivalent of US$700 to US$1,400—a drop in the bucket, in view of the fact that the rhino horns sell for ten times that amount on the black market.

Given the buzz of a burgeoning bribery and corruption circle in Nepal blended with the revelation that the rhino poachers were well connected and had no shortage of cash, it is not certain if this significant arrest will stop rhino poaching entirely. Nevertheless, the fast-paced developments in Nepal in 2007 indicate that there is certainly a light at the end of the tunnel, a light that may bring hope for the betterment of the people and the rhinos of Nepal, whose destinies are interlinked.

Yet at times I wonder: Is this light an opening for peace and prosperity in Nepal and a pathway for the rhinos' eternal survival? Or is it the light of a runaway train on a catastrophic head-on collision course?

Only Samaya, the invisible and the never-resting Hindu God of Time, knows the right answer. I am a mere mortal, blessed by the soul of a rhino.

SELECTED BIBLIOGRAPHY

Adhikari, T. R, Pradhan, N. M. B., & Poudel, N. (1999). *A strategy to combat poaching in Chitwan Valley*. Kathmandu, Nepal: An unpublished report to His Majesty's Government of Nepal. Department of National Parks and Wildlife Conservation.

Bajimaya, S., Baral, J., Chand, R., Rana, R., and Nepal, S. M. (1993). *A report on conservation of rhinoceros in and around Royal Chitwan National Park*. Kathmandu, Nepal: An unpublished report submitted to His Majesty's Government, Ministry of Forests and Soil Conservation.

Baum, Julian and Goldstein, Carl (1993). *Wildlife: Asia's untamed business*. (19 August 1993). *Far Eastern Economic Review*. 22–27.

Bhatt, N. (2003). Kings as wardens and wardens as kings: Post Rana ties between Nepali royalty and national park staff. In *Conservation and Society*. 1, 2. Thousand Oaks, CA/London/New Delhi, India: SAGE Publications.

Bista, D. B. (1976). *People of Nepal*. Kathmandu, Nepal: HMG Department of Publicity.

Byrne, P. (2001). *Gone are the days*. Huntington Beach, CA: Safari Press.

Caughley, G. & Mishra, H. R. (1968). *Wildlife and tourism: The rhino sanctuary*. Kathmandu, Nepal: An official report to the HMG/UNDP/FAO Trisuli Watershed Development Project.

Dinerstein, E. (2003). *The return of the unicorns: The natural history and conservation of the greater one-horned rhinoceros*. New York: Columbia University Press.

Dinerstein, E. (2005). *Tigerland and other unintended destinations*. Washington, D.C.: Island Press.

Dinerstein, E., Shrestha, S. R., & Mishra, H. (1988). Adoption in greater one-horned rhinoceros (*Rhinoceros unicornis*). *Journal of Mammalogy, 69*, 813–814.

Dinerstein, E., Shrestha, S. R., & Mishra, H. (1990). Capture, chemical immobilization, and radio-collar life for greater one-horned rhinoceros. *Wildlife Society Bulletin 18*, 36–41.

DNPWC. (2000). *Rhino count initial report*. Kathmandu, Nepal: His Majesty's Government of Nepal, Department of National Parks and Wildlife Conservation. Unpublished report.

DNPWC. (2006). *The greater one-horned rhinoceros: Conservation action plan for Nepal (2005–2011)*. Kathmandu, Nepal: His Majesty's Government of Nepal, Department of National Parks and Wildlife Conservation.

Fleming, R. L. Sr., Fleming, R. L., & Bangdel, L. S. (1976). *Birds of Nepal* (3rd. ed.). Kathmandu, Nepal: Nature Himalayas.

Foose, T. J. & van Strien, N. (Eds.). (1997). *Status survey and conservation action plan: Asian rhinos*. Gland, Switzerland: The World Conservation Union (IUCN).

Gregson, J. (2002). *Massacre at the palace: The doomed royal dynasty of Nepal*. New York: Miramax Books.

Gurung, C. P. (2005). *Rhino count report 2005*. A PowerPoint presentation of the World Wildlife Fund. Kathmandu, Nepal. WWF–Nepal.

Jnawali, S. R. (1995). *Population ecology of greater one-horned rhinoceros* (Rhinoceros unicornis) *with particular emphasis on habitat preference, food ecology, and ranging behavior of reintroduced population in Royal Bardia National Park*. Unpublished doctoral dissertation, Agricultural University of Norway.

Joshi, A. R. (1996). *The home range, feeding habits, and social organization of sloth bears* (Melursus ursinus) *in Royal Chitwan National Park, Nepal*. Unpublished doctoral dissertation, University of Minnesota, Minneapolis.

International Union for Conservation of Nature & International Resources Group. (2000). *Report on the regional meeting for India and Nepal of the IUCN/SSC Asian rhino specialist group*. Species Survival Commission and the International Rhino Foundation. Gland, Switzerland: Author.

Laurie, W. A. (1978). *The ecology of greater one-horned rhinoceros*. Unpublished doctoral dissertation, University of Cambridge, England.

Lekagul, B. & McNeely, J. A. (1975). *Mammals of Thailand*. Bangkok, Thailand: Kuruspha.

Lemkhul, J. (1989). *The ecology of a south Asian tallgrass community*. Unpublished doctoral dissertation. University of Washington, Seattle.

MacKinnon, K., Mishra, H., & Mott, J. (1999). Reconciling the needs of conservation and local communities: Global Environment Facility support for tiger conservation in India. In J. Seidensticker, S. Christie, & P. Jackson (Eds.), *Riding the tiger: Tiger conservation in human dominated landscapes*. Cambridge, England: Cambridge University Press.

Martin, E. B. (1979). *The international trade in rhinoceros products*. A report for the World Wildlife Funds (WWF) and the International Union for Conservation of Nature and Natural Resources. Gland, Switzerland: IUCN.

Martin, E. B. (1983). *Rhino exploitation: The trade in rhino products in India, Indonesia, Malaysia, Burma, Japan & South Korea*. Hong Kong: World Wildlife Fund–Hong Kong.

McDougal, C. (1977). *The face of the tiger*. London: Andre Deutsch.

Mishra, H. R. (1974). *Nature conservation in Nepal: An introduction to the national parks and wildlife conservation programme of His Majesty's government*. Kathmandu, Nepal: HMG Press.

Mishra, H. R. (1981). Gnade Fur den Tiger! Wir fingen einen "Morder." *Das Tier* (Germany), *Nr. 6*, 45–51.

Mishra, H. R. (1982). Balancing human needs and conservation in Nepal's Royal Chitwan National Park. *Ambio* (Sweden), *11*(5), 246–251.

Mishra, H. R. (1982). *Ecology of chital* (Axis axis*) in Royal Chitwan National Park: With comparison with hog deer* (Axis procinus*), sambar* (Cervus unicolor*) and barking deer* (Muntiacus muntjak*)*. Unpublished doctoral dissertation, University of Edinburgh, Scotland.

Mishra, H. R. (1983). Tourism and conservation of natural heritage: The Nepalese experience. *Proceedings of the Third International Asia-Pacific Travel Association (PATA) Tourism Heritage Conservation Conference*. Kathmandu, Nepal: PATA, Nepal Chapter.

Mishra, H. R. (1984). A delicate balance: Tigers, rhinoceros, tourists and park management vs. the needs of the local people in Royal Chitwan National Park. In J. A. McNeely & K. R. Miller (Eds.), *National parks, conservation and development*. Washington, D.C: Smithsonian Institution Press.

Mishra, H. R. (1984, July). Nepal. Ecologie Dans le parc des tueurs d'hommes. *Geo. Un nouveau monde: la Terre* (France), No. 65. 92–93.

Mishra, H. R. (1991). Operation Unicorn. A new home for the rhinos of Chitwan. *Shangri-La Royal Nepal Airlines In-flight Magazine, 2* (4), 52–60.

Mishra, H. R. (1994). South and Southeast Asia: Protecting nature. In J. A. McNeely, J. Harrison, & P. Dingwall (Eds.), *Regional review of protected areas*. Gland, Switzerland: IUCN.

Mishra, H. R. & Dinerstein, E. (1987). New zip codes for resident rhinos in Nepal. *Smithsonian Magazine, 18*, 66–73.

Mishra, H. R. & Jefferies, M. (1991). *Royal Chitwan National Park: Wildlife heritage of Nepal*. Seattle, WA: The Mountaineers.

Mishra, H. R., & Maskey, T. M. (1982). Zuruck indie
   Flusse. *Tier Grizmeks Sielmanns Tierwield* (Germany), *NR.6*,
   14–18.

Mishra, H. R. & Mierow, D. (1974). *Wild animals of Nepal.*
   Kathmandu, Nepal: Ratna Pustak Bhandar.

Mishra, H. R. & Wemmer, C. (1983, October). Abenteuer in
   Nepal's Chitwan National Park. Auf Nashornfang mit
   Elefanten. *Das Tier* (Germany), *Nr. 10.* 14–17.

Mishra, H. R., Wemmer, C., & Smith, J. L. D. (1987). Tigers in
   Nepal: Management conflicts with human interests. In R. L.
   Tilson & U. S. Seal (Eds.), *Tigers of the world: The biology,
   biopolitics, management, and conservation of an endangered species.*
   Park Ridge, NJ: Noyes Publications.

Mishra, H. R., Wemmer, C., Smith, J. L. D., & Wegge, P. (1992).
   Biopolitics of saving mammals in the wild: balancing
   conservation with human needs in Nepal. In P. Wegge (Ed.),
   Occasional Papers Series C. 9, 35. Aas, Norway: NorAgric
   Agricultural University of Norway.

Misra, N. (2001). *End of the line: The story of the killing of the royals in
   Nepal.* Delhi, India: Penguin Books India.

Nepal, S. K., & Weber, K. (1993). *Struggle for existence: Park-people
   conflict in the Royal Chitwan National Park, Nepal.* Bangkok,
   Thailand: Asian Institute of Technology.

Oldfield, H. A. (1880). *Sketches from Nepal: Historical and descriptive.*
   London: Allen.

Pellinck, E. & Upreti, B. N. (1972). *A census of rhinoceros in Chitwan
   National Park and Tamaspur Forests, Nepal.* Kathmandu, Nepal:
   FAO/UNDP National Parks and Wildlife Conservation
   Project.

Perry, A. (2002, May 13). Nepal. Reign of terror. Return to year
   zero. Nepal's Maoists rebels are murdering, beating, bombing
   and looting—all in the name of "protecting the people." *Time,*
   18–21.

Raj, P. A. (2006). *The dancing democracy: The power of the third eye.* Delhi, India: Rupa Books.

Schaller, G. B. (1967). *The deer and the tiger.* Chicago: University of Chicago Press.

Seidensticker, J. (1976). Ungulate population in Chitwan Valley. *Biological Conservation 10,* 183–210.

Shah, His Royal Highness Prince Gyanendra Bir Bikram. (1984). *Statement at the National Zoological Park.* Washington, D.C.: Smithsonian Institution.

Sharma, U. R. (1991). *Park-people interactions in Royal Chitwan National Park, Nepal.* Unpublished doctoral dissertation. University of Arizona, Tucson.

Smith, J. L. D. (1984). *Dispersal, communications and conservation strategies for the tiger* (Panthera tigris). Unpublished doctoral dissertation. University of Minnesota, Minneapolis.

Smythies, E. A. (1942). *Big game hunting in Nepal.* London: Thacker, Spink.

Stainton, J. D. (1988). *Forests of Nepal.* London: John Murray.

Sunquist, M. E. (1981). *The movements and activities of tigers* (Panthera tigris tigris) *in Royal Chitwan National Park.* Unpublished doctoral dissertation. University of Minnesota, Minneapolis.

Tamang, K. M. (1979). *Population characteristics of the tiger and its prey.* Unpublished doctoral dissertation. University of Minnesota, Minneapolis.

Thapa, D. (with Sijapati, B.). (2003). *A kingdom under siege: Nepal's Maoist insurgency, 1996 to 2003.* Kathmandu, Nepal: The Print House.

U.S. Fish & Wildlife Service. (1999). *Rhinoceros & tiger conservation act. Summary report.* Washington, D.C.:

U.S. Dept. of the Interior, U.S. Field and Wildlife Service, International Affairs.

Wemmer, C., Smith, J. L. D., & Mishra, H. R. (1987). The biopolitical challenge. In R. L. Tilson & U. S. Seal (Eds.), *Tigers of the world: The biology, biopolitics, management, and conservation of an endangered species*. Park Ridge, NJ: Noyes Publications.

World Wildlife Fund. (2001). *Terai arc: In the shadow of the Himalayas. A new paradigm for wildlife conservation*. Washington, D.C.: World Wildlife Fund–US.

Yonzon, P. (1994). *Count rhino 94. A report of the World Wildlife Fund Nepal Program*. Kathmandu, Nepal: WWF–Nepal.

INDEX

A

Africa, rhinoceros in, 30, 38
Aishwarya, Queen, 161–62
Akash (Maoist commander), 211
Asian rhinoceros. *See also* Rhinoceros; Royal Chitwan National Park, 24, 31
    ancestors of, 29
    in Bardia, 9, 187, 189, 198–99, 200, 203
    census of, 32–33, 36–37, 38–39, 42–43
    conservation agreement for, 210–11
    George's story, 89–91
    habitat in Chitwan, 54–56, 62–63, 79–80, 81
    horns of, 8, 35
    mating behavior, 3–4
    numbers of in Chitwan, 139, 188, 201–2, 205, 206–7
    poaching, 45–52, 206, 207, 208
    range of, 32

B

Ba, Buddha, 142–43, 145
Babur (Muslim ruler), 138–39
Bach, Barbara, 86
Badahur, Jung. *See* Rana, Jung Badahur

Badai (elephant driver), 108–9, 110–11, 118, 125, 134
Bala (rhino tamer), 124–25, 126, 127–28, 129–31
Baral, Ana Nath, 215
Bardia wildlife preserve. *See also* Royal Bardia National Park, 9, 133
Bass, Edward P., 131, 132, 133, 200
Bass, Ramona, 123, 131–32, 135
Basundhera, Prince. *See* Shah, Prince Basundhera Bir Bikram
Bhaggu (elephant driver), 165, 166, 167
Bhakta, Murli, 81
Bhelur trees, and rhinos, 36
Birendra, King. *See* Shah Dev, King Birendra Bir Bikram
Blower, John, 70–72
Botes (ethnic group), 28
Brahmin caste, 4–5, 100
Buddha, Lord, 147, 182
Budhathoki, Madhav Bahadur, 215

C

Cambodia, rhinos in, 31
Cat Loc Nature Reserve, 31

Caughley, Graeme, 32–33, 36–37, 38–43, 205
Chang-Block, Julia, 135
China, and rhino poaching. *See also* Taiwan, 45–46, 47–48, 50, 51
Chitwan National Park. *See* Royal Chitwan National Park
Clinton, President Bill, 50
Coapman, John, 82–86
Communist (Maoist) Party of Nepal. *See also* Maoists, 206
Connolly, Billy, 86
Conservation movement. *See also* Royal Chitwan National Park
  Bass's contributions to, 132
  and helicopter crash, xvi, 213–15
  importance of national parks, 64, 69
  in Nepal, ix–x, xxi–xxii
  and trafficking in endangered species, 46, 47, 49, 50
Convention on International Trade in Endangered Species of Wild Fauna and Flora (CITES), 46

D
Deuba, Prime Minister, 208
Dhirendra, Prince. *See* Shah, Prince Dhirendra Bir Bikram
Dinerstein, Eric, xvii, 200
Dipendra, Prince. *See* Shah, Prince Dipendra Bir Bikram

E
Edwards, Jim, 86
Elephants, 107
  elephant polo, 86–88
  handlers and drivers of, 93–95
  importance of in Chitwan, 92, 93
  mounting, 95–96
  and rhino calves, 105, 106
  and rhinos in Bardia, 198
Elizabeth I, Queen, 140
Emmanuel, King, 138
Endangered species. *See also* specific species
  and habitat destruction, 55
  trafficking in, 46, 48, 50, 51
Endau Rompin National Park, 32
Environmental Investigative Agency (EIA), 48

F
Fort Worth Zoo, rhinos for, 131–32, 133, 136
Fort Worth Zoological Society, 133

G
George V, King, 139
Giant giraffe rhinoceros, 29
Giris (ethnic group), 100
Gurung, Chandra Prasad, 147, 207
  and conservation agreement, 210
  death of, xvi, 213, 214
Gurung, Kuber, 111–12, 123, 124, 176
  moving rhinos, 187, 189, 192, 195, 197, 199
Gyanendra, King. *See* Shah Dev, King Gyanendra Bir Bikram

Gyanendra, Prince. *See* Shah,
    Prince Gyanendra Bir
    Bikram

H

Hainan, and rhino poaching, 51
Hekou, and rhino poaching, 51
Hemingway, Margaux, 86
Hillary, Edmund, 75, 150
Himalayan Mountains, 29
Hinduism
    karma in, 184
    letter *om*, 181
    Nagas sect, 17–18
    respect for nature, 202
    Shivaratri festival, 17, 18
    swastik symbol, 181
    and Tharus, 26–27

I

Ijima, Masahiro, xvi
India
    and Nepal's government, 209
    rhino hunting in, 138–39
    and rhino poaching, 45, 47
Indian rhinoceros. *See also* Asian
    rhinoceros, xii, 29, 139
International Union for Conserva-
    tion of Nature (IUCN), 46

J

Jabara, Jim, 201
Javan rhinoceros. *See also* Asian
    rhinoceros, 31
Joshi, Anup, xvii, 189–90,
    193, 194

K

Kalu (elephant driver), 165
Karma. *See also* Hinduism, 184
Kathmandu. *See also* Nepal, 16, 17
    Americans in, 18

Bagh Darbar palace, 154
    Narayanhiti Royal Palace, 150
    politics in, 148, 149
Khatri, Top, 191
Koirala, Girja Prasad, 208
Koshi Tappu (game reserve), 9
Kuanda, Kenneth, 38
Kumal (ethnic group), 28
Kumar, Kishan, 68, 69

L

Laos, rhinos in, 31
Leo, Pope, 137
Linlithgow, Lord, 139
Lissanevitch, Boris, 82, 83
Lockie, James, 60, 61

M

Mahato, Mallu, 78
Mahendra, King. *See* Shah Dev,
    King Mahendra
    Bir Bikram
Malaysia, rhinos in, 31–32
Malla, Sher Bahadur, 19
Man Bahadur (game scout), 119,
    121–22
Manuel I, King, 137
Maoists, in Nepal. *See also* Nepal,
    xix, 206–7
    peace deal of, 211, 215
    and rhino poaching, 207, 213
Martin, Esmond Bradley, xvii,
    47–48
Maskey, Tirtha Man, 51, 75
    and conservation
        agreement, 210
    death of, xvi, 213, 214
    moving rhinos, 207
    and royal hunt, 158, 159, 160,
        161, 176

Mingma Norbu Sherpa. *See*
    Sherpa, Mingma Norbu
Mishra, Hemanta R., ix, xi–xiii,
    xv–xvi, xxi–xxiii
    in Britain and University of
        Edinburgh, 57–62
    capturing baby rhinos, 107–8,
        109, 112, 113–22,
        125–26, 128–29
    and elephant polo, 86–88
    family and background of,
        11–19
    first wild rhino encounter, 1–4
    and George, 89–91
    and helicopter crash, 213–14
    international recognition
        for, 188
    and King Mahendra, 74–75
    and National Park and Wildlife
        Conservation Act,
        69–72
    and poachers, 51–54
    and Prem Rai, 95–97
    relocating rhinos, 187, 188–95,
        197–203
    and rhino census, 32–33, 36–37,
        38–43
    on royal hunt, 153–56, 157–66,
        167–68, 169–77
    and Sagarmatha (Mt. Everest)
        National Park, 75,
        150–51
    and shamanistic rites, 108,
        109–12
    and Smith, 97–99
    taming baby rhinos, 123–25,
        126–28, 129–31, 133–36
    and Tapsi, 5–10, 24

    and Tarpan ritual, x, 141–46,
        152, 179–85
    and tourism in Chitwan, 77,
        78, 79
    and villagers in Chitwan,
        62–63, 67–69, 79–80
    working with tigers, 80–81,
        92–93
    in Yellowstone, 63–65
Mishra, Sushma, 90, 141–42
Musahar (ethnic group), 28
N
Nagas sect. *See also* Hinduism,
    17–18
Nath, Neel, 52
National Park and Wildlife Con-
    servation Act, 69
National parks, importance of. *See*
    also specific parks, 64, 69
Natural Resources World Conser-
    vation Union, 46
Nepal. *See also* specific rulers;
    Royal Chitwan National
    Park, 147
    conservation agreement for
        rhinos, 210–11
    culture of Kathmandu, 16, 17
    deal with WWF for rhinos,
        131–32, 133
    early wildlife tourism in, 82–86
    ethnic groups in, 4–5, 28
    geography of, 24
    helicopter crash in, xvi, 213–14
    Maoist rebels in, xix, 205–7
    National Park and Wildlife Con-
        servation Act, 69–73
    numbers of rhinos in, xii,
        139, 205

political structure in, xviii–xix,
148–49, 208–10
preservation of temples and
monasteries, 202
Rana regime, 16–17, 148
resident Europeans and
Americans in, 37–38
role of sons in, 11
royal hunts in, 25, 45
Royal Palace Wildlife
Committee, xxi–xxii
Tarpan ritual, x, 141, 144–46,
175, 176–77, 179–85
US programs and habitat in,
55–56
wild animals in, xii

O

Om (Sanskrit letter). *See also*
Hinduism, 181
Ottaway, Jim, Jr., xvi, 214

P

Parsa Wildlife Reserve. *See also*
Royal Chitwan National
Park, 188
Pieffer, Tom, 37, 38
Pokhrel, Ramesh Chandra,
215, 216
Pompadour, Madame, 138
Poudal, Narayan, xvi, 210
Powell, Enoch, 61
Prachanda (Maoist leader), 206
Pradhan, P. B. S., 85
Prasad, Sharada, 16

R

Rahut, Ravi, 67
Rai, Prem Bahadur, 95, 96, 97
Raj, Shanta, 191
Ram Lotan, 91–92, 93, 94

moving rhinos, 190–91, 194
and rhino calf, 124, 125
and royal hunts, 101–5, 157,
158, 159, 160, 161, 162
Rana, Juddha Shamsher, 15,
26, 153
Rana, Jung Badahur, 16–17
protection for rhino, 45
Ranga, General, 152, 153, 154,
155, 158, 170, 174, 175
Rhinoceros. *See also* Asian
rhinoceros
classification of, 23–24
horns of, xv, 35, 140
importance of, xii, 203
mating behavior, 3–4
origin of word, 29–30
poaching and trade of parts,
45–52
royalty's fascination with,
137–41
senses of, 36, 114
species of, 24, 30–32
Rhinoceros unicornis. See Asian
rhinoceros
Rhinoceros unicornis fossilus. See also
Asian rhinoceros, 29
Royal Bardia National Park,
rhinos in, 9, 187, 197–201,
203, 207
Royal Chitwan National Park. *See
also* Mishra, Hemanta R.,
xi, xii, xvii, 24–25, 188
ancient climate change in, 29
arrest of staff, 212
conservation agreement with
Maoists, 210–11
establishment of, 75

ethnic groups in, 28
game scouts *(shikaris)* in,
     99–100
human-wildlife conflicts in,
     62–63, 80–81
living quarters in, 100
map of, xx
number of rhinos in, xii, 139,
     188, 201–2, 205, 206–7
rhino census in, 32–33, 36–37,
     38–39, 42–43
rhino habitat in, 54–56, 79–80
rhino poaching in, 51–54,
     212–13, 215–16
tourism in, 77–79, 82–86
traveling in, 4
Royal Shikar Reserve. *See also*
     Royal Chitwan National
     Park, 25

S

Sadhus. *See also* Hinduism, 17
Sagarmatha (Mt. Everest)
     National Park, 75
Sarki (caste), 180
Scott, Peter, 38
Selassie, Haile, 70
Shah, Prince Basundhera Bir
     Bikram, 83
Shah, Prince Dhirendra Bir
     Bikram, 166–67
Shah, Prince Dipendra Bir
     Bikram, xxi, 205
Shah, Prince Gyanendra Bir
     Bikram, 151–52
and national parks, xxii, 75, 77,
     150
and Tarpan ritual, 152, 154,
     155–56, 164–65, 173

Shah Dev, King Birendra Bir
     Bikram, x, 75, 95
death of, xxi, 205–6
naming rhino calves, 134
and Royal Chitwan National
     Park, 75, 188
and royal hunt, 161–66,
     167–68, 169–75
and Tarpan ritual, 141–42,
     143–46, 179, 182–84
Shah Dev, King Gyanendra
     Bir Bikram
conservation work of, xviii
and Maoist rebels, 208–9
Shah Dev, King Mahendra Bir
     Bikram, 73–75
and Bass family, 132
conservation work of, 43, 44,
     72–73
coup by, 148–49
hunting accident, 166–67
King Mahendra Trust for
     Nature Conservation,
     xviii, 188
resettlement program of, 55
Shah Dev, King Tribhuvan
     Bir Bikram, 148
Shah Dynasty. *See also* Nepal;
     specific rulers, 210
Shakti (taxidermist), 180
Shakya, Karna, 214
Shamsher, Juddha. *See* Rana,
     Juddha Shamsher
Sherpa, Mingma Norbu, 210
death of, xvi, 213, 214
Sherpa, Tenzing, 150
Shivaratri festival. *See also*
     Hinduism, 17

Shrestha, Narayani Prasad, 152
Singh, Gagan, 199
Smith, James L. David, 97–99
Smithsonian Institution, xviii, 92,
    95, 108
Som (poacher), 51–52
Starr, Ringo, 86
Stebbins, Henry, 73
Sukla Phanta (game reserve),
    9, 166
Sumatran rhinoceros. *See also*
    Asian rhinoceros, 31–32
Sunquist, Melvin Eugene, 93
Sushil, Brigadier (Little
    Uncle), 152
    and royal hunt, 157, 158, 159,
        160, 163, 164, 169–70,
        171–72
    and Tarpan ritual, 154–55,
        156, 184
Swamp deer, 55–56
Swastik symbol. *See also*
    Hinduism, 181
T
Taiwan, and rhino poaching, 46,
    48–52
Tamang, Harkha Man, 113–14
Tamang, Kirti, 96
Tamangs (ethnic group), 99–100
Taman Negra National Park, 32
Tapsi (elephant driver), 3, 4, 94,
    101–2, 203
    as elephant driver, 25–26
    and Mishra, 5–10, 24
    and rhino census, 39–41
    story of rhino's creation, 21–23
Tarpan ritual, x, 141, 144–46, 175,
    176–77, 179–85

Taylor, Charles, 60
Tenzing Sherpa, 150
Terai. *See* Royal Chitwan
    National Park
Thapa, Chiran, 152
Tharus (ethnic group), 4–5,
    26–28
    and Chitwan's rhino habitat,
        79–80
    and elephant driving, 95
    and shamanism, 108
    "stick dance" of, 78–79
Tigers
    in Chitwan, 80–81, 82, 84
    and habitat destruction, 55
    radio-collaring, 92–93
Tiger Tops. *See also* Coapman,
    John, 83–84, 86
Tilak (guard), 53–54
Tourism. *See* Royal Chitwan
    National Park
TRAFFIC (Trade Records
    Analysis of Fauna and
    Flora in Commerce), 46
Train, Russell E., 133
Tribhuvan, King. *See* Shah Dev,
    King Tribhuvan
    Bir Bikram
U
Ujung Kulon National Park, 31
United States
    and habitat destruction in
        Nepal, 55–56
    national parks in, 63, 64
    and rhino captive-breeding
        program, 189
    and trafficking in endangered
        species, 50

United States Operation Mission
(USOM), 55
Upreti, Bishwa Nath, 70–72
US Aid for International
Development (USAID),
55, 56
V
Vietnam, rhinos in, 31
W
Wangchuck, Deki, 49–50
Wangchuck, Queen Ashi Sangay
Choden, 214
Wangchuk, King Jigme, 50
Wemmer, Chris, xvi, 188–89
World Conservation Union,
xvii, 207

World Wildlife Fund, xviii,
175, 207
and baby rhinos, 131, 132, 133
Wynne, Toddy Lee, 82
Y
Yadav, Ram Prit, 81–82
and elephant polo, 86, 87–88
Yellowstone National Park,
63–65, 69
Yemen, and rhino horns,
47–48, 140
Z
Zambia, elephants in, 38